Passion for Excitement

By the same author

MARIE CORELLI:
The Woman and the Legend

IN THE STEPS OF GEORGE BORROW

OUIDA:
The Passionate Victorian

THE INDOMITABLE MRS. TROLLOPE

Lord Byron from a watercolor by William Blake.

Passion for Excitement

THE LIFE AND PERSONALITY
OF THE INCREDIBLE LORD BYRON

BY EILEEN BIGLAND

Coward-McCann, Inc. New York

MANUFACTURED IN THE UNITED STATES OF AMERICA

VAN REES PRESS • NEW YORK

À mon ami

GASTON BERLEMONT

et sa famille

Acknowledgment

The author's most grateful thanks are due to Sir John Murray, K.C.V.O., D.S.O., whose kindness enabled her to complete this book.

Contents

His misfortune is an habitual *passion for Excitement,* which is always found in ardent temperaments, where the pursuits are not in some degree organized.

LADY BYRON

in a letter to Augusta Leigh

If I could explain at length the *real* causes which have contributed to increase this perhaps *natural* temperament of mine, this Melancholy which hath made me a bye-word, nobody would wonder; but this is impossible without doing much mischief. I do not know what other men's lives have been, but I cannot conceive anything more strange than some of the earlier parts of mine. I have written my memoirs, but omitted *all* the really *consequential* and *important* parts, from deference to the dead, to the living, and to those who must be both.

LORD BYRON

from *Detached Thoughts,*
dated October 15th, 1821

Prologue

✱ ✱

Prologue in Missolonghi, April, 1824

FOR three days the sirocco had raged over Missolonghi, and although it was only just past midday the dirty, untidy room where Lord Byron lay was already growing dark. On either side of the bed Fletcher, the valet, and Tita Falciere, the gondolier of happier days, kept watch over their master; on the floor the two dogs, Lion and Moretto, sprawled among a litter of books, papers and soiled linen; in and out of the shadows the little Greek page, Loukas, wandered disconsolately with a trayful of coffee and olives which nobody wanted.

A particularly savage gust of wind sent the rain spattering against the windowpanes, and the sick man stirred uneasily. He was thirsty, he complained, so very thirsty, and while Fletcher supported his head he gulped down a concoction of lemon juice, cream of tartar and distilled water. From the far side of the bed Tita bent forward, imploring in a gabble of Venetian dialect that milord should allow the wise doctors to bleed him, but Byron turned fretfully away. He had no manner of use for that silly pair of doctors, Bruno and Millingen. Only yesterday he had told them he knew full well that the lancet killed more people than the lance and railed at them for their inefficiency and igno-

13

rance; now the knowledge that they had prevailed upon his servant to influence him—for how else could Tita have got hold of such a notion?—incensed him further.

"*They* tell me," he said suddenly to Fletcher, "that it is only a common cold, which you know I have had a thousand times."

Fletcher gave a little cough. He shared his master's opinion of the two doctors and was still smarting over their abrupt refusal of his plea that the more experienced Dr. Thomas should be fetched from Zante.

"I am sure, my lord, that you have never had one of so serious a nature," he said.

"I think I never had." Even in its weakness Byron's voice held a note of irony. He lay back with closed eyes, trying to forget the fever mounting in his blood, the intrigues, the frustrations, the disasters of the past three months, the lost prestige of the Government of Western Greece, the whole sad story of a campaign which had fizzled out. True, the immediate danger of Missolonghi's capture by the Turks had been averted, but the War of Liberation, the cause to which he had dedicated his mind, his fortune, his life, seemed lost before it had properly begun. He might never, he reflected wryly, fight that second Lepanto of his dreams. Worse, perhaps he who longed so ardently for battle might never fight at all.

"Fletcher," he whispered, "if I die in Greece what will you do with me?"

"My lord, what should we do but take you home?"

Byron moved his head as if in negation. "Why, it is not worth while to take such a body as this home." Then he paused, and the lines on his face deepened. "Perhaps," he added slowly, "perhaps on the whole, it would be better so."

The afternoon dragged on. The sick man dozed, seemingly unaware of whistling wind and beating rain. Tita nodded in his chair, Loukas ceased his prowling and crouched in a corner, Lion and Moretto slept. Only Fletcher remained wide awake, his gaze fixed on his master. For Fletcher was a sorely worried man. He was convinced that Lord Byron was dying and that those around him were either without the wit to recognize the fact or were deliberately ignoring it.

The sick man moaned a request for a drink and inquired for Parry, and Fletcher, with a disapproving air, sent Tita in search of him. The habit of nearly twenty years was strong, and whatever his private feelings he could not disobey the master he had served so long.

Parry's arrival seemed to revive Lord Byron in amazing fashion. He sat up in bed and carried on a lucid conversation for quite a time. Then, according to Parry's own account, he lapsed into melancholy:

"You have no conception of the unaccountable thoughts which come into my mind when the fever attacks me. I fancy myself a Jew, a Mohammedan, and a Christian of every profession of faith. Eternity and space are before me; but on this subject, thank God, I am happy and at ease. . . ."

After Byron's death, Parry wrote:

I had never before felt as I felt that evening. There was the gifted Lord Byron, who had been the object of universal attention . . . gradually expiring, almost forsaken, and certainly without the consolation which generally awaits the meanest of mankind, of breathing out his last sigh in the arms of some dear friend. His habitation was weather-tight, but that was nearly all the comfort his deplorable room afforded him. He was my protector and benefactor, and I could not see him whom I knew to have been so differently brought up thus perishing, far from his home, far from all the comforts due to his rank and situation, far, too, from every fond and affectionate heart, without a feeling of deep sorrow, such as I should not have had at the loss of my own dearest relation. The pestilent sirocco was blowing a hurricane, and the rain was falling with almost tropical violence. In our apartment was the calm of coming death, and outside was the storm desolating the spot around us, but carrying, I would fain hope, new life and vigour to some stagnant part of nature.

This evening was, I believe, the last time Lord Byron was calm and collected for any considerable period.

15

When Parry had gone Byron sank back exhausted, but while Fletcher fussed around him his lips curved in a faint smile. Poor Fletcher, he knew so well what he was thinking. He was wrong. For all his faults Parry was an honest fellow, and to talk with him had been a great relief. Not that Parry had understood one tenth of what he had said. Perhaps nobody could have understood ... nobody ... except, of course, himself.

He lay quietly, feigning sleep. For once he did not think of the Greek War; instead, his thoughts strayed back to England. He was at Newstead again and the snow was falling and the being who had meant more than anyone in the world to him was standing beside him watching the flakes drift down on the mere. .... He was in a London ballroom watching a thin, wild-eyed girl waltzing. ... He was a new boy at Harrow passionately resenting the cutting remarks of Henry Drury. .... He was a child limping up an Aberdeen street. ...

For many years Byron had not allowed himself to think of that child—but time was so short now and the child so important. For he **was the** reason behind the whole pattern of the past fifteen years.

Passion for Excitement

I

❋❋❋❋❋❋❋❋❋❋❋❋❋❋❋❋❋❋❋❋❋❋❋❋❋❋❋❋❋❋

For I Was Always Violent

THE Bath Assembly Rooms were crowded, as was usual during the season when fashionable folk descended on the city to take the waters, to dance, to make love, to vie with each other in the wearing of fanciful costumes. But on this particular evening, although the musicians had been playing the most enticing music for the past hour, people seemed strangely reluctant to begin the dance. Instead, they stood about in little groups, the ladies nodding and whispering behind their fans, the gentlemen conferring together in low voices. Then somebody nudged somebody else, the buzz of talk died, and everyone turned to face the doorway as a tall, exceedingly handsome man entered with a young woman on his arm. The central figures in the most savory scandal known for years had arrived.

The man was Captain John Byron, the woman Catherine Gordon of Gight, and they had just announced their forthcoming marriage.

It was not surprising that this news had thrown the fashionable world into a flutter. "Mad" Jack Byron, since his return from service with the Guards in the Americas, had proved himself one of the most dissolute and spendthrift young men of his age.

A creature of irresistible charm (as many poor girls had found to their cost) he had capped all previous indiscretions by eloping to the Continent with the wife of the Marquis of Carmarthen. Certainly he had married the lady when her husband divorced her, but the most terrible tales had been brought back by those who had encountered the couple in France or Belgium. "Mad" Jack had treated his poor wife abominably, leaving her to lead a miserable existence in primitive inns while he drank and rioted with harlots. He had taken all her money—she had been Amelia d'Arcy, Baroness Conyers in her own right—and gambled it away. Before she had fully recovered from the birth of their daughter, Augusta, he had insisted upon her accompanying him on a hunting expedition so strenuous that she had suffered a relapse and died. Finally—and to a society which rigidly observed certain conventions while condoning all kinds of moral laxity this was perhaps his most shocking sin—he had returned to England, handed the baby Augusta over to her mother's relations, and proceeded to woo Miss Gordon before, as you might say, his first wife was cold in her grave.

It was obvious, of course, that Jack Byron was after money. There was no other reason why anybody so debonair and attractive should wish to marry Catherine Gordon. Kitty, as she was called, was a rather squat young woman with an inordinate idea of her own importance and a habit of speaking in an uncouth Scots dialect. She bored everyone within reach with long stories about her descent from Scottish kings, flew into violent rages on the slightest provocation, and showed a dogged pertinacity in pursuing eligible young men who fled at her approach. To these unwilling suitors she gave details of the estates and fortune she had lately inherited from her father, George Gordon, who had been found mysteriously drowned in the River Avon.

According to contemporary accounts one or two older friends tried to dissuade her from the marriage, and were severely snubbed for their pains. Against Jack Byron she would not hear a word; moreover she insisted that fate had decreed she should marry him, and in proof of this produced an amazing story of how, when watching Mrs. Siddons playing Isabella in Southerne's *The Fatal Marriage* in Edinburgh, she had suddenly been so overwhelmed by emotion that she had fallen into a fit and been carried out screaming, "Oh, my Biron, my Biron!" At that time she had not even met Captain Byron in the flesh, so the only explanation was that theirs was a predestined marriage of twin souls.

Poor Kitty Gordon! It is easy to understand how she fell victim to the Byron charm. Despite her wealth she had had little education, she was strangely ignorant of the ways of the great world, she was acutely conscious of the fact that men avoided her, she had a head stuffed full of sentimental notions and she yearned for love.

As for Captain Byron, he must have heaved a prodigious sigh of relief when the marriage actually took place and he journeyed northward with his bride to her Aberdeenshire estates of Gight and Monkshill. Now that he had really won his prize there would be no more need for honey phrases and loving glances. All that Kitty needed to bring her to heel was a little persuasive argument—after all, who wanted tracts of windswept land, or salmon-fishings on the river Dee, or shares in the Aberdeen Banking Company, which was administered by a group of cold, tight-fisted Scots?

Bemused by her infatuation for her husband, Kitty Gordon spent 1785, the first year of her marriage, realizing portions of her inheritance for his benefit; and from the wedding day onwards Jack Byron treated his bride shamefully—a fact noted by the Aberdonians, who took pleasure in singing a scurrilous ballad in the streets whenever his presence in the city was known:

> Oh, whaur are ye' gaen, bonny Miss Gordon?
> Oh whaur are ye' gaen, sae bonny and braw?
> Ye've married, ye've married wi' Johnny Byron
> To squander the lands o' Gight awa'.

This youth is a rake, frae England he's come;
    The Scots dinna' ken his extraction ava';
He keeps up his misses, his landlord he duns,
    That's fast drawen' the lands of Gight awa'.

The shootin' o' guns, an' rattlin' o' drums,
    The bugle in woods, the pipes i' the ha',
The beagles a' howlin', the hounds a' growlin';
    These soundings will soon gar Gight gang awa'!

Neither the townsfolk nor the estate tenants had any manner of use for this penniless adventurer who had, in their opinion, enticed their Miss Gordon into marriage, and the knowledge of their dislike made him all the more determined to leave Scotland as soon as possible. This could not be done, however, without first cajoling his Kitty into parting with yet more of her property, so for a few brief months at the beginning of 1786 he made an effort to please her by curbing his wild ways, and she, slavishly grateful for his renewed attentions, ignored the advice of her kinsman, the Duke of Gordon, and of Colonel Duff of Fetteresso, and sold yet more land on the grounds that Captain Byron wished to live in France. By the summer her possessions had dwindled to the estate of Gight and she and her husband had departed for the Continent.

It is doubtful whether Captain Byron had ever intended to take his wife abroad: it is certain that she was an extremely unhappy woman during this brief sojourn. Her infatuation was wearing off and, although she still fondly hoped that her rake would reform, her natural ill-temper was reasserting itself. Scenes became distressingly frequent. He taunted her about her meanness and sneered about the "barbarian ancestors" of whom she was so proud: she retaliated by hurling abuse at the Byron family. What was there so wonderful, she demanded, about his father, an admiral who had been known while alive as "Foul Weather Jack" because of the number of shipwrecks attendant on his career? And wasn't he ashamed of his uncle, the fifth Lord Byron, who had once been arraigned before his peers after killing a kinsman and neighbor in a duel, and who now lived a life of seclusion at Newstead Abbey, his sole companions a village concubine and some tame crickets?

The rows grew in magnitude—and all the time Captain Byron required more and more money. It had been possible, while actually on the spot, to use high-handed methods with lawyers and men of business; but conducting a lengthy correspondence with them from France was a very different matter. By 1787 Kitty Byron was in despair. She was pregnant, she felt exceedingly ill, she was thoroughly homesick, and they had practically no ready money. Hitherto she had steadfastly refused to part with Gight: now she issued instructions that it was to be sold— and for the first time since her disastrous marriage, she showed some sign of common sense, for she stipulated that sufficient money to bring her in an annuity of about £150 a year was to be kept on one side. The remainder of the proceeds, of course, were to go to Captain Byron.

Sick at heart, yet still cherishing the illusion that fatherhood would transform her husband's character, Kitty Byron returned to England alone and took rooms at 16 Holles Street, London. There, on January 22nd, 1788, she gave birth to a son, George Gordon Byron.

❊ 2 ❊

Some time later in the same year Mrs. Byron took her son to Aberdeen, where she established herself in lodgings. Contrary to her hopes, her husband had shown markedly little interest in the child's arrival—there was still some of the Gight money to be squandered and he much preferred his gay French companions to his vituperative wife—and to this worry was now added another. Little Geordie, as she called him, had been born with a deformity and would, so the doctors informed her, always be lame.

23

In the light of present-day medical knowledge it seems probable that this lameness, which was to haunt Byron his life long and which obsessed his mother from the moment she was told of it, was "caused by hæmorrhage on to the surface of the infant's brain, the result of some delay in the establishment of respiration at the moment of birth." * Known as *Little's Disease*, this complaint produces an affliction known as "scissor-leg." "A child so injured walks clumsily and with difficulty, though the legs and feet are well formed. . . . The sufferer walks with a curious running gait, with a great appearance of effort, though only slow progress may be achieved. The body rises upon the toes and the knees are kept tightly pressed one against the other." Other results of the disease (also called spastic paraplegia) are epileptiform attacks—and it is well known that Byron suffered such attacks towards the end of his life.

But in the year 1788 such an explanation of lameness was unheard of in medical circles; and even if it had been, Mrs. Byron was the last person to have put any credence in it. No, her Geordie had been born with a "club foot" because his faithless, good-for-nothing father had so harried and hounded his poor mother before the birth that something had gone wrong.

Exactly what this something was Mrs. Byron did not specify, for the simple reason that she had no idea of the answer. Like many another woman she had transferred her affections from her husband to her baby son, and she was now fiercely determined to devote all her time and energy to the curing of her precious boy. Since she did not trust English doctors she made the move to Aberdeen, where she pestered every doctor (and every quack) with such success that even before Geordie had reached the age of three his poor small body had been submitted to various extremely painful experiments which failed to alleviate his condition. His legs were stretched, he was put in irons, his feet were encased in heavy surgical boots—and all the time his distracted

* The Mystery of Lord Byron's Lameness: H. Charles Cameron, *The Lancet*, March 31st, 1923.

mother rushed around the district telling her woes to every member of the Gordon clan and every old family friend she could find. Nor did she approach these good folk in gentle fashion. She wept, she hectored, she demanded until one by one they grew adept at evading her. The Duke of Gordon and Colonel Duff, who were the young Byron's godfathers, put up with her for a considerable time, but when they heard some of the slanderous remarks she had made about them they too withdrew.

As she sat in her shabby lodgings Mrs. Byron burned with resentment against the lot of them, and by way of giving vent to her feelings ranted away by the hour to her baby son, pouring into his uncomprehending ears her opinion of the ducal Gordons —"the *Seyton* Gordons, just a cadet branch"—and of the various county families who spurned her because she had fallen on evil days through no fault of her own. She conveniently forgot that she had insisted upon marrying Captain Byron despite all their protests, and when she had invented sufficient vile calumnies against them she took up her child and rocked him in her arms. He was her hope, her all.... He was destined for greatness.... Someday his name would be on everybody's lips....

And then one day her erring husband returned. The exact date is not recorded but it must have been in 1789 or 1790, and he made it brutally plain that his visit was not inspired by affection but by a need for hard cash. The scene which ensued was terrific, with Mrs. Byron shouting that she and her precious son were living in penury, and Captain Byron shouting back that if she did not raise money somehow he would be thrown into prison for debt, or worse. To drive his point home he then picked up the young Geordie and carried him off to the rooms he had taken in the city, declaring that the boy was a true Byron and that his place was with his father. Not unnaturally the child was so frightened by this sudden abduction that he screamed the night through and was sent back to his hysterical mother with the message that he was a "squalling brat." Somehow she raised a little money and the gallant Captain departed, speeded on his way by the threats of his creditors to have him arrested if he lingered in England. Although not yet forty years old he was worn out by his excesses, and in 1791 his wife received word that he had died in Valenciennes.

One might have expected Mrs. Byron's predominant feeling to be one of relief. In the six years of their marriage her husband had humiliated her in every possible way, dissipated her considerable fortune, and alienated the sympathy both of her family and his own. But whether she still loved the man, or whether his treatment of her had slightly unhinged her mind, the news of his death sent her into paroxysms of grief, and it was probably about this time that she began to seek solace for her misery in the whisky bottle. Whenever she felt her sorrows too great to be borne she took a little dram—never in public but in the privacy of her own room—and when the spirit sent a tingling glow through her she knew an urgency to tell somebody all the thoughts that thronged her mind. Unfortunately, there was nobody to tell except Geordie.

Much has been written about Byron's tragic heritage, but while I fully agree that this played a large part in his complex character I feel convinced that his childhood, spent with his garrulous, vindictive mother, played an even larger one. From babyhood onwards she fed his mind with stories in which it was impossible to distinguish fact from fiction.

To begin with, the stories were eulogies of his dead father. He must never forget that Captain Byron had been a brave soldier who had covered himself with glory while on active service. In society he had been the most handsome and popular man of his age and the horrible scandals spread about him were mere inventions made up by his rivals in the lists of love. It was quite untrue to say that he had seduced Lady Carmarthen and then killed her by his brutal neglect. He had been romantically in love with the lady (though it was inferred here that he had been far more deeply attached to his second wife). He had spent much time in

France because his Norman ancestry was strong within him, and he had made close friends with the aged Marshal Biron, Commandant of the French Guards, who was sure they had sprung from the same stock. And what wonderful stock it was! The de Buruns, as they were then, had come over with the Conqueror and were mentioned in the Domesday Book. One Ralph de Burun had been granted lands in Nottinghamshire and Lancashire by Edward I. On the dissolution of the monasteries Henry VIII had made a royal grant of Newstead priory and the surrounding lands to "Sir John Byron the Little, with the great beard," one of his most doughty and trusted friends; and in 1643 the ill-fated Charles I had created a Sir John Byron Baron Byron of Rochdale. Moreover, the stock had not weakened. Young Geordie must always remember that his grandfather, Admiral Byron, had won tremendous public sympathy after his ship had been wrecked in 1750, and that his great-uncle, the present Lord Byron, had been fully justified in killing the quarrelsome Mr. Chaworth in a duel. One day, she assured her son, he would revive—nay, outdo—all the glory his ancestors had achieved, for she could probe the future and she knew that some day he would be the sixth Lord Byron.

Over and over again did Mrs. Byron repeat these tales of Byronic valor to her son, and in addition she told him the history of the Gordons, reminding him that in his veins ran the blood of proud Scottish kings; and as the little boy limped along the wind-swept streets with his nursemaid he dreamed of the greatness which was assuredly going to come to him. He was a highly intelligent child and, probably because of his lameness, abnormally sensitive. Apart from the Gray sisters, two country girls who somehow put up with Mrs. Byron's tantrums and seem to have acted alternately as maids over a long period, his mother was the only person in his small world. He adored her and, alas, he believed implicitly every word she said. Buoyed up by her stories he even managed, temporarily, to forget his physical disability. When some well-meaning acquaintance said, "What a pretty boy! What a pity he has such a leg!" he merely laughed and answered, "Dinna' speak of it!"; and when he met a boy with a similar deformity he shouted gleefully to the nursemaid, "Come and see the two laddies with the twa club feet going up the Broad Street!"

Apart from his lameness young Geordie was a sturdy, plump child with wavy auburn hair, remarkably fine eyes, a determined chin, and a very white skin; and his handsome appearance led to many fulsome compliments from Aberdeen ladies. He appreciated these enormously, repeating them with gusto to his mother, so perhaps it was just as well that he shortly began attending a small mixed school where he had to rub shoulders with children of his own age. This establishment was kept by a Mr. Bowers, a small, dapper man known to everybody as "Bodsy," whose teaching ability seems to have been strictly limited since Byron wrote years afterwards that he "learned little there, except to repeat by rote the first lesson of Monosyllables—'God made man, let us love him'—by hearing it often repeated, without acquiring a letter." For a year he remained under "Bodsy's" care, but when it was discovered that he merely chanted the words like a parrot and was quite unable to read them, he was removed.

His next teacher was a Presbyterian minister named Ross, "a very decent, clever little Clergyman," and under his care Geordie quickly learned to read—and, what was perhaps more important, to become interested in history. He received, too, a thorough grounding in Calvinistic beliefs and doctrines which was to influence him for the rest of his life. At neither of these early schools did he form any close friendships with other children, although he joined in their games. He could not forget that he was a Byron, an aristocrat, a being apart.

But when the boy was about six years old his consciousness of grandeur received a rude jolt. With the passing of time Mrs. Byron's noisy grief over her husband's death had faded to an occasional mutter and she had become a martyr to self-pity.

Huddled by the smoky fire in her draughty sitting room she reflected on her tragic lot. Everyone had left her, she was perpetually short of money, she had done nothing to deserve such misery. And as she brooded so, anger began to stir in her. It had all been Jack Byron's fault. He had swept her off her feet with his fine promises and loving looks, and then he had cast her into the depths. Then there was that horrible old man at Newstead—no wonder they called him the "Wicked Lord"!—who ignored the existence of herself and her son.... Having fortified herself with two or three nips of whisky Mrs. Byron decided that she hated the Byrons, hated them....!

Soon the inevitable happened. The child came home one afternoon to a frenzied mother who told stories vastly different from her earlier ones. When at last she fell exhausted into her chair and started to weep he crept from the room in bewilderment. How could the gallant, handsome father of whose exploits he had heard so much suddenly turn into a savage bully? How could his great-uncle, who had done a Grand Tour of Europe and been appointed Master of Staghounds after his acquittal by his peers, suddenly become a mean, cruel old man known as the "Wicked Lord"? He worked these problems over and over in his small mind and came to the conclusion that these terrible new tales simply were not true. When his mother sought him out, still weeping, and strained him to her breast crying that he was her precious wee son, he made an instinctive movement of recoil. From that moment onwards he never fully trusted her.

It is doubtful if a sensitive little boy who had dreamed so much of his wonderful heritage would have forgotten his mother's outburst even if it had been an isolated incident. But Geordie had no chance to forget because Mrs. Byron's temper now seemed ungovernable and distressing scenes occurred with increasing frequency. Not only did she repeat her ravings about the Byron family; she taunted her child about his deformity. "Ye lame brat," she would shout, "get out o' my sight!" and very likely she would pick up some object and hurl it at him to aid his progress to the door. Half an hour afterwards she would be full of maudlin contrition and make bad worse by spinning him garbled accounts of the cause of his lameness. Exactly what she said to him is not known, but it became firmly implanted in his mind that she, and she alone, was responsible for the deformity which gave him so much pain and unhappiness. That he never forgave her is made clear in his drama, *The Deformed Transformed*, which opens with a mother saying to her son, "Out, hunchback!" and the son retorting, "I was born so, mother!" Even more significant is the answer he gives when she sneers that his back must bear its burden:

> It *bears* its burthen;—but, my heart!
> Will it
> Sustain that which you lay upon it, mother?
> I love, or, at the least, I loved you; nothing
> Save you, in nature, can love aught like me.
> You nursed me—do not kill me!

These lines show that despite her cruelty towards him Byron's hatred of his mother was, years after her death, still strangely tempered by love.

But at the age of six or seven he could not analyze his emotions. He was a confused and angry little boy, and when his mother raged and threw things at him he raged and threw things back at her. The scenes between them were deplorable, yet perhaps neither of them can be blamed. Geordie had suffered a great deal from the treatments devised by doctors who had tried in vain to cure his condition, and the knowledge that it was his parent who had made such suffering necessary was bitter indeed. Kitty Byron had never been a particularly stable character, and doubtless her wretched married life had increased her instability and caused her to seek refuge in the whisky bottle. One tragic fact stands out—it was she who inculcated the habit of violence in her son.

Byron in the costume of a Greek Legionnaire.
From a painting by Thomas Phillips.

Lady Caroline Lamb.   Lady Byron.

Countess Teresa Guiccioli from a drawing by Hayter.

❊ 3 ❊

Fortunately, as Geordie grew in stature, outside interests claimed more of his time and attention. There were summer holidays spent at Lochnagar, where the dark beauty of the lake set among frowning mountains made a deep impression on his mind. Here the child had a welcome respite from Mrs. Byron's tongue, for she was so busy trying to edge her way into the society of such nearby landowners as Lord Fife and Farquharson of Invercauld that she left him to the care of the sisters Gray. By now, owing to the death of the "Wicked Lord's" grandson, Mrs. Byron's wild assertion that her son was destined to become the sixth Lord Byron had unexpectedly come true, and as mother to the heir to a peerage she considered it her duty to mix once more with *suitable* people. Whether she succeeded in doing so is extremely doubtful, but at least her social aspirations kept her occupied and allowed her child to enjoy his holidays in peace.

It was necessary (in Mrs. Byron's opinion) for a prospective peer to learn Latin, and as this subject did not apparently come within Mr. Ross's curriculum, Geordie was sent to be coached in it. "I had," he wrote, "a very serious, saturnine, but kind young man, named Paterson, for a Tutor: he was the son of my Shoemaker but a good Scholar, as is common with the Scotch. He was a rigid Presbyterian also. With him I began Latin in Ruddiman's Grammar, and continued till I went to the 'Grammar School' (*Scotice* 'Schule'—*Aberdonice* 'Squeel'), where I threaded all the classes to the *fourth,* when I was recalled to England (where I had been hatched) by the demise of my Uncle."

One feels it likely that Geordie learned more than Latin from the saturnine Paterson. The Calvinistic beliefs already implanted would be strengthened and, since shoemakers were notoriously

Radical and presumably passed on their views to their sons, maybe the pupil would imbibe from the tutor certain ideas on Liberalism.

When Geordie was not quite eight years old he fell head over heels in love with a little girl named Mary Duff, a distant cousin, and this precocious attachment had, according to what he wrote in his Journal in 1813, a tremendous and lasting effect upon him. "I had and have been attached fifty times since that period; yet I recollect all we said to each other, all our caresses, her features, my restlessness, sleeplessness, my tormenting my mother's maid to write for me to her, which she at last did, to quiet me. Poor Nancy thought I was wild, and, as I could not write for myself, became my secretary. I remember, too, our walks, and the happiness of sitting by Mary, in the children's apartment, at their house not far from the Plain-stanes at Aberdeen, while her lesser sister Helen played with the doll, and we sat gravely making love, in our way. How the deuce did all this occur so early? where could it originate? I certainly had no sexual ideas for years afterwards; and yet my misery, my love for that girl were so violent, that I sometimes doubt if I have ever been really attached since."

Byron often exaggerated when recalling his early loves, but it seems clear from Tom Moore's biography that he thought of little save Mary for several months and was inconsolable when —owing to some indiscretion on the part of her mother—she was sent away to live with her grandmother at Banff. On the other hand John Cam Hobhouse, one of Byron's closest friends, penciled in his copy of Moore's *Life* that he was "acquainted with a singular fact, scarcely fit for narration but much less romantic and more satisfactory than the amour with Mary Duff." What this sinister-sounding fact was we have no means of telling. Byron may have confided the secret of some less innocent affair to his friend; he may equally well have invented some discreditable tale to shock the slightly pompous Hobhouse. What is definite is that the young Geordie was devoted to Mary, that

Mrs. Byron constantly twitted him about her, and that when he reached the age of sixteen she announced with malicious pleasure, "Oh, Byron, I have had a letter from Edinburgh, from Miss Abercrombie, and your old sweetheart Mary Duff is married to a Mr. Cockburn." The news had a disastrous effect on her son. "I really cannot explain or account for my feelings at that moment," he wrote, "but they nearly threw me into convulsions, and alarmed my mother so much, that after I grew better she generally avoided the subject—to *me*—and contented herself with telling it to all her acquaintance."

While he was still smarting over Mary's disappearance Geordie entered Aberdeen Grammar School, which consisted of some hundred and fifty boys. These were divided into five classes which were taught by four masters—the Headmaster managing somehow to attend to the two senior classes—and Paterson must have coached to good purpose for Geordie acquitted himself well in his lessons. Despite his lameness he ran in the game of "bases" and proved remarkably handy with his fists when offered some real or fancied taunt by a schoolfellow. On the whole, however, he was well liked by both masters and boys for, away from his mother, he was a lively, warm-hearted child with a great sense of fun.

Then on a day in 1798 he was summoned to the Headmaster's study and informed that as his great-uncle had died he was now Lord Byron. It was a solemn occasion but he rose to it with an aplomb seldom seen in a ten-year-old child. Gravely he accepted the slice of cake and glass of wine proffered by way of celebration and received his master's congratulations with a touch of hauteur before returning to his classroom. Later, however, at roll-call, when his name was read out with *"Dominum"* before it, the tears rushed to his eyes and he was so overcome that he could not answer *"Adsum."* Later still, trudging homewards through the gray streets he pondered the glories of his new position. He wasn't Geordie any longer; he was a *lord*. He would not live in cheap lodgings near Aberdeen's fish market any longer; he would live in a great, wonderful house called Newstead Abbey. He would travel the world, fight in battles, meet kings and princes, reach for the stars and hold them in his hand.

He found his mother in a whirl of packing and a state of wild excitement. She insisted upon calling him Byron forthwith and, as she darted round the room, regaled him with details of their immediate movements. They were to journey south to Nottinghamshire with all possible speed so that he might take up his inheritance. . . . The Earl of Carlisle had been appointed as his guardian; Mr. Hanson, the Byron family lawyer, would administer the estates of Newstead and Rochdale until he came of age. As he listened the young Byron's heart swelled within him. The future was going to be miraculous indeed.

❋ 4 ❋

To any pair less buoyed up by dreams than Mrs. Byron and her son the mere sight of Newstead would have been a grievous disappointment. The west front of the original Abbey Church, now literally falling to pieces, was joined on to a mansion built in Tudor times which was also in a ruined condition. The ground floor consisted of a succession of storerooms with high vaulted ceilings, and access to the house itself was provided by a flight of steps which led, by way of a hideous and gigantic porch, into the Great Hall. From this ran the West Corridor with windows overlooking the cloister garden, and beyond the corridor was an enormous Great Drawing Room. Both hall and drawing room were in a shocking state of disrepair, while the smaller rooms— particularly the bedrooms and kitchens—were even worse. The "Wicked Lord" had allowed the whole place to go to rack and ruin while he shut himself up in the Prior's Dining Room, a small apartment behind the hall, and amused himself with his concubine and his tame crickets. Moreover, he had felled and sold every tree on the surrounding parkland, so that the view from the windows was yet more depressing than the house itself.

But to Byron and his mother the derelict state of the place meant little—what satisfied them was that it was so vast. Their disillusionment only began when they interviewed Lord Carlisle —who not surprisingly took an instant dislike to Mrs. Byron and found his ward's Scots voice so uncouth he couldn't understand a word the child said. The nobleman announced coldly that there could be no question of *living* in Newstead as the place was totally uninhabitable and the estate so impoverished that the extensive repairs needed could not possibly be carried out. He added tersely that in his opinion the Rochdale lands were in as bankrupt a condition as the Newstead ones. Mr. John Hanson, the lawyer, was scarcely more cheering, but he did make a considerable effort to explain the situation. It would take several years to carry out improvements on both estates and until they were put right the income from them would necessarily be small. It was believed that there was coal underneath the Rochdale lands, but if this were so the negotiations for mining operations would take time. Meanwhile, he suggested that Mrs. Byron should take rooms in or near London, send her son to some suitable school, and allow them to try to find a tenant for the Abbey.

Mrs. Byron, as was her wont, behaved extremely badly. She wept, she ranted, she made the most outrageous suggestions about the dishonesty inherent in all lawyers, she accused Lord Carlisle of misrepresenting facts, she said the Rochdale coal mining should be started immediately. To her dismay she was then informed that there was litigation in progress over Rochdale since the late Lord Byron had indulged in such complicated manuevers with the property that there was some doubt whether it was still part of the young lord's inheritance. After further argument she agreed reluctantly to send Byron to Dulwich Grove School the following term and to take rooms somewhere in its vicinity.

For a brief spell, however, Byron knew the joy of living in Newstead. It was late autumn: the wind scudded across the treeless park, to whip the gray waters of the mere into little waves; the huge, echoing, draughty house was cold and uncomfortable. But the boy did not even notice such things. For him Newstead was peopled by the ghosts of those long-dead Byrons who had fought so nobly, and for hours on end he would stand in the Prior's Dining Room gazing up at the mantelpiece which displayed the arms of "little Sir John with the great beard." This was his very own home. When he was a man he would live here (no matter what Lord Carlisle or Mr. Hanson said) and for his private rooms he would choose the two at the top of the spiral stairway leading from the Gallery, because from the windows of the larger one he could see in the foreground the entrance court with its hexagonal fountain and in the distance the wind-ruffled mere.

While her son dreamed Mrs. Byron bustled round the neighborhood looking up such old friends and acquaintances of the Byron family as she could summon to mind. At most houses her welcome was a cool one, partly because the "Wicked Lord" had quarreled with nearly everyone in the district, and partly because the people she called on did not like the look of this blowsy, breathless female who gushed to them about her dear brilliant boy. Being an arrant snob she persisted with her efforts and was delighted when Mrs. Parker, who had been born Charlotte Augusta Byron, showed signs of friendship. Mrs. Parker had two little girls, Augusta and Margaret, about the same age as Byron, and much to his mother's satisfaction he condescended to play with them.

It was to Mrs. Parker, indeed, that Byron wrote his first letter:

Newstead Abbey, Nov. 8th, 1798

DEAR MADAM:

My Mamma being unable to write herself desires I will let you know that the potatoes are now ready and you are welcome to them whenever you please.

36

She begs you will ask Mrs. Parkyns if she would wish the poney to go round by Nottingham or to go home the nearest way as it is now quite well but too small to carry me.

I have sent a young Rabbit which I beg Miss Frances will accept off and which I promised to send before. My Mamma desires her best compliments to you all in which I join.

I am, Dear Aunt, your sincerely, BYRON.

I hope you will excuse all blunders as it is the first letter I ever wrote.

Two years later Byron fell in love with Margaret Parker with all the fervor he had displayed over Mary Duff. She inspired his first dash into poetry and, as with all his early loves, her memory stayed with him. "I have long forgotten the verses, but it would be difficult for me to forget her," he wrote. "Her dark eyes! her long eye-lashes! her completely Greek cast of face and figure!" Both Margaret and her sister died of consumption while Byron was at Harrow and, according to him, "Margaret coloured through the paleness of mortality to the eyes" when somebody mentioned his name to her shortly before her death. But in 1798 there was no lovesick sighing and suing and the children played happily together while Mrs. Byron played the Lady Bountiful as though tumbledown Newstead was a rich and flourishing estate.

January came all too soon, and with their departure from Newstead the uneasy truce between mother and son broke down. As usual Mrs. Byron was at fault. Lord Carlisle was one of the few people for whom she had a wholesome fear, so she duly deposited Byron at Dulwich Grove, where he had a bed in the study of Dr. Glennie, the Headmaster. She herself stayed near at hand—too near—and began a campaign of interference. She wrote copious notes to Dr. Glennie about various aspects of education—a subject on which she was totally ignorant. She exasperated the poor man by reminding him continually that, because of his *rank*, her son merited treatment quite different to that given to other boys. She called in the middle of school hours and insisted loudly that Byron must be allowed out for the rest of the day.

Byron had hated his mother for her behavior to him in Aberdeen: now, for the first time, he was deeply ashamed of her. He had not wanted to go to Dulwich Grove, and he had resented Dr. Glennie's dictum that he had to go back to the beginning in Latin in order to study it "in one of the forms prescribed by English schools"; but after an initial sulkiness he had settled down fairly well. Now his mother had to blunder in and upset everything. And it was all so humiliating. Why, only the other day a schoolfellow had said to him, "Byron, your mother is a fool," and he had been obliged to answer, "I know it!" It was of no use to remonstrate with her either—he had tried to do so and the result had been a tempestuous scene which outdid in violence any they had had in earlier days.

For the two years he remained at Dulwich Grove his mother was a constant menace to Byron's peace of mind. He never knew when she was going to appear in Dr. Glennie's study with a shrill demand that he should forsake his books and sally forth with her on some expedition, usually a social one for she dearly loved introducing "my son, *Lord* Byron," to her various acquaintances. Terrified lest she lost her temper in front of the Headmaster, Byron accompanied her reluctantly and sat in gloomy boredom while she and her companions indulged in tittle-tattle. But there was one call they made which more than compensated the boy for the tedium he usually endured among his mother's friends. They went to see Lady Holderness, with whom lived Byron's half-sister Augusta. It was a curious visit for Mrs. Byron to make, because she had long ago vowed that the family of the first Mrs. Byron were a worthless lot and that the two children of "Mad Jack" should never meet. But since her son's succession to the title her social ambitions had led her to change her ever erratic mind about many things (as witness her wooing of the Parkers) and she had lately decided to cultivate all the Byron relations.

Lady Holderness, Augusta's maternal grandmother, disliked Mrs. Byron at sight—a dislike which was fully reciprocated. Politeness, however, had to be observed, so while the two ladies exchanged pleasantries the young folk conversed at the far end of the room. Augusta was about fifteen—almost a young woman in those days. She had large dark eyes and a sweet full mouth, dark curly hair and a well-shaped head set delicately on a long slender neck. Byron was entranced by her appearance, but he was even more captivated by her low melodious voice, her delicious sense of fun, the way her hands fluttered as she talked. She called him "Baby B."—from any other lips the name would have infuriated him—and he thought it delightful. They laughed and talked and laughed again and Byron would have stayed happily beside her all day had not his mother told him sharply it was time to leave. All the way back to Dulwich she railed against Lady Holderness, but for once her son did not hear her. He was thinking of the wonderful bright being he had just left. Never before had he met anyone whose ideas fitted in so well with his own, whose charm was so potent. And she was his *sister*—was not "sister" the loveliest word in the language? Oh, it was wonderful to have a sister of one's very own!

❋ 5 ❋

In 1801 Byron was sent to Harrow, where the redoubtable Dr. Joseph Drury had been Headmaster for some seventeen years, and for some time the boy was acutely miserable. At Dulwich Grove he had been someone of importance: at Harrow, surrounded by young aristocrats, he was made to feel inferior— and it was not a sensation he enjoyed. His lameness tried him sorely, and in an effort to overcome it he neglected his books and concentrated all his energies on boxing, cricket and swimming. He imagined that he had shaken off his mother's influence but

39

he was entirely wrong. She had given him false ideas of grandeur, she had shown him the value of hatred as a weapon, she had taught him violence—and she had performed her task so well that these attributes were now part of his character. If a master reprimanded him he was arrogant and insolent; if a schoolfellow offended him he immediately challenged him to a fight. His particular enemy was his tutor, Henry Drury, and very early in his Harrow career Dr. Drury was obliged to write to Mrs. Byron, "My son and Lord Byron have had some disagreements; but I hope that his future behavior will render a change of Tutors unnecessary?"

The tutor was not changed; but it is worth noting that Byron frequently invoked the aid of the mother he was supposed to hate in an effort to bring about that change. As late as May 1st, he wrote her a passionate epistle denouncing Henry Drury.

Byron had broken a rule by speaking in church to the boy next to him, and after the service Mr. Drury had ignored Byron and taken the other boy to his study—

> ...where he abused me in a most violent manner, called me *blackguard,* said he *would* and *could* have me expelled from the School, and bade me thank his *Charity* that *prevented* him; this was the Message he sent me, to which I shall return no answer, but submit my case to *you* and those you may think *fit* to *consult.* Is this fit usage for any body! had I *stole* or behaved in the most *abominable* way to him, his language could not have been more outrageous. What must the boys think of me to hear such a Message ordered to be delivered to me by a *Master?* Better let him take away my life than ruin my *Character....*

There was much more in the same strain and Byron closed his letter with an urgent plea that his mother write to Dr. Drury. "If you do not take notice of this," he added dramatically, "I will leave the School myself; but I am sure *you* will not see me *ill-treated;* better that I should suffer anything than this. I believe you will be tired by this time of reading my letter, but, if you love me, you will now show it. Pray write me immediately.'

I shall ever remain, Your affectionate Son." A postscript contained the words, "God bless, bless you."

This was scarcely the letter of an unloving son and, needless to say, it was one Mrs. Byron was delighted to receive. Fortunately there were two reasons against immediate action on her part. The first was that she had already found her usual nuisance tactics to be worthless so far as Dr. Drury was concerned, since that wise man knew exactly how to deal with problem parents. The second was that she was now living at Burgage Green in Southwell, a market town near Newstead, a long coach journey from her aggrieved child. She did, however, write him a great deal of ill-advised nonsense and shouted her opinion of Henry Drury round Southwell drawing rooms.

Her efforts were wasted. By the time her letter reached Harrow the volatile Byron had lost interest in the affair and was absorbed in another of more importance. One of his most cherished possessions was a bust of Napoleon Bonaparte, his romantic hero, and when news came of the First Consul's plans for conquering the East he had to defend this treasure from several indignant schoolfellows who wished to smash it. He won the battle and his scornful descriptions of his opponents as "rascally time-servers" brought him the admiration of a group of younger boys, among them being the Duke of Dorset, the Earl of Clare, the Earl de la Warr, and John Wingfield. For the remainder of his stay at Harrow these children were his devoted slaves, fighting with each other for the privilege of fulfilling his least behest. Byron behaved towards them rather after the manner of a Sultan distributing favors to the ladies of his harem— and perhaps, who knows, their relationship may have been tinged with the homosexual ideas which often accompany adolescence. Certainly he wrote in his Ravenna journal in 1821: "My school friendship were with *me passions* (for I was always violent)," and of Lord Clare he remarked he had loved him "better than any *male* thing in the world."

Now that he was surrounded by friends Byron found Harrow

a vastly more pleasant place, and while he had several brushes with Mark Drury he quite forgot his animosity towards Henry and became sincerely attached to him. He was still somewhat lethargic about his studies but, despite his lameness, played cricket and took a great interest in boxing. Swimming, however, was his favorite sport and one in which he excelled.

But in contrast to happy schooldays there were holidays at Burgage with a mother whose temper was ever uncertain and a tenant at Newstead whose behavior had given Byron great offense. He was Lord Grey de Ruthyn and in 1803 he had rented the Abbey for a term of five years. At first Byron had been a frequent visitor to the home he loved, but within twelve months some serious rift had occurred. Exactly what happened is not known, but in his copy of Moore's *Life* John Cam Hobhouse scribbled in the margin, "A circumstance occurred during this intimacy which certainly had much effect on his [Byron's] future morals," and Byron himself threw out dark hints in letters to his sister Augusta:

> I am not reconciled to Lord Grey, *and I never will*. He was once my *Greatest Friend*, my reasons for ceasing that Friendship are such as I cannot explain, not even to you, my Dear Sister, (although were they to be made known to any body, you would be the first,) but they will ever remain hidden in my own breast.

Mrs. Byron was extremely indignant with her son for quarreling with their influential tenant and not only flew into one of her celebrated rages when he refused to discuss the matter but thereafter nagged him on the subject in public. Whether or not there had been any attempted seduction of the boy, the humiliation his mother caused him over the affair must have been well-nigh intolerable and his continued silence on the matter was wholly admirable.

When Mrs. Byron had exhausted herself and everybody else by her outbursts on the Lord Grey quarrel she retired to sulk— and to commune with the whisky bottle—and for the remainder of that particular holiday she sat huddled in her chair, a morose figure who ignored all attempts to improve her mood. But by the long summer vacation of 1804 she was again in fighting trim and this time she accused her son of banding her bitterest enemies into a league against her. It was his fault that Lord Carlisle refused to see or write to her. It was thanks to his scurrilous tales that Mr. Hanson the lawyer gave her the merest pittance as an allowance (at the time she was a great deal better off than she had been since she sold her own property). Worst of all, he was exchanging letters with that cat Augusta, in whose veins ran the quintessence of the vile Byron blood (this was followed by the usual tirade against Mad Jack and his forebears).

Byron could scarcely be blamed for shutting himself into his room and pouring out his woes to his sister.

> No captive Negro, or Prisoner of war, ever looked forward to their emancipation, and return to Liberty with more Joy, and with more lingering expectation, than I do to my escape from this maternal bondage, and this accursed place, which is the region of dullness itself, and more stupid than the banks of Lethe, though it possesses contrary qualities to the river of oblivion, as the detested scenes I now witness, make me regret the happier ones already passed, and wish their restoration.

He had always been highly sensitive: now he grew abnormally so, for when his mother was not attacking the Byron family she poked cruel fun at his personal appearance. As a small child he had been plump but since entering his teens he had become really stout—a condition he hated and did his best to remedy by living on fruit and vegetables and the swallowing of powerful purges each night. With calculated venom Mrs. Byron drew the attention of all her acquaintances to his size, adding that she thought it positively ludicrous that he should waste so much time on the care of his small plump hands (of which he was inordinately proud) when he couldn't stop biting his nails.

One sometimes wonders if Mrs. Byron's vicious remarks were not at least partially responsible for the death of a calf-love affair which occurred about this time. When away from his Harrow adorers Byron was extremely susceptible to feminine wiles, and during his holidays at Burgage he had fallen madly in love with Mary Chaworth, a girl a year or two his senior. The Chaworths lived near by at Annesley Hall and it was a relative of theirs who had been killed in a duel by the "Wicked Lord"—a piece of history which fed fuel to Byron's fire. How wonderful it would be, he thought, if by the union between himself and Mary the long-standing family feud could be wiped out and his great-uncle's deed forgiven. He thought of his beloved as "the Morning Star of Annesley," haunted her mother's drawing room where he stood silent in a corner staring at her out of dreamy eyes, wrote poems to her, cherished a lock of her hair, and went through agonies every time she looked at anyone else. His love was practically inarticulate, but on the rare occasions when he summoned up the courage to address his divinity his mother's voice would boom some slighting reference to his figure.

Years afterwards Byron gave his friends an exaggerated account of his sufferings over Mary Chaworth, insinuating that he had never recovered from her spurning of his love; but there is no doubt that he did suffer greatly at the time and that his torment was accentuated by his mother's behavior. Perhaps too, if Mrs. Byron had held her peace, he might have been spared the unkindest cut of all—the knowledge that his Morning Star had alluded to him contemptuously as "that fat boy."

Byron went back to Harrow in the January of 1805 wrapped in misery over his failure to win Mary's affection, and when he heard of her marriage to Jack Musters, a dissolute local squire, he gave vent to his feelings in eight pathetic lines:

> Hills of Annesley, bleak and barren,
>   Where my thoughtless childhood stray'd,
> How the northern tempests, warring,
>   Howl above thy tufted shade!

Now no more, the hours beguiling,
Former favourite haunts I see;
Now no more my Mary smiling
Makes ye seem a heaven to me.

By Easter, however, he had recovered sufficiently to enjoy the company of John and Elizabeth Bridget Pigot, who also lived at Southwell. (In her old age Elizabeth recollected him as a "fat, bashful boy with his hair combed straight over his forehead"). And by July he was writing in high feather to Augusta, telling her he had just been up to Cambridge to enter himself at Trinity College and inviting her to Speech Day at Harrow. "... but for *Godsake* bring as few women with you as possible. ...*I beg, Madam,* you may make your appearance in one of his Lordship's most *dashing* carriages, as our Harrow *etiquette,* admits of nothing but the most *superb* vehicles, on our Grand *Festivals.*"

Setting aside Mary Chaworth's defection Byron had cause to feel happy that summer term. He had played in the Eton and Harrow match and although Harrow was "most confoundedly beat" he made eleven runs in the first innings and seven in the second despite his handicap of lameness. The mere fact of having been chosen for his school eleven did much to raise his spirits, and his group of young favorites were loud in their admiration of his achievement. Moreover, much as he had enjoyed the latter part of his stay at Harrow he was exhilarated by the knowledge that in a few short weeks he would cease to be a schoolboy, a role which had long irked him. To be sure there were still the summer holidays to live through before he went up to Cambridge, but he had no intention of spending the whole ten weeks at Burgage and indulged in a little pardonable duplicity by telling his mother that school did not break up until August 6th when, in fact, the real date was July 31st.

He wished to spend these stolen few days with friends in London so that he might see his half-sister, and he even enlisted the aid of Mr. Hanson, begging him to "connive at this deception." But Mrs. Byron, while extraordinarily foolish in many ways, had an uncanny faculty for scenting out her son's little ruses and wrote to say that she proposed to visit London herself during the first week in August. Poor Byron had to cancel his plans and was at Burgage by August 4th. He had, however, managed to squeeze in a visit to Augusta, a fact quickly discovered by his mother who immediately lost her temper. She had always disliked Augusta simply because she was the child of Mad Jack's first marriage: now she saw her as a potential rival. Byron was seventeen and once he was up at Cambridge, where she could not watch his every movement, he would grow away from her and come under the influence of this detestable girl who was his only other close relative. Unable to control her jealousy she made the long summer days hideous with her ceaseless recriminations. How dared Byron sneak off to see his sister behind her back? Why did he and Augusta exchange so many letters? Had he no feeling for the mother who had lavished such loving care upon him?

Her tirades had their usual depressing effect. Byron's high spirits vanished and melancholy overcame him. He was aware by now that his mother's attacks on the Byron family owed a great deal to her powers of invention, but there was enough truth in them to cause him grave unease and, try as he might, he could not shake off the conviction that he was destined to suffer his life long for the sins of his fathers. Only the previous year he had written to Mrs. Byron, "I will carve myself the passage to Grandeur, but never with Dishonour"; but no echo of those words came to him as he brooded over his fate, and what drove him almost to despair was the knowledge that his sister, that innocent creature of sweetness and light, must share in the Byronic doom. Escape for either of them was out of the question —but if they were together, if they were able to turn to each other whenever danger threatened, surely their lot would be eased? As he listened to his mother's diatribes Byron determined that so soon as he attained his majority he and Augusta would live at Newstead, two against the world.

His plans were fantastic, but he was an unhappy boy of seventeen and he craved affection and understanding. He was also lonely—because apart from his young admirers at Harrow he had no really close friends—and he did not realize that if he had been in a position to invite Augusta to share Newstead with him straight away she would have crowed with laughter, called him her "Baby B.", and dismissed the notion as preposterous. For Augusta, brought up fondly and carefully by her grandmother Lady Holderness, had no conception of the fears which haunted her half-brother. Pretty, feckless, always inclined to take the line of least resistance, she sent soothing replies to Byron's anguished letters (poor "Baby B.", he exaggerated so!) and turned back to enjoyment of country-house gaieties and the companionship of a dashing but dissolute cousin, Colonel George Leigh of the Tenth Dragoons.

Byron had no such solace, but as September merged into October he knew a slight lifting of the gloom which had enwrapped him. In two weeks, in a week, he would be in Cambridge—but even as he supervised his packing, bade farewell to the Pigots and a few other friends, and made arrangements for his black and white Newfoundland dog, Boatswain, to be looked after by a trusted servant, two words echoed through his mind: Augusta—Newstead—Augusta—Newstead. . . .

II

❋❋❋❋❋❋❋❋❋❋❋❋❋❋❋❋❋❋❋❋❋❋❋❋❋❋❋❋❋

The Myrtle and Ivy

CAMBRIDGE life proved so exhilarating that Byron soon forgot the dreary months at Burgage Green and his presentiment of doom. He found it entirely delightful to be treated like a man and not a schoolboy, to be able to give supper parties, to be free to go hither and thither as he pleased, to be greeted deferentially by tradespeople who called him "my Lord" with every breath and hastened to supply his lavish orders. He had his rooms redecorated and filled with new furniture; he laid in a stock of rare vintage wines; he purchased a fine gray horse and when riding it wore a gray coat and white hat; he bought books galore and on November 6th he wrote ecstatically to Augusta that his rooms were "*Super*-excellent," that he was allowed £500 a year and a manservant, and that he felt as "independent as a German Prince who coins his own cash, or a Cherokee Chief who coins no cash at all, but enjoys what is more precious, Liberty."

Many an undergraduate before and since Byron's day has been intoxicated by the first heady draught of freedom and has shortly awakened with an appalling hangover. But Byron was no normal youth. He was hyper-sensitive and extremely vain; he had been brought up by a coarse and ignorant mother who had dinned snobbism into him since babyhood; he held within him the seed of genius. Consequently his mental drunkenness lasted for several weeks, during which his behavior became ever more extravagant, his efforts to attract attention ever more pathetic.

He boxed in seven waistcoats and a greatcoat in an effort to get his weight down. In order to conceal his lameness he developed the habit of standing still at any gathering and gazing at the assembled company with an expression of ineffable disdain which he assumed because he imagined it suited his features. He used finicky little gestures when he talked so that people might notice his hands and he bored everybody within reach with snatches of the Byron family history.

His fellow students had no manner of use for such eccentricities. They thought him both bumptious and vulgar and pointedly refused his invitations, while John Cam Hobhouse (afterwards his closest friend) was heard to remark that any man who wore riding-kit to match his horse was beyond the pale.

At first Byron simply could not believe in his own unpopularity. Why, at Harrow he had always been surrounded by a group of adorers! But when people turned their backs ostentatiously as he approached he at last realized the truth—he was not wanted. In a mood of savage resentment he retreated to his rooms, where he stood by the windows alternately biting his nails and drumming on the panes. He was discovering that freedom had no savor if one was lonely, and in his misery he turned to Edward Long, the only friend of Harrow days who was available.

But Edward was a studious youth. He did not approve of Byron's nocturnal habits, or of the drinking of quantities of claret. His idea of a pleasant evening was to sit at his table with his nose buried in a book—and he expected his friend to do likewise. Byron grew quickly bored with this pursuit but, although he did not realize it at the time, it produced one excellent result. While Edward studied, Byron wrote verse.

And then he met John Edleston, a chorister who came from a lowly home. "His *voice* first attracted my attention," wrote Byron, "his *countenance* fixed it, and his *manners* attached me to him for ever." Edleston, a delicate boy already in the early stages of consumption, was overwhelmed by the kindnesses showered on him by his new friend and accorded him a doglike devotion so much to Byron's taste that he promptly forgot his ideas of life of seclusion with Augusta at Newstead and declared that he and Edleston would spend the rest of their lives together in an idyllic relationship which would put Pylades and Orestes "out of countenance."

It was a highly sentimental attachment, but although Byron afterwards vowed that he had been utterly absorbed in his love for the timid Edleston, at the time the company of his protégé did not mitigate his sense of loneliness. He could not forgive the unfriendly attitude of his fellow undergraduates: he could not forget the blissful contentment of the days when he had been surrounded by Dorset, Clare, Wingfield and the rest. He who had exulted in his new-found liberty but a few brief months before now mourned the fact that he was "no longer a boy."

His wretchedness was increased by a severe letter from Mr. Hanson, to whom he had applied for an advance on his allowance. In this the lawyer pointed out various extravagances and said coldly that no further money would be forthcoming until the due date. Byron was furious. It did not occur to him that, having no idea of the value of money, he had spent a whole year's income within a few weeks. He replied with a long, grandiloquent and absurd epistle in which he not only upbraided Hanson for deceiving him but assured him that "not even the Shadow of dishonor shall reflect on *my* Name, for I will see that the Bills are discharged; whether by you or not is to me indifferent, so that the men I employ are not the victims of my Imprudence or your Duplicity."

Mr. Hanson remained unmoved by these high-sounding words, and while bills descended like snowflakes Byron was further worried by a series of vituperative letters from his mother, who demanded that he should curb his expenditure and dismiss his manservant and threatened to come to Cambridge herself if he did not obey her orders. Exasperated beyond endurance Byron flounced off to London at the end of the term, took rooms at 16 Piccadilly, interviewed moneylenders, and wrote begging Augusta to act as joint security with him in raising seven or eight hundred pounds which he would repay on attaining his majority.

Whether she agreed to this proposal or not we do not know, but Byron's financial affairs grew steadily worse over the next three years and by the time he came of age his debts were around £12,000.

❋ 2 ❋

It was not until 1807 that Byron succeeded in making friends with the three men who had cold-shouldered him during his first term, John Cam Hobhouse, Scrope Berdmore Davies, and Charles Skinner Matthews. Up to this time he had lived doucely enough—though his natural extravagance caused him to spend far too much on living expenses, clothes, sparring partners, and dogs. Edleston was still in favor and touched his patron deeply by presenting him with a little cornelian heart. *Hours of Idleness*, a collection of his verses, was being prepared for publication by a Mr. Ridge of Newark.

But under the ægis of Hobhouse, Davies and Matthews life changed suddenly, gloriously. They were a gay, talented trio possessed of sufficient money to indulge their many whims and they introduced Byron to the most intriguing round of dissipations. With them he visited London and Brighton, where he gambled heavily and had a succession of affairs with ladies of the town. With them he attended rowdy, drunken parties at Cambridge. With them, in short, he learned how to live for the first time and he enjoyed it immensely.

51

All too soon Byron was so deeply in debt that he was forced to retreat temporarily to Burgage and Mrs. Byron with the excuse that he was seriously unwell. To Hanson, however, he wrote the truth.

> The Fact is I remain here because I can appear no where else, being *completely done* up. *Wine* and *Women* have dished your *humble Servant*, not a *Sou* to be *had;* all *over;* condemned to exist (I cannot say live) at this *Crater* of Dullness till my *Lease* of *Infancy* expires. To appear at Cambridge is impossible; no money even to pay my College expences.

He added that by violent exercise and fasting he had reduced his weight by eighteen pounds, an achievement which caused a rumor that he was in a decline to fly around Southwell drawing rooms.

Despite his bitter complaints Byron's sojourn at Burgage had its lighter moments. Now that he was older he had become adept at evading his mother's tantrums, and when he was not engaged in his weight-reducing activities he was playing in amateur theatricals with his good friends the Pigots; or visiting a clergyman, the Rev. John Becher, who gave him wholesome advice about his poems; or going over to Newark to interview Mr. Ridge about *Hours of Idleness.* But after his taste of debauchery, life at Southwell was unconsciously dull and by early summer either Mr. Hanson or some moneylender must have come to his assistance for he was back at Cambridge and making arrangements to stay up at Trinity another year. "At this moment," he wrote to Elizabeth Pigot, "I write with a bottle of claret in my *head* and tears in my *eyes;* for I have just parted with my '*Cornelian*,' who spent the evening with me.... I certainly love him more than any human being, and neither time nor distance have had the least effect on my (in general) changing disposition."

These brave words did not endure. Young Edleston left Cambridge to start work with a London merchant and Byron gallivanted off with his new friends. Moreover, he gave the precious cornelian heart to Elizabeth as a trifling keepsake.

The Pigots, both brother and sister, were astonishingly loyal to Byron, more loyal perhaps than he deserved. They entertained him constantly when he was obliged to be at Southwell; they were of great assistance in his dealings with Ridge; they kept an eye on his animals (particularly Boatswain) and wrote him long accounts of them. He rewarded them with long descriptions of his London dissipations, reiterated how much he loathed Southwell, and made the condescending remark that "the intelligence of London life cannot be interesting to you, who have rusticated all your life." And when *Hours of Idleness* appeared in London bookshops he wrote to Elizabeth that "a man whose works are praised by *reviewers*, admired *by duchesses*, and sold by every bookseller of the metropolis [surely a pardonable exaggeration], does not dedicate much consideration to *rustic readers.*"

But if Byron was at his most unlikable with the Pigots he was at his most lovable with Hobhouse, Davies and Matthews. Quick-witted, with a tremendous sense of the comic, he could be an enchanting companion when he chose and while his friends laughed at some of his eccentricities—as when he bought a tame bear and led it through Cambridge—they not only liked him but genuinely admired his gifts.

Others, unfortunately, did not admire them so much. In February, 1808, the *Edinburgh Review* published a scathing indictment of *Hours of Idleness.*

> As an author [wrote Byron to Hobhouse] I am cut to atoms by the E—— Review. It is just out, and has completely demolished my little fabric of fame. This is rather scurvy treatment from a Whig Review, but politics and poetry are different things, and I am no adept in either. I therefore submit in Silence.

And as if to emphasize his unconcern he went on:

> Last night at the Opera Masquerade, we supped with seven whores, a *Bawd* and a *Ballet Master*, in Madame Catalini's apartment behind the Scenes, (of course Catalini was not there). I have some thoughts of purchasing Dégrille's pupils: they would fill a glorious Haram.

53

But although Byron scoffed at what he called these "paper bullets of the brain" he was inwardly very sore indeed with the *Edinburgh Review* for he considered it had ridiculed him—and probably because of his deformity he could not bear to be laughed at. Alone in his rooms in the small hours he began to plan the revenge which eventually appeared under the title *English Bards and Scottish Reviewers.*

In the April of 1808 Lord Grey de Ruthyn left Newstead, and after his graduation Byron spent an agitated time settling into his ancestral home. The house was in even worse condition than when he had first seen it and, as usual, he was "cursedly dipped." However, with the assistance of the Rev. John Becher he did try to make a few rooms habitable—including the suite at the top of the spiral stairway leading from the Gallery, which he had long dreamed of making his own. Over the mantelpiece in his bedroom he hung a baroque mirror, and in the window recess with its views across the bare park to the mere he placed a round table at which he could write. But the dominant feature of the room was a bed specially made to his own design. It had a double-tiered cornice of gilded bamboo, from which hung thick olive-green curtains looped up with black and red cords. An inner layer of curtaining was of green chintz with a fantastic pattern of Chinese pagodas and African palm trees, and from each of the four corners of the tester winked a massive gilded coronet.

It mattered not to Byron that the greater part of his home was in ruins, that there were few servants, that the kitchens were a mass of rubble. At last he was living in his own house and was his own master—for Mrs. Byron, much against her will, had been denied access to Newstead and was still living at Burgage Green.

In the autumn Hobhouse came to stay with him and, having seemingly put away childish things since leaving Cambridge, the two young men spent a strangely decorous few weeks, shooting during the day and dining out around the neighborhood in the evening. Hobhouse also hunted but Byron, never a good horseman despite heroic efforts, wisely stayed at home putting the finishing touches to his *English Bards,* an excellent satire in eighteenth century style. The only event which marred their peace was the death of Boatswain on November 10th. Byron went into paroxysms of grief, declaring that he had "lost his only friend," and gave orders the dog was to be buried in the garden vault, which marked the site of the original high altar.

But Byron's main preoccupation that autumn was the planning of an Eastern tour the following year. After gravely informing Mr. Hanson that he wished to study Asiatic policy and manners he added, "I am young, tolerably vigorous, abstemious in my way of living," and went on to give a remarkably ingenious explanation of how much money such a tour would save. Mrs. Byron could be housed at Newstead during his absence, his horses could be sold, and there would be no necessity to purchase a house in London. Of course, there were his debts to be settled, but once this was done he could live very cheaply while abroad.

Fortunately, there was at last every hope that Byron's Rochdale property would prove extremely valuable. Mr. Hanson agreed to the Eastern tour and Byron wrote to Augusta, who had married Colonel Leigh the previous year and had just given birth to a daughter, that his pecuniary affairs were in a far better state than he or anybody else had hoped.

> Mrs. Byron I have shaken off for two years, and I shall not resume her yoke in future, I am afraid my disposition will suffer in your estimation; but I can never forgive that woman, or breathe in comfort under the same roof. I am a very unlucky fellow, for I think I had naturally not a bad heart; but it has been so bent, twisted and trampled on, that it has now become as hard as a Highlander's heelpiece.

Poor Byron was entirely wrong. His heart was always to remain extremely vulnerable.

In the January he came of age and shortly afterwards went up to London to take his seat in the House of Lords. It was not the most successful of occasions, for Byron, ever ready to imagine a slight, was convinced that his guardian, Lord Carlisle, was deliberately insulting in manner towards him. In consequence he behaved very badly, looking extremely bored and giving the Lord Chancellor (Lord Eldon) the haughtiest of bows before sprawling on one of the Opposition benches to the left of the throne instead of sitting primly on one of the Government benches. His fellow peers stared in disapproval. They thought his manner uncouth, to say the least, and young men who wrote verse were always suspect.

It was a relief to return to Newstead and plunge into preparations for his journey; for Hobhouse had decided to accompany him and they were to sail for Falmouth in June or July. But before then there were many things to be done. Byron had commissioned one of the foremost miniature painters of the day to depict his Harrow friends and he wished the collection completed before his departure. Then Mr. Hanson sent the bad news that it was impossible either to sell the Rochdale estate or work the coal there for a long time to come, and Mrs. Byron took hysterics and wailed they would all be ruined if her wicked son persisted in his wild ways. Finally Byron decided to give a farewell house party at Newstead for his Cambridge friends and this resulted in a scandal which set the ladies of Southwell agog for months, for he hired monastic habits from a theatrical costumier and the whole company, dressed in these, dined and wined for the better part of a night, occasionally toasting their host whom they had elected as Abbot. There were other incidents too which got bruited abroad. Charles Matthews had threatened to throw Hobhouse out of the window and there had been a disgraceful brawl. A maidservant had fled screaming across the park. The young men had quaffed wine—oh, gruesome thought!—out of a *skull*.

It was no wonder that before Byron sailed he had a scene with his mother which surpassed all earlier ones, and it was not surprising that he waited until he was at Falmouth to write her a dramatic farewell:

> As to money matters, I am ruined—at least till Rochdale is sold; and if that does not turn out well, I shall enter into the Austrian or Russian service—perhaps the Turkish, if I like their manners. The world is all before me, and I leave England without regret, and without a wish to revisit anything it contains, except *yourself*, and your present residence.

But in his heart Byron was conscious of an overwhelming sadness. He had dreamed so long of the niche he was destined to occupy in the great world, and that world had refused him his due, treated him with disdain.

❋ 3 ❋

Bankrupt or not, Byron was determined to travel in a style befitting a young nobleman of ancient lineage. The year before he had been obliged to dismiss his manservant for dishonesty (much to his chagrin Mrs. Byron had been right in her opinion of him) and in his place had engaged the lugubrious but faithful Fletcher, who was to remain with him through so many vicissitudes. The rest of his retinue consisted of a German servant recommended by Dr. Butler of Harrow, Robert Rushton, his sparring partner, and a lad named William. In time each one of these was to prove more of an encumbrance than a help, but on their arrival at Falmouth Byron surveyed them with pride, a feeling not shared by his traveling companion.

John Cam Hobhouse was an excellent friend for Byron, especially at this particular period. He was a young man with both feet firmly planted on the ground, and while he had rioted with the best of them at Cambridge and had no objection to the seeking of amorous or other adventures during the forthcoming voyage, he had definite ambitions in life which he meant to fulfill.

His ultimate object was to enter the political arena; his immediate one to write a travel book, and he had no intention of being diverted from either purpose. Already he showed signs of the pompousness which was to distinguish him in later life, and his attitude toward Byron was that of an indulgent elder brother. The "dear fellow" was a trifle wild, perhaps, but he would soon settle down.

They set sail from Falmouth on July 2nd, reaching Lisbon some four days later; and as they passed up the Tagus Byron's reaction was that of a delighted child. The Tower of Belem, the Monastery of São Jeronimo, the first glittering view of Lisbon crowned by the castle of São Jorge, filled him with ecstasy. True, he recoiled from the stench and filth in the narrow, hilly city streets, but his stay there was brief and soon he and Hobhouse moved out to Cintra, some fifteen miles from the capital.

It was Byron who called Cintra a "glorious Eden" and even today, when one climbs the winding path between the great cork trees to the Castle of the Moors, one appreciates that description. The sheer beauty of the place, with its woods, flowers and tinkling fountains, its view over the plain of Colares to the Tagus and the sea, entranced him; and as he wandered through Cintra Palace (where he particularly admired the mosaic ceiling with a pattern of magpies devised by a Portuguese monarch as a deterrent to the court ladies' chattering tongues) he reflected on the long, savage history of "this purple land, where law secures no life."

From Aldea Galbega, near Lisbon, Byron and Hobhouse rode nearly four hundred miles to Seville, where they lodged for a few days in the home of two Spanish maiden ladies. The elder, Donna Josepha, took a great fancy to Byron and invited him to stay and share her apartment, an offer which momentarily alarmed him since he was unused to this direct approach. Donna Josepha, however, laughed heartily at his embarrassment, snipped off a lock of his hair and gave him in return a tress of her own almost three feet in length. Byron was an inveterate collector of locks of hair (it was then a fashionable pastime) but it is difficult to determine exactly why he sent Donna Josepha's luxuriant tress to his mother for safe keeping, for any charge more calculated to arouse that lady's ire it is hard to imagine.

From Seville the travelers went to Cadiz, then to Gibraltar— called by Byron "this cursed place"—where they took the packet for Malta. Staying on the island at the time was Mrs. Spencer Smith, wife of the British Minister at Stuttgart, and to this extraordinary woman Byron fell such an easy victim that he gave her a yellow diamond ring of which he was especially fond. According to John Galt "he affected a passion for her, but it was only Platonic"; but there is no doubt that he believed every word she told him about her astonishing history. An Austrian by birth, she incurred the wrath of Bonaparte because she played "a part in some conspiracy," was imprisoned by him, escaped, and then went through the most hair-raising perils. Even in Malta, so she assured Byron, she was pursued by the Emperor's spies. Byron was so impressed that he made her the "Florence" of his *Childe Harold*, and it is more than likely that she had something to do with his challenge to duel with a Captain Cary just before he left the island.

Apparently the duel did not take place and when, on September 21st, Byron stepped aboard the brig-of-war *Spider* bound for Prevesa on the Albanian coast, he had already forgotten Mrs. Spencer Smith. Indeed he was, as Hobhouse remarked, an altogether different creature from the moody young man who had left England a brief ten weeks before. Extremely susceptible to beauty, he had reveled in each moment of their travels; had reveled also in the complete sense of freedom he had hitherto tried so vainly to attain. There was no Mr. Hanson to plague him with tales of financial disaster, no Lord Carlisle to make him aware of his many shortcomings. There was no Mrs. Byron to crouch like an obese witch in the background (and although he wrote her a number of letters, one feels, from study of them, that these were penned with the purpose of flaunting his new-found independence). Even Augusta, New-stead and the Byronic doom had become shadowy and unreal.

In short, Byron was really happy for the first time in his life, and as the ship bore him eastward he looked forward eagerly to Turkey, the land which had long ago captured his imagination. Nor was he disappointed. Albania was at that time a province of the Ottoman Empire, and from Prevesa Byron and Hobhouse rode for three days through the bleak mountains to Yanina, the capital, in order to present their credentials to the Governor, Ali Pasha. They found he was "with his army in Illyricum, besieging Ibrahim Pasha in the castle of Berat," but that he had left instructions that the "Englishman of rank" was to be provided with a house and treated as an honored guest.

It was just the sort of welcome to appeal to Byron. He rode the Governor's magnificent horses, inspected the ornate palaces, rode surrounded by slaves to visit a Greek monastery, and finally undertook a nine-day journey to Tepaleen far in the interior, where the Governor waited to greet him. He never forgot the scene which met his eyes as he rode into Tepaleen at sunset.

> The Albanians, in their dresses, (the most magnificent in the world, consisting of a long *white kilt*, gold-worked cloak, crimson velvet gold-laced jacket and waistcoat, silver-mounted pistols and daggers,) the Tartars with their high caps, the Turks in their vast pelisses and turbans, the soldiers and black slaves with the horses, the former in groups in an immense open gallery in front of the palace, the latter placed in a kind of cloister below it, two hundred steeds ready caparisoned to move in a moment, couriers entering or passing out with the despatches, the kettle-drums beating, boys calling the hour from the minaret of the mosque, altogether, with the singular appearance of the building itself, formed a new and delightful spectacle to a stranger. I was conducted to a very handsome apartment, and my health enquired after by the vizier's secretary, *à-la-mode Turque.*

His introduction to Ali Pasha (to impress whom he donned a "full suit of staff uniform, with a very magnificent sabre") pleased him still more. The Governor, a squat, enormously stout man with light blue eyes and a white beard, received him standing, a singular honor from a Mohammedan. He had already been told by the British Minister that Byron came of a noble family, but said that he could have drawn that conclusion from his own observation, because his visitor had "small ears, curling hair, and little white hands." His manner was gentle and dignified, although he was renowed as a tyrant given to violent cruelties, including the roasting of rebels, and was nicknamed the "Mohammedan Napoleon." Powerful and lawless, he preferred the English to the French and spurned all Bonaparte's attempts to woo his aid by promising to make him King of Epirus. Towards Byron he adopted a most kindly attitude, making him princely gifts and insisting that he regard him as a father while he remained in Turkey—a proposal Byron was only too delighted to accept.

Ali Pasha certainly treated Byron handsomely. He introduced him to his two small grandsons, who had "painted complexions like rouged dowagers, large black eyes, and features perfectly regular"; he provided him with an Albanian soldier as personal guard; gave him letters of introduction to his son Vely Pasha, Governor of the Morea; and ordered one of his own galiots and an escort of fifty men to take him to Patras. He also allowed him to see a good deal of Albania, then a country little known to Western travelers, and Byron was particularly intrigued by the lowly position of the women, who did all the work while their men made war, and were "complete beasts of burden."

The voyage to Patras did not materialize, since Byron and his party nearly lost their lives in a Turkish warship while proceeding down the Albanian coast from Prevesa. A sudden storm sprang up, whereupon the captain burst into a torrent of weeping and scurried below deck, most of the crew following his example. The sails were split and the mainyard shivered; and poor Fletcher was so overcome that he implored his master to save him from a "watery grave" and let him return to his loving wife in England. Byron, always exhilarated by personal danger

61

or hardship, wrapped himself in an immense Albanian cloak and lay down philosophically on the deck—a course which was fortunately justified as the ship ran aground on the coast. He had no wish, however, to repeat this experience so decided to journey overland to Missolonghi and across the gulf to the Morea.

Vely Pasha proved as hospitable as his father, and after a pleasant stay Byron and Hobhouse crossed the Gulf of Lepanto to land at the foot of Parnassus and visit Delphi before proceeding to Athens. Portugal and Spain had lured Byron by their beauty, Albania had reawakened in him all his old dreams of martial splendor, Greece induced in him a sense of homecoming that was to haunt him his life long. Even as Hobhouse hurried him on a little fussily, urging that time was growing short and that they had yet to visit Smyrna, the Troad and Constantinople, he vowed to himself that he would return to Attica.

In truth, Hobhouse was anxious to remove his impressionable young friend from the influence of Teresa Macri, the coppery-haired "Maid of Athens," who presented him with one of her braided tresses and filled his mind with wildly romantic notions. For Hobhouse, while delighted with the change wrought in the dear fellow's character since leaving Falmouth, was a shade disconcerted by the *abandon* with which he threw himself into amorous adventure.

Byron left Athens "dying for love" not only of Teresa but also of her two sisters, Mariana and Katinka; but revived somewhat when they reached Smyrna and went on to the Troad, where he lost his way when riding in a "cursed quagmire of the Scamander, who wriggles about as if the Dardan virgins still offered their wonted tribute," admired Mount Ida, inspected the barrows said to contain the remains of Achilles, Antilochus and Ajax, and found the snipe-shooting excellent.

The end of April, 1810, found the pair at Sestos, and on May 3rd Byron swam the Hellespont, a feat which he retailed gleefully to his mother, Henry Drury, Francis Hodgson and other friends.

This morning I *swam* from *Sestos* to *Abydos*. The immediate distance is not above a mile, but the current renders it hazardous;—so much so that I doubt whether Leander's conjugal affection must not have been a little chilled in his passage to Paradise. I attempted it a week ago, and failed,—owing to the north wind and the wonderful rapidity of the tide,—though I have been from my childhood a strong swimmer. But, this morning being calmer, I succeeded, and crossed the "broad Hellespont" in an hour and ten minutes.

In the letter to his mother he added a little wistfully, "You know the story of Leander, but I had no *Hero* to receive me at landing"; but there is no doubt that his achievement gave Byron profound and lasting satisfaction. Debarred from taking part in various sports, in water he was in his true element, for here his lameness ceased to be a handicap.

He and Hobhouse explored Constantinople, then traveled together as far as the island of Zea where they bade each other a sentimental farewell, halving a little posy of wild flowers between them. Hobhouse was bound for Malta and England; Byron for another extended tour of Greece, the land which had captured his heart.

❊ 4 ❊

Now began the period which was to stand out in Byron's memory as the happiest he had ever known. He was devoted to Hobhouse and genuinely grieved by his departure, but there had been times of late when he had felt a little irked by his friend's criticisms of his behavior. Hobhouse did not understand the violence of his emotions—he had frowned, for example, upon Byron's affectionate patronage of Nicolo Giraud, the handsome young brother-in-law of Lusieri, the painter employed by Lord Elgin in Athens—and his attitude towards affairs of the heart was too conventional. That Hobhouse was fully aware of these feelings was made clear in the marginal notes he afterwards scribbled in his copy of Moore's *Life*, for when Moore hinted that the poet was bored with his friend and welcomed the Zea parting Hobhouse retorted that Tom Moore "had not the remotest guess at the real reason, which induced Lord Byron to prefer having no Englishman immediately and constantly near him" during his Levantine sojourn.

There seems little doubt that Byron was bi-sexual. At Harrow there had been his group of "favorites"; at Cambridge John Edleston; and in Greece not only Nicolo but several charming adolescents and a curiously pathetic lad whom Byron called Eustathius whom he met again, either by accident or design, shortly after Hobhouse's departure. From Zea Byron had returned to Athens, where the Marquis of Sligo suggested they should journey together as far as Corinth, an invitation Byron was too weak to refuse. The nobleman traveled in style with numerous English servants, a painter, a captain and a "gentleman misinterpreter (who boxes with the painter.)" The ride to Corinth was singularly uncomfortable, the Marquis proved a bore, and Fletcher, "with his usual acuteness, contrived to run his damned clumsy foot into a boiling tea-kettle."

Small wonder that Byron was soothed and delighted when, having bade the Sligo party a joyous good-bye, he encountered Eustathius, who vowed he loved his patron so much that it was his intention to follow him back to England. To Fletcher's horror Eustathius insisted on riding horseback clad in abbreviated Greek garments, with his ringleted hair hanging down his back and a parasol held in one hand to protect his complexion from the sun. Byron, however, was highly amused and took his quaint protégé with him to Patras, where they stayed in the house of Mr. Strané, the English Consul, and had such an almighty quarrel that their host intervened and told Byron he was a fool to spoil the boy. This rebuke was sufficient to make Byron redouble his efforts to effect a reconciliation, but Eustathius remained inconsolable and after a parting which contained "as many kisses as would have sufficed for a boarding school, and embraces enough to have ruined a county in England," he retired temporarily to his father's house.

Next day he was back again full of contrition and swearing eternal devotion. Would the noble lord grant his plea and allow him to journey to Tripolitza and Athens with him? Pleased with this capitulation Byron gave him a green eyeshade to replace the parasol and a dose of sal volatile to cure a headache; then turned his attention to Vely Pasha, who was so delighted at the renewal of their acquaintance that he made him a present of a fine horse and invited him to meet him at Larissa where they would "eat, drink and go a-hunting."

Vely Pasha shared Eustathius's longing to become Byron's lover. Much to the poet's embarrassment he kept throwing his arm around his neck and squeezing his hand during their interviews; and he flabbergasted Strané (who was interpreting) by suggesting that it was only right and proper, since they were both young men, that they should live together. As the Governor was twice his age and had a beard reaching down to his middle even Byron recoiled from such a proposal, explaining that he must return to Athens, and begging his friend to accept a sporting gun as a parting gift.

With Fletcher, a motley collection of servants that included a Tartar among them, and the now beaming Eustathius, Byron set off for Athens "amidst the usual creaking, swearing, loading and neighing of sixteen horses and as many men." The restless side of his nature loved travel, the indolent side loathed it, and by the time he reached Tripolitza he was in no humor to put up with the capricious Eustathius who, having won his way, was growing increasingly impertinent. Moreover, the poor boy was subject to epilepsy and this distressing complaint so unnerved Byron that he sent him back to his home.

But when he reached it Athens more than rewarded him for the discomforts of the journey. He lodged in the Capuchin Convent (*sic*) near the Acropolis, where the jovial Father Abbot had a "school" of six young and beautiful youths, three being Catholic and three Greek. One of them was Hobhouse's *bête noire*, Nicolo Giraud, who constituted himself Byron's Italian tutor, but the lessons were continually interrupted by the other five "Ragazzi" who also adored Byron and clamored for his company. It was like being at Harrow all over again! Through the long summer days the seven laughed and talked, ate fruit and pelted each other with stones, swam in the Piraeus and played practical jokes. Their enjoyment was heightened by the spectacle of the stalwart Albanian women who did the Convent washing spending their leisure sticking pins into the wretched Fletcher's behind, while the behavior of Byron's servants, who drank Zean wine by the skinful and were experts in the seduction of any woman they met, also afforded them much amusement.

It was an idyllic existence and one which Byron appreciated to the full. It could have happened, he told himself, nowhere else but in Greece, the land where responsibility was unknown and the clear heady air tasted like wine on the tongue. "What with the *women* and the *boys*," he wrote slyly to Hobhouse, "we are very disorderly. But I am vastly happy and childish.... Intrigue flourishes: the old woman, Teresa's mother, was mad enough to imagine I was going to marry the girl; but I have better amusement."

During these months of August and September Byron had little contact with anyone outside the Convent. Lord Sligo was in Argos, and he shunned other Western Europeans with the exception of Lusieri, with whom he arranged to go on a tour of Attica—accompanied, of course, by young Nicolo. But one day when he had ridden down to the Piræus for his usual swim he did encounter the celebrated Lady Hester Stanhope, who had first seen him diving off the mole as her ship entered the harbor. Byron did not admire "that dangerous thing a female wit," and was incensed when she told him that she had got the better of Hobhouse at Malta in some argument about Naval affairs.

66

From this, of course [he wrote to John Cam], I readily inferred the contrary....She evinced a similar desire to *argufy* with me, which I avoided by either laughing or yielding. I despise the sex too much to squabble with them, and I rather wonder you should allow a woman to draw you into a contest, in which, however, I am sure you had the advantage, she abuses you so bitterly. I have seen too little of the Lady to form any decisive opinion, but I have discovered nothing different from other she-things, except a great disregard of received notions in her conversation as well as conduct.

Not surprisingly, Lady Hester returned Byrons dislike with interest, and described him to her friend Dr. Meryon:

A strange character. His generosity was for a motive, his avarice for a motive; one time he was mopish, and nobody was to speak to him; another, he was for being jocular with everybody. Then he was a sort of Don Quixote, fighting with the police for a woman of the town; and then he wanted to make himself something great....At Athens I saw nothing in him but a well-bred man, like many others....He had a great deal of vice in his looks—his eyes set close together and a contracted brow.... The only good thing about his look was this part [here she drew a finger under her cheek and down the front of her neck], and the curl on his forehead....Oh, Lord! I am sure he was not a liberal man, whatever else he might be.

Toward the end of September Byron, with Nicolo, went back to Patras to consult Mr. Strané on some matter of business, and there fell sick with fever—"five days bed-riding with Emetics, glysters, Bark, and all the host of Physic"; and before he was fully recovered had to attend to Nicolo, who went down with the same complaint. He was half chagrined, half relieved, to find that Vely Pasha had hurried off to Albania to aid his father as the latter was being violently attacked by his old enemy Ibrahim Pasha. In the absence of his Turkish friend there was little to hold him in the Morea, and after a half-hearted attempt to purchase the island of Ithaca (where presumably he intended to reside surrounded by his "Ragazzi") he returned to Athens.

67

In November he could stand poor Fletcher's miseries no longer and packed him off to England.

> The perpetual lamentations after beef and beer, the stupid, bigoted contempt for every thing foreign, and insurmountable capacity of acquiring even a few words of any language, rendered him, like all other English servants, an incumbrance. I do assure you, the plague of speaking for him, the comforts he required (more than myself by far), the pilaws (a Turkish dish of rice and meat) which he could not eat, the wines which he could not drink, the beds where he could not sleep, and the long list of calamities, such as stumbling horses, want of *tea*!!! etc., which assailed him, would have made a lasting source of laughter to a spectator, and inconvenience to a master.

So Byron wrote to his mother, but despite this tirade one's sympathies lean towards Fletcher. For eighteen months he had trailed through Europe at Byron's heels. He had put up with indigestible foods, bugs, fleas, storms at sea and the outrageous teasing of the Albanian washerwomen. He had endured Byron's tantrums, the wild rages of Greek, Albanian and Tartar fellow servants, and the insufferable behavior of youths such as Eustathius. He was entitled to a long rest and one hopes he got it during his voyage home.

In the March of 1811 Byron wrote to Hobhouse:

> Ever since my fever in the Morea in September ... my health has been changing in the most tramontane way. I have been fat, and thin (as I am at present) and had a cough and the catarrh and the piles and be damned to them, and I have had pains in my side and left off animal food, which last has done me some service. But I expect great things from the coming summer, and if well and wealthy shall go to Jerusalem, for which I have a firman.

He did not go to Jerusalem. To begin with he was short of money, having lent a considerable sum to some unnamed friend; long-delayed letters from Hanson disclosed an alarming state of affairs and he was terrified of having to sell Newstead; finally he had known in his heart that his Convent life could not last and much as he loved it he felt ambition stir in him again. Reluctantly, therefore, he said good-bye to the Father Abbot and the "Ragazzi" (the farewell with Nicolo was particularly poignant) and set sail for Malta, leaving there for England on June 2nd in the frigate *Volante*.

❋ 5 ❋

For the two years of his absence from England Byron and melancholy had been strangers; but on board the *Volante* melancholy came back and in an unsuccessful effort to counteract it he wrote long letters to his friends. To Hobhouse:

> I am accompanied by two Greek servants, both middle-aged men. My own antiquities consist of four *tortoises*, and four *Skulls*, all taken out of ancient sarcophagi. . . . I shall first endeavour to repair my irreparable affairs, and it seems I must set out for Lancashire, for I shall have neither coals nor comfort till I visit Rochdale in person.

To Mrs. Byron he wrote in sterner strain.

> . . . I return to it [England] with much the same feelings which prevailed on my departure, viz. indifference; but within that apathy I certainly do not comprise yourself, as I will prove by every means in my power. You will be good enough to get my apartments ready at Newstead; but don't disturb yourself, on any account, particularly mine, nor consider me in any other light than as a visitor. I must only inform you that for a long time I have been restricted to an entire vegetable diet, neither fish nor flesh coming within my regimen; so I expect a powerful stock of potatoes, greens, and biscuit; I drink no wine. . . . My prospects are not very promising . . . indeed, by Hanson's last advices, I have some apprehension of finding Newstead dismantled by Messrs. Brothers, etc., and he seems determined to force me into selling it, but he will be baffled. . . . I have brought you a shawl, and a quantity of attar of roses, but these I must smuggle, if possible. . . .

69

Through all Byron's letters written from the *Volante* there runs a note of fear—fear of the responsibilities he was about to assume, fear of criticism, fear of his mother, above all fear of the destiny he once more believed he could not escape. Curled up in his favorite corner of the deck, his hand clenched against his cheek, he thought desperately of Greece, that land of eternal youth.

❋ 6 ❋

Byron arrived home in the latter half of July and immediately drove to London, and one of his first callers at Reddish's Hotel in St. James's Street was the middle-aged Robert Charles Dallas, a distant family connection who had seen *English Bards and Scottish Reviewers* through the press. To Dallas Byron gave his paraphrase of Horace's *Art of Poetry*, saying eagerly that in his opinion it was good satire and should prove a worthy successor to his previous volume. Dallas walked off with the manuscript, read it overnight, and returned to breakfast the following morning in a state of "grievous disappointment" which, however, he was wise enough to conceal. He had found the work dull and unoriginal, so over the meal he asked carelessly if the poet had nothing else to show him. Byron answered equally carelessly that he "had occasionally written short poems, besides a great many stanzas in Spenser's measure" about the countries he had visited. Apparently these verses had been read by Lord Sligo, who had been the reverse of complimentary about them, and their author scarcely thought it was worth Dallas's while to look at them. He could, however, take them away with him if he chose—but let him concentrate on getting the Horace paraphrase published, for Byron had no doubt that satire was his forte.

Dallas scurried off with the manuscript and when he settled down to read it he was overwhelmed. Surely there had been nothing like this romantic autobiography of a young poet before! Hastily he sent Byron a scribbled note:

> You have written one of the most delightful poems I ever read. If I wrote this in flattery, I should deserve your contempt rather than your friendship. I have been so fascinated by *Childe Harold* that I have not been able to lay it down. I would almost pledge my life on its advancing the reputation of your poetical powers, and on its gaining you great honour and regard....

Byron received this note just as he was setting out to visit Henry Drury at Harrow, and it was not until July 23rd that he saw Dallas again and rather grudgingly—for he was tremendously busy with Mr. Hanson and he did not really believe in the worth of the work—gave him permission to seek a publisher. The manuscript was in the hands of Mr. John Murray of Albemarle Street when Byron received a letter from Newstead informing him that Mrs. Byron was seriously ill. He set off immediately but during his journey the following day he had a message saying she was dead.

According to report, she had been so incensed on opening one of the many large bills Byron had run up while he was refurbishing the Abbey two years earlier that she had flown into such a violent rage she had suffered some sort of seizure.

It was a tragic homecoming, and as he posted north to the Abbey Byron forgot all the quarrels which had devastated his life since childhood, all her unforgivable taunts about his lameness, all her coarse abuse of the Byron family. She was his mother, the person nearest to him in all the world, and now she had died alone without the presence of her son to ease her passing. On his arrival he swept past the servants gathered on the steps with bowed heads and went straight to his mother's room. For hours he sat by her bedside in the dark, sobbing uncontrollably. "Oh, Mrs. By," he said to her maid, "I had but one friend in the world, and she is gone!"

Mrs. Byron died on August 1st, and while Byron still kept vigil beside her body he had news that his gay, delightful friend

Charles Skinner Matthews had drowned horribly while bathing in the river near Cambridge. Ropes of water-weed had twined themselves round his arms and legs and though he had made a series of desperate, breast-high leaps he had been unable to free himself from their coils. And as if this second blow were not enough a third one fell almost simultaneously when Byron learned that John Wingfield, one of his Harrow adorers, had died of fever in Portugal.

It was no wonder that Byron, who was superstitious to a degree, felt that he was accursed and that the Byronic doom was responsible for these tragedies. Hobhouse was not available so on August 7th he sent an impassioned plea to Scrope Davies:

> Some curse hangs over me and mine. My mother lies a corpse in this house; one of my best friends is drowned in a ditch. What can I say, or think, or do? I received a letter from him the day before yesterday. My dear Scrope, if you can spare a moment, do come down to me—I want a friend.... Come to me, Scrope, I am almost desolate—left almost alone in the world—I had but you, and H., and M., and let me enjoy the survivors whilst I can....

To Hobhouse he wrote that he was so bewildered by the shocks he had sustained that he could not "reduce himself to reason" by any occupation, frivolous or otherwise.

> There is to me something so incomprehensible in death, that I can neither speak nor think on the subject. Indeed, when I looked on the mass of corruption which was the being from whence I sprang, I doubted within myself whether I *was*, or she *was not*. I have lost her who gave me being, and some who made that being a blessing. I have neither hopes nor fears beyond the grave, yet if there is within us "a spark of that Celestial fire," Matthews has already mingled with the gods.

On the day of his mother's funeral Byron refused to accompany the cortège to the cemetery at Hucknall Torkard. Instead, he stood on the Abbey steps watching the procession move slowly down the drive and, before it was out of sight, turned on his heel and curtly ordered Robert Rushton to bring the boxing gloves to the Great Hall. For a time he boxed with savage intensity, but presently he snatched the gloves from his hands and limped upstairs to his own apartments, there to remain in solitude for the rest of the day reading and re-reading a scurrilous attack on himself and his family which had appeared the previous March in a paper called *The Scourge*.

The author of the article in question was one Hewson Clarke, a journalist who had incurred Byron's wrath by his unfavorable review of *Hours of Idleness* and by some verses entitled *Lord B . . .n to his Bear*. By way of revenge he had alluded to Clarke in *English Bards* as a money-grubbing scandalmonger:

> A would-be satirist, a hired Buffoon,
> A monthly scribbler of some low Lampoon.....

Nothing daunted, Clarke had retorted in *The Scourge:*

> It may reasonably be asked whether to be a denizen of Berwick-upon-Tweed be more disgraceful than to be the illegitimate descendant of a murderer; whether to labour in an honourable profession for the peace and competence of maturer age be less worthy of praise than to waste the property of others in vulgar debauchery; whether to be the offspring of parents whose only crime is their want of title, be not as honourable as to be the son of a profligate father, and a mother whose days and nights are spent in the delirium of drunkenness; and, finally, whether to deserve the kindness of his own college, to obtain its prizes, and to prepare himself for any examination that might entitle him to share the highest honours which the university can bestow, be less indicative of talent and virtue than to be held up to derision and contempt of his fellow-students, as a scribbler of doggerel and a bear-leader; to be hated for malignity of temper and repulsiveness of manners, and shunned by every man who did not want to be considered a profligate without wit, and trifling without elegance.

There was just enough truth in the article to hurt, and when Byron had been shown it on his return to England he had been so furious that he had gone straight to the Attorney-General and said he was going to take immediate proceedings. But that legal luminary pointed out that Byron himself had provoked the attack and that, moreover, the libel had been published several months before. Byron had abandoned the idea of a libel suit but the affair had rankled in his mind and now, with Mrs. Byron's death, it assumed almost monstrous proportions—for did it not center his thoughts on the very thing he wished to forget, his stormy family history?

Then on August 12th Byron sat down to compose his will, a document so extraordinary that Mr. Bolton, the local lawyer to whom it was entrusted, was utterly upset by the reading of it. To begin with Byron insisted that his body was to be buried in the Newstead garden-vault "without any ceremony or burial service whatever...and it is my will that my faithful dog (Boatswain) may not be removed from the said vault." A tablet inscribed with name and age only was to be erected by his "particular desire." The agitated Bolton wrote timidly suggesting that the funeral clause should be removed and that his Lordship should write it in a letter to his executors, John Cam Hobhouse and Scrope Davies. Byron was adamant. The clause must stand.

> With regard to the few and simple directions for the disposal of my *carcass*, I must have them implicitly fulfilled, as they will, at least, prevent trouble and expense; and (what would be of little consequence to me, but may quiet the conscience of the survivors) the garden is *consecrated* ground.

In the will itself Byron left the sum of seven thousand pounds, "to be paid from the sale of Rochdale, Newstead or elsewhere to Nicolo Giraud of Athens, subject of France, but born in Greece," when he attained the age of twenty-one years.

Hobhouse might well have had something tart to say about this legacy had he known of it; but Hobhouse had become a captain in the militia and was on his way to Ireland. Mr. Bolton saw nothing unusual in the bequest but was extremely distressed by his noble client's use of the word "carcass" and by his wish to be buried beside Boatswain.

Fortunately, Scrope Davies arrived to jolt Byron out of his melancholy; but the visit was not altogether a success. Davies was a happy-go-lucky young man with a tremendous zest for worldly pleasures, and while he was sincerely grieved about Matthews's death he certainly did not wish to spend his evenings in morbid discussion of the tragedy. Nor could he understand Byron's distress over the loss of his mother, for during their Cambridge days he had heard that lady's son express vastly different opinions. Wingfield he had not known at all, so he grew bored when Byron launched into eulogies of him and did his level best to turn the conversation to lighter topics—the gambling at Crockford's, the latest *bon mot* of his friend George Brummell, the splendid banquet given by "Prinny" at Carlton House when the great table had been decorated with a gleaming silver fountain from which flowed a stream of clear water. But Byron remained sunk in apathy and seemed completely disinterested in news of the great world, interrupting Davies's highly amusing stories with some lugubrious remark about one or other of his recent bereavements: and Davies cut his visit as short as he decently could.

> Scrope is a pleasant person [Byron wrote to Hobhouse], he laughs with the living, though he don't weep with the dead, yet I believe he would do that also, could it do them good service, but good or bad we must endeavour to follow his example, and return to the dull routine of business or pleasure, though I fear the more we see of life, the more we shall regret those who have ceased to live—we will speak of them no more.

Byron did make an effort to talk less of the dead, but they remained perpetually in his thoughts and not even the cheering news that Mr. John Murray was delighted with *Childe Harold* roused him from his depression. He invited a Harrow friend, John Claridge, to stay but found him grown into a dreary, stupid young man who clung to him like a limpet and, unlike Davies, considerably outstayed his welcome. To escape from his dull guest Byron spent a great deal of time in his bedroom. Here he would sit for hours before the baroque looking glass, gazing at his reflection, twisting his head this way and that in order to achieve a particularly telling pose. But in the midst of his Narcissus-like appreciation of his own beauty he would remember his unbearable loneliness. Should he end it all? he wondered, and sometimes his hand strayed to a tiny phial of hemlock he had brought home; then memories of Greece would crowd into his mind and he would prowl around his room with his curious half-limping, half-gliding gait, thinking of the gay, laughing boys at the Capuchin Convent, the purple slopes of Hymettus, the glory of the wine-dark sea, the incomparable beauty of the Ionian islands rising white from the indigo waters.

He was relieved when Claridge at last took his departure and emerged from his solitude to box with Robert Rushton—wearing a Turkish pelisse in an effort to reduce his weight and chewing tobacco or gum mastic to stave off pangs of hunger. There were bouts of amorous dalliance with the maidservants, and days when he devoted himself to the care of his tortoises, mastiff and hedgehog, and evenings when he sat up late quaffing wine from his skull-cup. But always around him in the vast, tumbledown house, were ghosts he could not banish. His financial affairs were in their usual chaos, he could not ride as he had sold his horses before leaving England in 1809, he could not shoot as he had given away his sporting guns to various Greek and Turkish acquaintances. He could only try to fill the empty days with the writing of verse and letters.

Once again his thoughts reverted to Augusta, with whom he had been corresponding again since Mrs. Byron's death. Her improvident husband, Colonel Leigh, spent his life journeying from race meeting to race meeting, leaving his poor wife to struggle with ailing children, unpaid bills and a never-ending stream of creditors at their Six Mile Bottom home near Newmarket. Things were in an even worse state than usual and Augusta had a vague idea of bringing her family to stay at Newstead. Byron immediately urged her to do so though he added:

I don't know what Scrope Davies meant by telling you that I liked Children. I abominate the sight of them so much that I have always had the greatest respect for the character of Herod. ...I must marry to repair the ravages of myself and prodigal ancestry, but if I am ever so unfortunate as to be presented with an Heir, instead of a *Rattle* he shall be provided with a *Gag*.

The proposed visit did not materialize because Augusta could not face the two-day coach journey with a nurse and babies; but Byron continued to write to his sister about the necessity for him to find a bride. "If I can't persuade some wealthy dowdy to ennoble the dirty puddle of her mercantile blood,—why—I shall leave England and all its clouds for the East again." With his natural indolence, however, he made no attempt to search for a suitable wife and by October, when he visited his Rochdale estates with Mr. Hanson, he was far more interested in financial problems than in matrimony. Work was to be started on the coal mines, but these could not be expected to yield much profit for several years and the initial expenses would be £10,000, while Byron was forced to raise mortgages to settle his debts of some £20,000.

Then, on his return to Newstead, he was again plunged into deepest gloom by a letter from John Edleston's sister, informing him of her brother's death. "My friends fall around me," he wrote to Dallas, "and I shall be left a lonely tree before I am withered. Other men can always take refuge in their families; I have no resource but my own reflections, and they present no prospect here or hereafter, except the selfish satisfaction of surviving my betters."

For all Byron's love for Newstead he was wretchedly unhappy there that summer and autumn of 1811. He was, he complained, "really, wretchedly, ridiculously, fine-ladically *nervous*"; he flew into gusts of wild rage when his Greek servants smashed the crockery or Fletcher made some more than usually obtuse remark. When he sat alone over his wine in the Prior's dining room he could positively imagine that across the table sat his great-uncle, the Wicked Lord, leering at him in diabolical fashion. Then, on one of those sudden impulses to which he was so prone, he decided to take rooms in London:

> But let this pass—I'll whine no more,
> Nor seek again an Eastern shore;
> The world befits a busy brain,—
> I'll hie me to its haunts again.
> But if, in some succeeding year,
> When Britain's 'May is in the sere,'
> Thou hear'st of one, whose deepening crimes
> Suit with the sablest of the times,
> Of one, whom Love nor Pity sways,
> Nor hope of fame, nor good men's praise...
> One rank'd in some recording page
> With the worst anarchs of the age,
> Him wilt thou *know*—and, *knowing*, pause,
> Nor with the *effect* forget the cause.

For once he was glad to leave his home. The influence of the Wicked Lord had become terrifyingly real.

✻ 7 ✻

Byron did not go direct from Newstead to London. He broke his journey for a few days at Cambridge, where he enjoyed the company of Scrope Davies and Francis Hodgson and forgot his melancholy at a series of dinners, after one of which he helped to put Davies to bed "in a state of *outrageous* intoxication." Soothed by this brief encounter with his friends Byron traveled to London on October 28th, and took rooms at No. 8 St. James's Street.

His stay started auspiciously. There were many consultations with Mr. Murray and Dallas about *Childe Harold*—which to Byron's indignation had been alluded to by the man in Murray's bookshop as *Child of Harrow's Pilgrimage!*—and the poet was immensely gratified to learn that the great William Gifford, editor of the *Quarterly Review* and the *Anto-Jacobin*, had been tremendously impressed by his work and regarded it as a poem equal to any "of the present age."

Then before he had been a week in London he received an invitation from Samuel Rogers to dine at his house in St. James's Place and meet Thomas Moore. Five years earlier, when Moore used the pseudonym "Thomas Little," he had challenged Francis Jeffrey of the *Edinburgh Review* to a duel. But when he arrived at Chalk Farm for the duel Moore was arrested and taken to Bow Street, where it was found that only his pistol was loaded with ball. The affair received much publicity and when Byron wrote *English Bards* he made an allusion to "Little's leadless pistol" which so infuriated Moore that he wrote a long letter to Byron challenging him to meet him and give him satisfaction. But Byron was in Greece and the letter was not forwarded, and by the time of his return Moore's anger had cooled and he was a sedate married man. He had been further mollified by a most polite letter from Byron and had expressed a desire to meet him.

Rogers was a little anxious as to how the two poets would react to each other and invited Thomas Campbell as the remaining guest. Byron was more anxious still, for this was his first introduction to literary London and he wanted desperately to create a good impression. Being Byron, however, he could not resist overacting the part of the eccentric young nobleman and when the four sat down to table he ostentatiously refused soup, fish, mutton and wine, saying he never touched any of them.

The sharp-eyed Rogers wrinkled his dome-shaped forehead. What then, he asked, did Lord Byron live on?

"Nothing but hard biscuits and soda water," answered the poet.

Unfortunately neither of these commodities was available, so Byron dined on mashed potatoes liberally sprinkled with vinegar. However, Moore was captivated by the "pure spiritual" pallor of his skin, by his auburn curls, and by his somber appearance (he was still in deep mourning for his mother), while Rogers, though thinking him affected, admired his conversational powers:

> My guests stayed till very late [he recorded] discussing the merits of Walter Scott and Joanna Baillie. Some days after, meeting Hobhouse, I said to him, "How long will Lord Byron persist in his present diet?" He replied, "Just as long as you continue to notice it."

It was a pity that Byron went straight from Rogers' house to a club in St. James's Street, where he was observed enjoying a large plateful of meat and vegetables, for this action was promptly reported to his host.

But the meeting between Byron and Moore marked the beginning of a long, close friendship. Moore admired Byron for his beauty, his extraordinarily vivid mind, and his air of distinction. Byron admired Moore for his quick wit, his volatile ways, and the fact that his songs and verses had won him the entrée to the closely guarded homes of the Whig aristocracy—whose doors were still closed to Byron, despite his ancient lineage. The two saw a good deal of each other through November and December and discovered they had much in common, though Moore was pardonably upset when they drove to Sydenham to see Campbell and Byron insisted on keeping a brace of loaded pistols on the carriage seat beside him!

Apart from his growing friendship with Moore, Byron's first months in London were as lonely as his months at Newstead had been. Solitary, he passed the time reading in his rooms, and took most of his meals at the Alfred, an extremely decorous club. Occasionally he saw Dallas and an acquaintance whom he found an intolerable bore, James Wedderburn Webster, but he shunned the gaming clubs and the gay coffeehouses he had liked so much in his undergraduate days. The mood of doom was still upon him and it was without regret that he left the inhospitable capital to spend Christmas at Newstead. With him he took two friends, Francis Hodgson and William Harness, who had been one of his intimates at Harrow. Both were prospective clergymen and they had many a long religious argument with their host, during which they tried vainly to wean him from the Calvinistic dogmas he had been taught in his Aberdeen childhood.

That Christmas was certainly the quietest Newstead had known since Byron had taken possession of his home. There were no fantastic drinking parties, no orgies as there had been in the days of Hobhouse, Matthews and Scrope Davies; although there seems little doubt that the host privately amused himself with a pretty maidservant called Susan, who shortly rewarded him by quarreling violently with Robert Rushton and getting entangled with a local swain.

By mid-January Byron was back in London. He had lately developed political ambitions and was engrossed in the preparation of his maiden speech in the House of Lords. He resolved to oppose the Frame-Breaking Bill which was to be introduced by Lord Liverpool, and to give him his due it was a subject about which he knew a considerable amount, since it was only the previous November that the Luddite riots among the unemployed stocking-weavers of Nottingham had broken out and the military had been called in to quell the disturbance. The workers had smashed the frames which, to their way of thinking, would keep them out of employment for good, and they were filled with a bitter resentment against the employers who were beginning to introduce all kinds of machinery.

Byron took immense pains over his speech and learned it off by heart. In it he pointed out that even in the most backward provinces of Turkey he had not seen "such squalid wretchedness as I have seen since my return, in the very heart of a Christian country." He opposed the bill not only because of the misery it would cause but also because of its "palpable injustice and certain inefficiency," and he warned the government of the ghastly consequences should the bill be made law. It was a very able speech and was warmly received—although Byron's sense of the dramatic caused him to deliver it in a very theatrical tone of voice—and he was quite overwhelmed by the congratulations showered upon him as he left the chamber. He was especially gratified when Lord Holland approached him with words of praise, for in a misguided moment he had attacked the Hollands in *English Bards* and as a result Holland House, center of the most brilliant intellectual society in England, was barred to him.

But now that Lord Holland had gone out of his way to congratulate him Byron sent him an advance copy of *Childe Harold* together with a strangely humble letter.

> Your Lordship, I am sorry to observe today, is troubled with the gout; if my book can produce a *laugh* against itself or the author, it will be of some service. If it can set you to *sleep*, the benefit will be yet greater; and as some facetious personage observed half a century ago, that "poetry is a mere drug," I offer you mine as a humble assistant to the *eau médicinale*.

At last it seemed that the world was beginning to appreciate his worth. "I have had many marvelous eulogies," he wrote to Hodgson, "repeated to me since, in person and by proxy, from divers persons *ministerial*—yea, *ministerial!*—as well as oppositionists." Once again melancholy was forgotten. Byron was on the crest of the wave.

III

✿✿✿✿✿✿✿✿✿✿✿✿✿✿✿✿✿✿✿✿✿✿✿✿✿✿✿✿✿✿

Childe Harold

CHILDE HAROLD was published early in March and practically
overnight its author sprang to a fame that even he had
never dreamed of in his most euphoric moments. Within three
days the first edition was sold out and Mr. Murray's shop was
besieged by clamorous customers who vowed they would go to
any lengths to obtain a copy of the poem, while Byron himself
received invitations and letters by the score from people who
hailed him as the leader of the Romantic movement in literature.

The reasons behind this sudden and immense popularity were
not far to seek. Ever since the turn of the century Europe had
been beset by war and although Englishmen had been able to
travel abroad to an extent unknown in later conflicts their jour-
neyings had been limited and their interests restricted. They
were conscious, therefore, of a yearning towards the romantic
and found that *Childe Harold* satisfied this in a most remarkable
way. Moreover, their own country was in a state of upheaval;
people were restless and discontented and in Byron's flamboyant
verses they discovered an escape from their present woes and a
hope for the future. Finally, they were intrigued beyond measure
by the personality of *Childe Harold* himself, and were convinced

that the cynic who described his youthful sins and indiscretions with such devastating frankness was really the author.

To a certain extent they were right in this premise. In rough drafts of the poem the hero was alluded to as "Childe Burun," and there is no doubt that Byron had drawn to a considerable extent on his own experiences when writing it. But he had done more than draw upon them; he had embellished and embroidered them out of recognition, and in the process a character had emerged who was part himself and part the Wicked Lord, that forebear who seemed to him the archetype of all the reckless Byron line.

Wherever Byron went men and women—particularly women—crowded around to catch a glimpse of this astonishingly handsome young nobleman who had so captivated the public fancy. They agreed with the description of Sir Thomas Lawrence, who wrote of his features that "the forehead [was] clear and open, the brow broadly prominent, the eyes bright and *dissimilar*, the nose finely cut and the nostril *acutely* formed— the mouth well-formed, but wide, and contemptuous even in its smile, falling singularly at the corners, and its vindictive and disdainful expression heightened by the massive firmness of the chin." They admired his auburn curls and small white hands, his rather foppish dress which displayed too many lace ruffles, his expression of haughty sadness as if he were surveying a strange world of which he could not possibly approve.

About his lameness the wildest rumors flew around London. He had a club foot . . . he had *two* club feet . . . he had actually a cloven hoof, only to be expected in one of *Childe Harold's* propensities.

Byron was an opportunist and he seized his fame with both hands. All the mannerisms cultivated at Cambridge and practiced before the baroque looking glass at Newstead returned in exaggerated form and gave rise to a great deal of talk, some of it ill-natured. Observers were not to realize that his poses and attitudes were designed to disguise the deformity he hated so much, and many people felt repelled by him. These included Lady Granville, who shrewdly remarked that she had "no wish for any further intimacy with him. His countenance is fine when it is in repose, but the moment it is in play, suspicious, malignant, and consequently repulsive. His manner is either remarkably gracious and conciliatory, with a tinge of affectation, or irritable and impetuous, and then I am afraid perfectly natural."

The adulation he received pleased Byron enormously, for curiously enough he wanted to be a man of the world first and a poet second. Despite the chaotic state of his money affairs he insisted that the faithful Dallas should take the £600 which Mr. Murray had given for the copyright of *Childe Harold*, and he himself made no profit from his poem. What really interested him was the fact that he had successfully stormed the bastions of London society and thus justified all the garbled prophecies of greatness dinned into him by Mrs. Byron in his childhood.

Yet he was never wholly at ease in drawing rooms. There was his cursed lameness to remember; there was his innate suspicion of his fellow men which caused him to search always for the hidden barb beneath the honeyed word; there was his sense of destiny—no matter what he did he could never overthrow the Byronic doom. Only in the company of a few cronies such as Hobhouse, Scrope Davies or Moore, could he be a jovial, natural companion.

In the days immediately following *Childe Harold's* publication, however, Byron preened himself on the invitations which poured in from Lady Holland, Lady Jersey, Lady Westmorland and other hostesses of the time; and in the background Samuel Rogers congratulated himself on being one of the first to discover this singular young man and spent most of his time attending to the requests of ladies who positively *had* to make the poet's acquaintance. Always he was the guest of honor and as he made an effective entry—pausing in the doorway with a royal air—he heard the awestruck murmur of "Byron ... Byron ... Byron ..." running around the room.

2

Among the first to beg Samuel Rogers for an introduction to the poet was Lady Caroline Lamb, a young woman who had literary aspirations of her own. Born Lady Caroline Ponsonby, daughter of the Countess of Bessborough and niece of Georgiana, Duchess of Devonshire, she had emerged from a wild childhood to become an erratic, headstrong girl with a brilliant tongue and a flair for the outrageous. In 1803 she had married the agreeable and cynical William Lamb, eldest surviving son of Lord and Lady Melbourne, and since then had scandalized London by her daring behavior. William was a complaisant husband, genuinely fond of his madcap wife and tolerant of her many vagaries; but her parents-in-law viewed her escapades with alarm. Lady Melbourne, a woman of great charm and character, tried to inculcate some sense of discretion into her William's wife, but Caroline, with her huge dark eyes, her "fawn-flaxen" mop of curls, and her slender, appealing grace, paid no attention to admonitions or pleas. She remained the same "wild, delicate, odd, delightful person," dashed enthusiastically into every new craze, lived in a perpetual turmoil, and alternately spoiled or neglected her only child, Augustus Frederick, who was an imbecile.

Caroline and William Lamb occupied an upper floor of Melbourne House in Whitehall, and here the young woman pursued her crazy career, playing ball with her pages (occasionally she was known to don their uniforms), entertaining an extraordinary mixture of guests, and flying into tantrums when opposed in any way. Not so long before, she had caused immense concern by her flirtation with Sir Godfrey Webster, son of Lady Holland by her first marriage. From this admirer she had accepted a dog as a present, and the animal had attacked and bitten her small son, much to Lady Melbourne's wrath. When remonstrated with,

86

Caroline burst into a tempest of weeping, promised to dismiss Sir Godfrey, and explained to her doubting mother-in-law that during their honeymoon at Brocket Hall William had "called me Prudish, said I was straitlaced, amused himself with instructing me in things I need never have heard or known." She added that William's teaching had "undermined the few virtues I ever possessed" and caused her to develop an unholy interest in the world's wickedness.

By the spring of 1812 the atmosphere of Melbourne House was stormy indeed. On the ground and first floors Lady Melbourne, outwardly serene but inwardly fuming, held innumerable functions which everybody who was anybody, from the Prince Regent to Sheridan, attended. Upstairs Lady Caroline— "dressed, or rather *not* dressed, so as to excite universal attention, and authorize every boldness of staring"—gave waltz parties at which her friends practiced this new and intoxicating dance just imported from the Continent.

Naturally, Lady Caroline was fascinated by *Childe Harold*, but Samuel Rogers was not anxious to act as intermediary between the poet and herself, and murmured unhappily that she would like neither Byron's club foot nor his pernicious habit of biting his nails. A few days later, however, when she entered Lady Westmorland's drawing room she saw Byron standing at its far end, surrounded by a crowd of adoring women. She suffered her hostess to lead her towards them and then, on an impulse, swung on her heel and began chattering eagerly to some other guests.

The snub was unmistakable and it wounded Byron to the quick. On the instant he decided that he would teach Lady Caroline a much-needed lesson at the first opportunity, and when he shortly met her at Lady Holland's and was introduced to her formally he said in a biting voice, "This offer was made to you the other day—may I ask why you declined it?" He then gave her what his feminine admirers called his "under look" and in a low tone asked if he might call upon her. She gave rather cool permission but as she turned away her heart was beating madly and in her mind echoed the words she had written in her diary upon first seeing him. "Mad, bad and dangerous to know...."

Byron's original intention may have been to put Lady Caroline in her place, but he very soon changed his tactics. The morning after the encounter at Holland House he called upon her and sent up his name by the flunkey. Caroline had just returned from a ride in the park "filthy and disheveled" and was talking to Moore and Rogers when she heard that the poet was downstairs. Without excuse to her guests she fled from the room, and Byron was greeted by Rogers with the remark, "Here has Lady Caroline been sitting in all her dirt with us, but as soon as you were announced, she fled to make herself beautiful."

Despite himself Byron felt flattered. His snobbism had always made him regard the "Devonshire House clique" as the most fashionable and glittering in London—and here was its bright particular star doing him signal honor! From that moment he began to woo his Caro Lamb with a fervor he was soon to regret. He asked if he might see her in private, and thereafter he visited Melbourne nearly every day, undeterred by her disturbed mother's warning that her heart was already given elsewhere. He took her a rose and a carnation with the remark, "Your Ladyship, I am told, likes all that is new and rare—for a moment." He put out every ounce of his charm in an effort to beguile her, he wrote her ardent letters, he talked to her for hours in his soft, persuasive voice.

At Lady Caroline's waltzing parties Byron stood glowering in a corner. Since he was unable to dance himself he disliked watching others do so and, moreover, he took the Oriental view that beautiful young women should remain mysterious, elusive creatures and not display their charms in public. Very soon he told Caroline that if she wished to keep his affection she must forswear the waltz, and so infatuated was she that she promptly banished her gay young friends and paid off the musicians. "He liked to read with me," was her ingenuous comment, "and stay with me out of the crowd. Not but what we went about together everywhere, and were at last invited always as if we had been married."

Here Lady Caroline was guilty of an overstatement. It was she who maneuvered that they should be invited together, and by May Byron was growing irritated by her cloying attentions:

> I was soon congratulated by friends on the conquest I had made, and did my utmost to show that I was not insensible to the partiality I could not but perceive. I made every effort to be in love, expressed as much ardour as I could muster, and kept feeding the flame with a constant supply of *billets doux* and amatory verses.

For a little while Caroline had made Byron happy. She had fed his vanity and she had provided him with the lavish affection for which he craved. But he hated being monopolized by any one person and he wanted to be free to enjoy the fame which had come to him so suddenly, to go out and about as he pleased, to savor his new and delicious life to the full. But everywhere he went there was Caroline waiting to seize his arm with a proprietary air, to indulge in whispered conversations, to upbraid him for some fancied slight; and it was with a sense of relief that he saw her off to the country in the third week of May.

Without Caroline life was sweet. He spent entrancing evenings at Holland House, where he listened to such noted wits as "Conversation" Sharp, Henry Luttrell, J. P. Curran and Sydney Smith, met "Monk" Lewis, nicknamed after his famous novel, and made friends with Sheridan—"poor dear Sherry."

> He had a sort of liking for me [wrote Byron long afterwards], and never attacked me—at least to my face. . . . It occasionally fell to my lot to see him home—no sinecure, for he was so tipsy that I was obliged to put on his cock'd hat for him: to be sure it tumbled off again, and I was not myself so sober as to be able to pick it up. . . .

Byron also saw a great deal of Lady Melbourne with whom, oddly enough, he had formed a close friendship, and derived much satisfaction from the hundreds of letters he received about *Childe Harold*. On June 2nd, he, his heir Captain George Byron, and Hobhouse went down to Newstead to spend a care-free holiday, but on the 10th a page arrived with an impassioned scrawl from Lady Caroline demanding that he return to London forthwith. Had Byron ignored this summons he might have saved himself much trouble, but he had not yet reached the stage of exasperation at which he was to make a ruthless attempt to break the relationship.

He found Lady Caroline in a most hysterical frame of mind. If he attended a gathering to which she was not invited she waited on the pavement for him till the small hours and forced her way into his carriage. When he took refuge in his rooms she dressed herself up as a page and arrived with some fictitious message. If he eluded her successfully she fled to Samuel Rogers' house, and when he returned from some party he would find her flitting mothlike up and down his garden "waiting for me to beg that I would reconcile them."

At the beginning of the affair Lady Caroline had piqued Byron's vanity by sheering away from him at Lady Westmor-land's: now she piqued it by making him appear a figure of fun. The whole of London rang with the scandal and by July 2nd he was forced to agree to Hobhouse's suggestion and leave town for a few days. It was a measure which proved ineffectual, for both Caroline and her mother bombarded poor Hobhouse with notes and entreaties; and in addition Byron was extremely harassed over money matters and had come to the sad conclusion he would have to sell Newstead. Between sending soothing epistles to his lady love and enduring stormy interviews with Hanson, the poet was at his wit's end by August, when Lady Caroline staged a scene before which all her earlier efforts paled.

Her family had determined that she should be removed to the Bessboroughs' home in Ireland, and on August 12th Lady

Bessborough drove from Roehampton to Melbourne House to argue with her erring daughter. Lady Caroline was in a violent temper and not only refused to listen but spoke to Lord Melbourne "so rudely, so disrespectfully" that her flustered parent left the room in search of Lady Melbourne. While she was gone Caroline screamed to her father-in-law that she was about to elope with Byron, whereupon he told her he did not think for a moment that Byron wanted her but that she could "go and be damned!" To his dismay she immediately dashed out of the room, down the staircase and out of the front door at such speed that nobody had a chance to stop her. Lady Bessborough summoned her carriage and drove round "in every direction I thought she could have gone," and when her search proved vain she and Lady Melbourne drove to Byron's lodgings in St. James's Street. He, however, had no news of the truant and spent the next few hours in a fearful state of agitation, wondering what this latest vagary might portend. Not until evening did a hackney coachman arrive with a message to say that Lady Caroline had left a message for his Lordship at her mother's house in Cavendish Square.

By bribery Byron discovered from the man that the lady had hidden in a Pall Mall chemist's shop on leaving Melbourne House, and had then hailed him to drive her past "the first turnpike off the stones." He had taken her to Kensington, where she had first pawned an opal ring for twenty guineas and then sought refuge in the house of a surgeon to whom she told a garbled story about having run away from her family. Her intention, she added, was to journey to Portsmouth and there board the first ship to sail—no matter where its destination.

In Byron's complex nature there was a strong streak of common sense. Without more ado he had himself driven to Kensington, where he announced that he was the lady's brother. Caroline wept, raved and threatened, but Byron was adamant and though he had almost to drag her into the carriage he managed to transport her to Cavendish Square. Here a tearful Lady Bessborough awaited them—but it was Byron who eventually persuaded the now exhausted Caroline to return to Melbourne House, where the tolerant William agreed to forgive her.

But by the following morning Caroline, so to speak, had got her second wind. At one moment she was sobbing in remorse for her stupid action; at the next she was screaming that she was pregnant and that if she was forced to travel she would suffer a miscarriage. Her behavior had such an effect on Lady Bessborough that the poor lady fell to the floor in a fit in her carriage, and the news of her escapade spread round the town like wildfire, even the Prince Regent declaring that he had never heard such a thing in his life and that "Lord Byron had bewitched the whole family."

So far as Lady Caroline's running away was concerned Byron was entirely innocent; but around him eddied rumor and counter-rumor. Never of stable temperament and always affected nervously by scenes, he most unfortunately hinted to Lady Bessborough that the affair with her daughter could never have come to anything because of dark and dreadful episodes in his earlier life. Whether he meant his former dalliance with ladies of the town and maidservants, or whether he was referring to his Harrow, Cambridge and Grecian friendships with handsome youths we do not know, but it is certain that the Prince Regent had conceived a "shocking notion" about him and that from this time on he seemed to take a perverse delight in destroying his own reputation.

While Lady Caroline was still filling Melbourne House with her lamentations Newstead was put up for sale at Garroway's Coffee House on August 14th, and the loyal Hobhouse (who had returned penniless from Ireland and whose capital at the moment amounted to one guinea and sixpence) carried the bidding for the Abbey up to 113,000 guineas. This, however, was below the reserve price so Byron had to consent to both Abbey and farms being bought in. Personally he was relieved, for the last thing he wished to do was to sell his home, but the shortage of money continued to harass him and when he heard in the beginning of September that Caroline was actually in Ireland he decided that he would go to Cheltenham to recuperate and to write a prologue for the reopening of Drury Lane Theatre, which had been shut since a bad fire in 1809. He had been asked to write this by Lord Holland, a gentleman he was always ready to oblige, but it was definitely not a very successful piece of work.

* 3 *

The previous March, when his affair with Lady Caroline was yet in the innocuous stage, Byron had met her cousin by marriage, Annabella Milbanke, at Melbourne House. She was the daughter of Lady Melbourne's brother, Sir Ralph Milbanke, and heiress to a wealthy uncle, Lord Wentworth, and she was as unlike the usual débutante of her day and age as could possibly be imagined. Brought up by indulgent, middle-aged parents, Annabella had early determined to become a scholar and during her London stay she found far more pleasure in visiting museums and attending lectures than in the gay social round. She had many suitors but spurned them all—including Augustus, son of the Duchess of Devonshire, a lady who described her as "good, amiable, and sensible, but cold, prudent, and reflecting."

Annabella had read *Childe Harold* and been impressed by it, but when she first saw Byron she avoided an introduction to him partly because she considered him "rather too much of a mannerist," and partly because Lady Caroline, whom she detested, was making such a fool of herself over him; but at the same time she confided to her diary that although she could not "be captivated by that Genius which is barren of blessings" she would rather like to talk with the poet.

The opportunity came at a party of Lady Cowper's, where

the serious young bluestocking discussed the work of a shoe-maker poet she was interested in and took Byron to task for some of the sentiments expressed in *Childe Harold*. Rather amused, yet attracted to this grave, sweet-faced girl who seemed so concerned as to his moral welfare, Byron vowed that he was truly sorry for the evil he had done and asked her abruptly, "Do you think there is one person here who dares look into himself?" It was a remark which appealed to Annabella, who again had recourse to her diary, noting that he was a "very bad, very good man" sadly in need of reform, and that his statement that he "had not a friend in the world" had so moved her she had determined "to be a devoted friend to this lone being."

Annabella was unaware that it was Byron's habit to dwell upon his friendless state (at the time he had more friends than ever in his life before); nor did she realize that his nature had a darker side. She was a born reformer and she conceived, with an exhilarating sense of adventure, that it was her duty to turn the melancholy and libertine poet into a normal, cheerful human being. For his part Byron saw Annabella as an heiress who might well be considered as a bride.

Through Caroline Annabella sent him some blank verse she had written. He replied that he considered Miss Milbanke's poems "smooth and pretty," but that an author friend of his thought them brilliant. He asked Caroline to "convey as much of this to Miss M. as you think proper," but added, "I have no desire to be further acquainted with Miss Milbanke; she is too good for a fallen spirit to know, and I should like her more if she were less perfect."

He did not know that when Annabella returned to her home at Seaham she carried in her mind an idealistic portrait of him; indeed in the terrific fuss and scandal caused by Caroline he forgot her very existence. Only when the Lambs had departed to Ireland and he was enjoying a rest in Lord Holland's Chel-tenham home did he think of her again. As usual he was "cursed dipped"; in retrospect Annabella seemed all that was desirable;

94

the idea of marriage was an eminently suitable one. He therefore wrote Lady Melbourne a long letter setting forth his reasons for the break with Caroline and that there was someone he had wished to marry had not the affair intervened.

> The woman I mean is Miss Milbanke; I know nothing of her fortune, and I am told that her father is ruined, but my own will, when my Rochdale arrangements are closed, be sufficient for both.... I know little of her, and have not the most distant reason to suppose that I am a favourite in that quarter. But I never saw a woman whom I *esteemed* so much....

Lady Melbourne wrote back asking if Byron were sure of himself, and when he replied that he was she consented to approach her niece on his behalf.

Many a girl, even in the year 1812, would have found it unromantic to be proposed to through the medium of an aunt, but Annabella promptly sat down and penned a lengthy epistle which opened by saying that she felt Lord Byron could never become the "object of that strong affection which would make me happy in domestic life," and that she considered pride had twisted his outlook although "his love of goodness in its chastest form, and his abhorrence of all that degrades human nature, prove the uncorrupted purity of his moral sense." She then listed the virtues she would expect to find in a husband and ended with a definite refusal of his proposal.

But by October 12th, when her reply at length reached Byron, he had already become enamored of somebody else, so he wrote impudently to Lady Melbourne, "She deserves a better heart than mine. What shall I do—shall I advertise?"

✳ 4 ✳

With Miss Milbanke safely disposed of—he was really rather glad as he "never was enamored"—Byron turned his whole attention to his new love, Lady Oxford. Twice his age, erudite, witty and sensuous, she was to him both mistress and mother. With her and her charming children (known as the "Harleian Miscellany" since nobody was quite sure whether Lord Oxford had fathered them all or not) Byron spent the winter at Eyewood in Herefordshire. The house was warm and peaceful. It was indeed the sort of home which Byron had always longed for and never known, and his "Aspasia" was beautiful, gentle and kind. "She resembled," he told Lady Blessington years afterwards, "a landscape by Claude Lorraine, with a setting sun, her beauties enhanced by the knowledge that they were shedding their last dying beams."

Byron's nerves had been in a shocking state after the Lady Caroline affair: the months spent with Lady Oxford soothed them, but even the peace of Eyewood was disturbed by wild letters from Ireland. Byron, terrified lest his inamorata should carry out her threats of returning to England, wrote gentle replies full of "the greatest absurdities," but by November his patience was exhausted and when she sent him an abusive epistle saying she had heard "such things, such double things of his saying and doing," the cruel streak in him came uppermost. "Correct your vanity which is ridiculous and proverbial," he wrote savagely, "exert your Caprices on your new conquests and leave me in peace."

Lady Caroline was distracted and, having no least idea of Byron's latest affair, wrote to her "Dearest Aspasia" begging her to tell Lord Byron that she truly loved him and would not hurt him for the world. By way of answer she received a curt note in Byron's handwriting: "Our affections are not in our power—mine are engaged"—and the missive was sealed with Lady Oxford's private signet, an intaglio portraying Cupid in a two-horse chariot which she knew very well.

Lady Caroline had long been ill-balanced: the knowledge that Lady Oxford and Byron were lovers temporarily turned her brain. William Lamb brought her back to England and deposited her at the country house of her cousin, Harriet Granville, who was shocked by "her poor careworn face" and seriously alarmed by her ungovernable moods. Poor Caroline, wildly excited one moment and in the depths of despair the next, insisted she must have a final interview with Byron, an idea her husband and mother-in-law at last agreed to. They stipulated, however, that a third party should be present. With deliberate cruelty Byron suggested Lady Oxford, but fortunately that lady refused so the interview was put off and Caroline sent down with her maid to Brocket Hall.

Here, on a bitter December day, she staged an auto-da-fé. A great pyre was stacked in the park, a group of village girls were given white muslin dresses and instructed to dance around it, and into the flames Lady Caroline cast a wax effigy of her lover, all his letters, a ring and chain he had given her, and a copy of *Childe Harold*. As she performed this task she chanted some verses of her own composition:

> See here are locks and braids of coloured hair
> Worn oft by me, to make the people stare;
> Rouge, feathers, flowers, and all those tawdry things,
> Besides those Pictures, letters, chains, and rings...
> Burn, fire, burn, while wondering Boys exclaim,
> And gold and trinkets glitter in the flame....

Even in his Eyewood seclusion Byron heard about the auto-da-fé, heard also that Lady Caroline's pages had new buttons with 'Ne Crede Byron' on them, a parody on his family motto which infuriated him; and when in a few weeks' time she committed a barefaced forgery by writing a leter in imitation of his hand to John Murray demanding to be given a miniature of the poet he had in his possession, he wrote to Lady Melbourne remarking that her action was "flat Burglary."

Having achieved the miniature Lady Caroline relapsed into comparative calm but—and it would have pleased her had she known of it—her deplorable conduct had shattered the halcyon peace of Eyewood. Byron was once more restless and irritable, and in February he and Lady Oxford drove up to London, where he took rooms in Bennet Street, St. James's. Byron was much exercised because a Mr. Claughton, who had made an offer for Newstead, was unable to complete the purchase price, and he seems to have vented his ill-temper on his Aspasia for when they visited the Princess of Wales that lady wrote to Lady Charlotte Campbell that

> Lady Oxford, poor soul, is more in love this time than she has ever been before. She was with me the other evening, and Lord Byron was so cross to her—his Lordship not being in a very good mood—that she was crying in the anteroom.

Byron had planned to go to Sicily with the Oxfords in the spring of 1813, but probably owing to shortage of money on his part the expedition was postponed. He stayed on in London while Lady Oxford returned to Eyewood. Presumably the rages of her young lover had proved a little too much for her, because she broke a small blood-vessel and remained in a low state for several weeks. By the time Byron rejoined her in April it was clear that their idyll was coming to an end.

Byron still had political aspirations—though Hobhouse mistrusted his enthusiasm and rightly thought the dear fellow's knowledge of politics a superficial one—and when he came back to London in May he visited Surrey Gaol to see Leigh Hunt who, with his brother, had been fined and sentenced to two years' imprisonment for a libel against the Prince Regent. Hunt, however, made light of his incarceration and had transformed his cell into a parlor which contained a piano as well as shelves of books, while Mrs. Hunt and their several children were also installed in the prison.

Meanwhile money worries were accumulating. Claughton still could not find the capital to buy Newstead, so Byron instructed the long-suffering Hanson to sell horses, books, pictures —"every moveable that is mine, and can be converted into cash," and went off to spend a final ten days with Lady Oxford at Maidenhead. He then accompanied her to Portsmouth, but returned before her ship sailed to face what was destined to be the most fateful summer of his life.

✳ 5 ✳

Byron's correspondence with his half-sister Augusta had practically ceased in 1812 because she had deeply disapproved of Caroline Lamb. In March 1813, however, she had appealed to him for money, and he had been genuinely distressed by his inability to help her. Augusta, who had remarkably elastic spirits, went on muddling along somehow until June, when even she had to acknowledge defeat since the house at Six Mile Bottom was surrounded by angry creditors. Several of her relations—notably her half-brother and sister by her mother's first marriage to Lord Carmarthen, the Duke of Leeds and Lady Chichester—were wealthy, but not unnaturally they had grown tired of helping Colonel Leigh; so she sent her little girls to stay with friends and rather timidly suggested to Byron she should come to him for a short visit.

Byron was delighted and on June 26th she arrived at Bennet Street to find that the brother she had scarcely seen for twelve years had grown into a handsome, charming young man who wore his fame with a casual air and greeted her as if they had parted only yesterday. There was no constraint between them. Within an hour they were talking nineteen to the dozen and before the day was out Augusta felt completely at home. She and Byron shared the same likes and dislikes, laughed at the same jokes, poked together through the drawers stuffed full of sentimental mementoes sent to him by feminine adorers, and giggled happily over trinkets, locks of hair, and ardent love letters.

Augusta was twenty-nine years old and had never been voted
a beauty, but there was about her an indefinable charm. Her
head, with its crown of dark curly hair, was beautifully set on a
long graceful neck, her eyes held an expression of wistfulness,
and her mouth had a delicious half-pout. Like her brother she
was given to gesticulating with her hands, and while she was apt
to dress a little fussily, adorning herself with bangles, brooches
and filmy scarves, these things somehow suited her. From her
grandmother, Lady Holderness, she had imbibed a sort of surface piety which led her to give prayer books to the poor and
talk at times in a vaguely high-souled way that Byron afterwards
alluded to as "Augusta's damned crinkum-crankum"; but she
had a tremendous sense of fun and was, at heart, amoral, her creed
being that one might do as one pleased provided one did not
hurt anyone else.

Byron found her even more lovable than he remembered
her. Other women—yes, even Lady Oxford—seemed convinced
there was something demonic about him: his "dear Goose"
regarded him as an enchanted playmate as simple and childish
as herself. She understood him as nobody else had ever done
and in her company he enjoyed functions which otherwise would
have bored him. Together they went to Almack's Masque, to a
reception given by Lady Davy, wife of the renowned chemist,
to parties galore, and on each occasion he felt prouder of his
sister.

It was left to Caroline Lamb to disturb his new-found serenity.
The scene was Lady Heathcote's ballroom and Lady Caroline
arrived in a "dreadful bad humor." Catching sight of Byron she
hissed at him, "I presume I may waltz *now?*"

"With everybody in turn," he answered cheerfully. "You
always did it better than any one. I shall have a pleasure in
seeing you."

Lady Caroline whirled away with her partner, but as Byron
was escorting Lady Rancliffe into the supper-room she suddenly

approached him and pressed something sharp into his hand, saying, "I mean to use this."

Byron replied, "Against me, I presume?" disengaged his hand and walked on, hoping that nobody had overheard her words.

Not until four o'clock in the morning did he learn from Lady Ossulston that the young woman had wounded herself with either a piece of broken glass or a knife and that her fellow guests had shouted for help. Then Lady Melbourne had held her arms, but when she released her Lady Caroline had produced a pair of scissors and dug them into her hand.

Byron immediately wrote to Lady Melbourne that he was at a loss to know what had happened.

> Lady Ossulstone looking angry (and at that moment ugly), delivered to me a confused kind of message from you of some scene—that is all I know, except that with laudable logic she drew the usual feminine deduction that I "*must* have behaved very ill"... I should have returned to her [Caroline] after her *doorway whisper*, but I could not with any kind of politeness leave Lady Rancliffe to drown herself in wine and water, or be suffocated in a jelly dish, without a spoon, or a hand to help her; besides if there was, and I foresaw there would be, something ridiculous, surely I was better absent than present.
>
> This is really insanity, and everybody seems inoculated with the same distemper. Lady Westmorland says, "You must have done something; you know between people in your situation, a word or a look goes a great way," etc., etc. So it seems indeed—but I never knew that *neither* words nor looks—in short, downright, innocent, vacant, indefinable *nothing*, had the same precious power of producing this perpetual worry.

But for once his "dear Lady M." did not entirely take his side. She was mortified by her daughter-in-law's crazy behavior, but she also blamed Byron for being the cause of it, and when she received scores of letters from friends who offered their sympathy and inquired anxiously if poor Lady Caroline had really been "at last carried out by several people actually in a strait waistcoat" she felt her cup of misery was full. True, her "Sweet

William" had again forgiven his erring wife but she knew that this final scandal was one which could not be lived down.

And as if these feline scratches were not enough to bear, the newspapers took up the story. Lady Caroline's dress had been soaked in blood.... She had raved like a madwoman.... She had severely wounded herself twice—thrice—*four* times in all.

Worst of all was *The Satirist*, which headed its article with a quotation from *Rejected Addresses*:

> With horn-handled knife
> To kill a tender lamb as dead as mutton

and went on to say that at Lady Heathcote's ball "Lord B ... n" had

> ... seemed to lavish his attention on another fair object. This preference so enraged Lady C.L.b. that, in a paroxysm of jealousy, she took up a dessert knife, and stabbed herself. The gay circle was, of course, immediately plunged in confusion and dismay, which, however, was soon succeeded by levity and scandal....

Byron was distraught by the whole affair. Everywhere he went he was treated to sly digs on the subject; Lady Melbourne was displeased with him; the newspapers had made unforgivable references to his lameness. In his despair he turned naturally to Augusta, the one person in the world who understood him; and through the summer days they grew ever closer together.

In her silliness—for in many ways she was a silly woman—Augusta hid a certain innate wisdom. Being herself a Byron she knew the family history, knew also of her brother's unhappy childhood; but although she was furiously angry with Caroline Lamb she refrained from allusions to her and carried on with her usual absurd prattle. Even in these dark days she made Byron laugh—and that, to her pagan mind, was the all-important thing.

It is doubtful if Augusta saw the pit that was opening before them. A volatile creature of primitive emotions, she took no heed of past or future but simply lived for the day. But Byron not only saw the pit but firmly believed in the darker recesses of his mind that it had been dug by fate to encompass his damnation. There was no question of escape; what was more, the lawless part of him did not really wish to escape but to plunge into the abyss in defiance of the world.

Once he had written:

> For he through Sin's long labyrinth had run
> Nor made atonement when he did amiss....

and now, as he sought the sleepy mother-comfort he had never known from this sister who seemed to embody every feminine virtue he had ever desired, the thought of sin stole into his mind again.

The question of whether Byron and Augusta were guilty of incest or not is one which has troubled the world of letters for some hundred and forty years. There is not and there never can be a definite answer of "Yes" or "No." Byron was a past-master in the art of innuendo both in letters and conversation, and for that reason many people have dismissed his references to Augusta from 1813 onwards, pointing out that he said equally terrible things about other people which had no foundation in fact. But if one studies these references closely one finds something which rings true, which obliges one to believe that there was a secret in his life he could never forget, and that that secret concerned his relationship wtih Augusta.

These references apart, the subsequent behavior of both Byron and his sister seems inexplicable if their relationship was an innocent one. If so, could he have written to her that she had left him "utterly incapable of *real* love for any other human being—for what could they be to me after you?"; could she have made the hysterical semi-confessions she did to Lady Byron after he had left England for good?

If there was indeed a guilty relationship between them (and there seems remarkably little doubt about it) was it such a terrible thing as many people have tried to make out? Incest is revolting, but in this particular case perhaps it was less disgraceful than is commonly supposed. Byron was an extraordinary man in whom all sorts of good and bad qualities were perpetually at war. He was a puritan and yet a rake; he was impulsive yet had a hard streak of common sense; he was a bundle of superstitions yet did not believe in faith; he was attached to his friends yet betrayed their confidences; he was generous to a fault yet guilty of sudden meannesses; he was soft-hearted yet cruel and violent; and above all he was haunted by the Byronic doom.

It was a doom he felt he had to share—and with whom else could he share it than with Augusta, who had the same blood as his own?

There were many other episodes in Byron's stormy career which seem far more discreditable than his relationship with Augusta, and one can surely understand how it was that the pair drifted together in that July of 1813. They had not seen each other for many years and the discovery of their mutual affection had an uplifting effect. Then came the disgraceful behavior of Lady Caroline, and Augusta assumed the role of comforter—a dangerous part to play opposite one of Byron's temperament. His gratitude gave way to passion, and with passion marched an overwhelming longing to cling for ever to this dearest of beings.

The consequences were to be disastrous beyond belief, but for a few weeks the two were happy in their Bennet Street retreat. Byron was again in the highest of spirits—he laughed uproariously when Lady Caroline sent him a "most tempting basket of fruit" from the country with a letter of apology; he made his peace with Lady Melbourne; he managed to stop a proposed duel between Lord Foley and Scrope Davies; he called upon Mme de Staël, who had recently come to London with her eldest son, her daughter Albertine, and her handsome but unacknowledged second husband, M. de Rocca; and he temporarily abandoned his Spartan diet of biscuits and soda water for a succession of rich dinners after which, he wrote to Moore, "my head aches with the vintage of various cellars, and my brains are muddled as their dregs."

It was a mood which could not endure, and the first hint of its passing was given on August 22nd in the postscript of an epistle to Moore. "... the fact is," he wrote, "I am at this moment in a far more serious, and entirely new, scrape than any of the last twelve months—and that is saying a good deal. It is unlucky we can neither live with nor without these women."

To Lady Melbourne, however, Byron was more explicit. He confided in her that he proposed to leave England and take Augusta with him. The mere prospect of such a move filled her with alarm, for she realized exactly how the world would view their departure, and she wrote the poet a long letter in which she pointed out the consequences which must inevitably follow if he took this fatal step. He would be ostracized by society. His sister would lose husband, children and reputation. His crime would never be forgotten or forgiven.

Much to Lady Melbourne's relief Byron replied on August 31st that his sister had returned to Six Mile Bottom, and that since he himself was still in London he could assure her that her kind and *"unanswerable"* letter had "as yet had all the effect you could wish"; but she was again thrown into a state of agitation a week later when she received a dramatic note saying that he was going to the country and would write to her if "nothing very particular occurred." He would not see her before he left lest she persuade him to give up his journey, and if anything *did* happen doubtless she would hear of it—but not from him, although wherever he was he would remain her faithful friend.

Fortunately, the visit to Augusta had no dire results, but Byron returned from it in a nervous, dissatisfied frame of mind which induced him to accept an invitation from James Wedderburn Webster to visit him at Aston Hall, Rotherham. It was the house, not its rather boring occupant, which lured him, for it had belonged to Lady Carmarthen, and Mad Jack Byron had once lived there; but when he arrived he was immediately intrigued by his delicate hostess, Lady Frances Webster, a "pretty, pleasing woman," very shy and, according to her pompous, boring husband, "very like Christ!" (a remark which sent Byron into shrieks of laughter).

Emotionally exhausted, out of love with romance for the moment, Byron found the quiet atmosphere of Aston soothing. He made no attempt to flirt with Lady Frances, but amused himself with writing long and witty letters to Lady Melbourne, who had now received him back into the fold and was urging him to find a new love—his hostess or her sister Lady Catherine Annesley for preference. Byron replied that he had grown "so good, or so indolent" that he could not be bothered, added that the Webster children only screamed "in a low voice," and regaled her with ribald accounts of Webster's jealousy of his wife.

He had also reopened a correspondence (directly this time) with Annabella Milbanke, who had lately been most distressed by a rumor that he had behaved exceedingly badly towards the "young man" who had bought Newstead and had written to her aunt asking if the report were true. Byron had answered through the same medium that Mr. Claughton was not young and had deliberately made a contract he was unable to honor, thus forcing the owner of Newstead to take legal action; this reply had so pleased and relieved the strange young woman that she sent him by way of thanks "one of the longest letters in the world, containing some of the longest words in the English language." In this she informed him that she was the victim of a hopeless love for another but that she wished to establish "an unreserved friendship" between him and herself. She begged him, however, to keep their correspondence a secret, except from her parents. This request entertained Byron hugely and needless to say he at once wrote to Lady Melbourne, enclosing a "word-portrait" which Annabella had sent him of her ideal husband.

...I shall say nothing because I do not understand it; though I dare say it is exactly what it ought to be.... She seems to have been spoiled—not as children usually are—but systematically Clarissa Harlowed into an awkward kind of correctness, with a dependence upon her own infallibility which will or may lead her into some egregious blunder. I don't mean the usual error of young gentlewomen, but she will find exactly what she wants, and then discover that it is much more dignified than entertaining.

Byron returned to London, but early in October he again visited Aston, ostensibly to collect a poodle Webster had promised him but really, one surmises, because he could not forget that "soul of melancholy gentleness," Lady Frances. On this occasion he could not resist living up to his reputation of being the most dangerous rake in London, and when he found himself alone with his hostess in the billiard room he not only made her a pretty speech but wrote her a *billet doux* which she "deposited not very far from her heart." "Take it once," he wrote to Lady Melbourne, "I have made love, and if I am to believe mere *words* (for there we have hitherto stopped), it is returned."

There was something about Byron which drew the most unexpected qualities from those with whom he came in contact. To his bewilderment, almost to his alarm, the decorous Lady. Frances changed suddenly into an ardent woman who wrote him passionate letters telling of her love, and Byron—who by this time was thinking in terms of duels and elopements—invited the Websters and Lady Catherine to stay with him at Newstead, where he hoped to bring the affair to a head. Unfortunately on the first evening, so he told Lady Melbourne,

...after deep and drowsy potations, I took it into my head to empty my *skull cup*, which holds rather better than a bottle of claret, at *one draught*, and nearly died the death of Alexander—which I shall be content to do when I have achieved his conquests. I had just sense enough left to feel that I was not fit to join the ladies, and went to bed, where, my valet tells me, that I was first convulsed, and afterwards so motionless, that he thought, "Good night to Marmion."

On recovering from his indisposition Byron arranged to meet Lady Frances in one of Newstead's many disused rooms at two o'clock in the morning. She greeted him with the words, "I am entirely at your *mercy*. I own it. I give myself up to you. I am not *cold*—whatever I seem to others; but I know that I cannot bear the reflection hereafter. Do not imagine that these are mere words. I tell you the truth—now act as you will."

In all his experience of love-making Byron had never been confronted with such a situation. There were no protests, no scenes; only this pathetic speech delivered with an air of sad resignation. There was "something so very peculiar in her manner," he wrote to Lady Melbourne, that he simply could not carry out the conquest he had planned so carefully.

> And yet I know not whether I can regret it, she seems so very thankful for my forbearance—a proof, at least, that she was not playing merely the usual decorous reluctance, which is sometimes so tiresome on these occasions.

On October 19th Byron and Webster left Newstead for London, and from her window Lady Frances watched their departure before crossing to her writing desk. For an hour or more she sat there, the tears welling in her eyes, writing to her lover; and when she had finished she cut off two of her fair curls and placed them in the envelope with her letter. For her the parting had been a "moment of torture" and with her last glance at "that too dearly cherished countenance" she had known "the true horror of separation."

Meanwhile Byron was sitting silently in his corner of the coach, his pistols at his side. He was already angry with himself for not seizing his opportunity but he was still determined to flee the country with Lady Frances if she would consent to such a proposal. Beside him Webster—to whom, either on impulse or from a sense of guilt, he had just lent a thousand pounds which he could ill afford—chattered inanities until he happened to notice his companion's scowling face. "For God's sake, my dear B.," he exclaimed, "what are you thinking of? Are you about to commit murder? or what other dreadful thing are you meditating?" Byron murmured that he had always felt sure he would someday be attacked and that he was thinking of possible footpads or highwaymen; but in truth his thoughts were back in Newstead with his "little proselyte" who had turned so swiftly into his "little *white* penitent."

✳ 6 ✳

As soon as Byron was back in Bennet Street he set to work on a new poem—"all convulsions end with me in rhyme." Since he always wrote at terrific speed this was soon in the hands of the printers, but the actual composition of the verses had effectively turned his thoughts from Lady Frances and it is to be feared that the letters she wrote him were not appreciated as they deserved. Byron was always irked by what he called the "foolish trophies" of love affairs; moreover, egged on by Webster, he was vaguely thinking of marrying Lady Catherine Annesley, and while he was not really serious about the idea her sister's passionate protests irritated him.

He preferred Augusta and Lady Melbourne as correspondents, though he took a kind of perverse pleasure in the lengthy sermons with which Annabella Milbanke still provided him. She seemed so genuinely distressed about his melancholy and he was distinctly flattered when she told him she felt he lived on a lonely peak "surrounded by admirers who could not value you, and by friends to whom you were not dear." By the end of October, however, he was growing a trifle bored by her effusions and hinted to Lady Melbourne that he was not going to answer the latest one; but Annabella was a tenacious young woman and promptly wrote again to tell him that she did not think so highly of his powers of reasoning as he did of his powers of imagination. Perhaps, she added haughtily, he would inform her if her letters were unacceptable.

Byron answered a week later, asking if she would accept a copy of his new poem, *The Bride of Abydos*. He added that he trusted she would not think he intended to present himself as one of her many suitors. "I have taken exquisite care to prevent the possibility of that," he wrote rather ominously; and at the end of November he noted in his journal:

> Yesterday, a very pretty letter from Annabella, which I answered. What an odd situation and friendship is ours!—without one spark of love on either side, and produced by circumstances which in general lead to coldness on one side, and aversion on the other. She is a very superior woman, and very little spoiled, which is strange in an heiress—a girl of twenty—a peeress that is to be, in her own right—an only child, and a *savante*, who has always had her own way. She is a poetess—a mathematician—a metaphysician, and yet, withal, very kind, generous, and gentle, with very little pretension. Any other head would be turned with half her acquisitions, and a tenth of her advantages.

In most of his letters of this period Byron gave the impression that he was living like a recluse in Bennet Street; but the journal he kept spasmodically from mid-November until the next spring revealed a very different picture.

> Two nights ago I saw the tigers sup at Exeter 'Change. Except Veli Pasha's lion in the Morea,—who followed the Arab keeper like a dog,—the fondness of the hyena for her keeper amused me most. Such a conversazione!—There was a hippopotamus, like Lord Liverpool in the face; and the "Ursine Sloth" had the very voice and manner of my valet—but the tiger talked too much. The elephant took and gave me my money again—took off my hat—opened a door—*trunked* a whip—and behaved so well, that I wished he were my butler. The handsomest animal on earth is one of the panthers; but the poor antelopes were dead. I should hate to see one *here:*—the sight of the *camel* made me pine again for Asia Minor. "*Oh quando te aspiciam?*"

In more somber mood he wrote that the previous night he had finished *The Bride of Abydos*.

> I believe the composition of it kept me alive—for it was written to drive my thoughts from the recollection of—
> "Dear sacred name, rest ever unreveal'd."
> At least, even here, my hand would tremble to write it.

The subject of the poem, significantly enough, was the love between a boy and girl who believed themselves to be brother and sister. The belief proved a mistaken one but their love ended in death.

His days were filled with visits from "Monk" Lewis, Dallas, Hodgson and other friends, with calls upon Mme de Staël and various London hostesses, with dinner parties, theater parties, and visits to the eating house of Tom Cribb, the boxing champion. He took the liveliest interest in the doings of "that Anakim of anarchy—Bonaparte," for whom he had an intense admiration, though he didn't want him in England.

> ...I should not wonder if he banged them yet. To be beat by men would be something; but by three stupid, legitimate-old-dynasty boobies of regular-bred sovereigns—O-hone-a-rie! It must be, as Cobbett says, his marriage with the thick-lipped and thick-headed *Autrichienne* brood. He had better have kept to her who was kept by Barras....

He greatly enjoyed dining with Lady Holland—where else could he hear such good conversation?—but he took great exception to her habit of placing a—

> ...damned screen between the whole room and the fire. I, who bear cold no better than an antelope, and never yet found a sun quite *done* to my taste, was absolutely petrified, and could not even shiver. All the rest, too, looked as if they were just unpacked, like salmon from an ice-basket, and set down to table for that day only.

But Byron suffered for the dinners he ate at Holland House and elsewhere—and this is not surprising in view of the fact that he alternately starved and gorged. A heavy meal induced the most dreadful nightmare from which he shuddered awake in a violent sweat, or upset his ill-treated liver so much that he developed acute bilious headache. In the depression following such an attack he thought gloomily of his vanishing youth for to him—

> ... the myrtle and ivy of sweet two-and-twenty
> Are worth all your laurels, though ever so plenty.

He was, he confided to his journal,

> ... *ennuyé* beyond my usual tense of that yawning verb....
> When one subtracts from life infancy (which is vegetation),—
> sleep, eating, and swilling—buttoning and unbuttoning—how
> much remains of downright existence? The summer of a dormouse.

❋ 7 ❋

It was late December or early January when Augusta came back to London, and on January 17th she and Byron set off for Newstead in a coach "really as large as the cabin of a 74," and, Byron considered, "meant for the Atlantic instead of the Continent"; and as soon as they arrived the snow began to fall so thickly that within a few hours the great gaunt old house was completely isolated.

It was a strange interlude which Byron never forgot. It was the fulfillment of his boyish dream of Augusta ... Newstead. They were alone in the empty, echoing Abbey, and outside the walls the snow formed a soft but impenetrable barrier between themselves and the world. They were happy, they laughed over the ridiculous old jokes which only they could understand, they watched the snowflakes gleefully and hoped they might go on falling so that peace would not be disturbed.

Before he left London Byron had received a letter from his old love, Mary Chaworth Musters, begging him to visit her when he came to Nottinghamshire. She had separated from her husband, who had been "playing the Devil with all kinds of vulgar mistresses," and she was living in a cottage with a woman companion. But he, who had told so many friends that he had never recovered from the blow of her marriage, made no attempt to renew the friendship. For the first week the snow stopped him; but even when the road was passable once more he did not go to see her although he wrote Lady Melbourne that Augusta had been urging him repeatedly to call before he left the county. Mary Chaworth belonged to the past and at the moment he was entirely wrapped up in the present.

In the first week in February Mr. Claughton arrived to discuss the completion of his purchase of Newstead, and on the 10th Byron and Augusta parted, she bound for Six Mile Bottom and he for London, where he found—

> ...all the newspapers in hysterics, and town in an uproar, on the avowal and republication of two stanzas on Princess Charlotte's weeping at Regency's speech to Lauderdale in 1812. They are daily at it still;—some of the abuse good, all of it hearty. They talk of a motion in our House upon it—be it so.

The stanzas in question had appeared anonymously in 1812 and were addressed to the Prince Regent's daughter who, upon hearing her father abuse his former Whig friends at a Carlton House banquet, had begun to sob so violently that she had been sternly told to retire.

> Weep, daughter of a royal line,
>   A Sire's disgrace, a realm's decay;
> Ah! happy if a tear of thine
>   Could wash a father's fault away!

> Weep—for thy tears are Virtue's tears—
>   Auspicious to these suffering isles;
> And be each drop in future years
>   Repaid thee by thy people's smiles!

In January 1814 John Murray had published Byron's latest poem, *The Corsair*, and attached to it were the *Stanzas to a Lady Weeping*. The Tory press, which had no love for the poet, launched a series of vitriolic attacks upon him. The *Courier* ran no fewer than nine articles devoted to Byron's character and pointed out that in *English Bards* he had attacked the very people for whom he now professed friendship. "We have, we should hope," their journalist remarked severely, "sufficiently exposed the audacious levity and waywardness of Lord Byron's mind." The *Morning Post* printed frightening verses about him and made most objectionable references to his lameness; other papers joined in the fray; and although the fate of the whole of Europe was trembling in the balance there was more space devoted to Byron's eight lines than to Napoleon. "I really begin to think myself a most important personage...," he told Lady Melbourne. "I think you must admit that mine has been an odd destiny."

Gradually the storm died down and Byron and Hobhouse—who had lately returned to London—indulged in an orgy of theater going, especially enjoying the performances of Edmund Kean in *Richard III* and *Hamlet*. They also dined together at the Cocoa Tree and other clubs, and had lengthy discussions on the European situation, with Byron backing Napoleon and voicing his dislike of "the dull, stupid old system—balance of Europe—poising straws on kings' noses instead of wringing them off."

On March 7th Byron attended a very peculiar wedding which he himself had helped to arrange. He gave away Mary Anne, eldest daughter of Hanson, his lawyer, at her marriage to the weak-witted Earl of Portsmouth. It was an affair which did no credit to either the poet or the Hanson family, for the bridegroom was in no fit state to know his own mind, and later on his relatives brought a lawsuit to inquire into his sanity at the time. More shocking still was a story (quoted by Lord Lovelace) of how Byron, while escorting the bride up the aisle, asked her if she remembered the occasion several years earlier when he had seduced her.

A month later Lady Melbourne was disturbed to receive a letter from Byron informing her that he had been staying with Augusta,

> ...where I swallowed the D...l in ye shape of a collar of brawn one evening for supper (after an enormous dinner too), and it required all kinds of brandies, and I don't know what besides, to put me again in health and good humour....I left all my relations—at least my niece and her mamma—very well. L(eigh) was in Yorkshire; and I regret not having seen him of course very much. My intention was to have joined a party at Cambridge; but somehow I overstaid my time, and the inclination to visit the University went off....

Lady Melbourne had every cause for alarm. She was aware that Augusta was expecting another child at any moment, and in the light of what she suspected had happened the previous summer she thought it entirely crazy of Byron to choose this particular time for his first visit to Six Mile Bottom—especially with Colonel Leigh absent from home. Nor did she believe that he had ever had any intention of going on to Cambridge; that sentence was merely put in to allay her fears.

But in his new rooms in Albany, which he had rented from Lord Althorpe, the cause of her anxiety was scribbling in his journal:

> Out of town six days. On my return, found my poor little pagod, Napoleon, pushed off his pedestal;—the thieves are in Paris. It is his own fault. Like Milo, he would rend the oak; but it closed again, wedged his hands, and now the beasts—lion, bear, down to the dirtiest jackal—may all tear him. That Muscovite winter *wedged* his arms;—ever since, he has fought with his feet and teeth. The last may still leave their marks; and "I guess now" (as the Yankees say) that he will yet play them a pass. He is in their rear—between them and their homes. Query—will they ever reach them?

There was no mention of his stay at Six Mile Bottom; no reference to her who must have been uppermost in his mind; but next day when the news of Napoleon's abdication came through and an excited Hobhouse rushed in to ask him to go over to Paris Byron said evasively that his plans were so uncertain he would not join his friend. And on April 15th Augusta gave birth to a daughter named Elizabeth Medora Leigh, a girl whose short and bizarre life was to be in the true Byronic tradition.

To Lady Melbourne, who had apparently either seen or written to him, Byron wrote ten days later:

> Oh! but it is "worth while," I can't tell you why, and it is *not* an *Ape*, and if it is, that must be my fault; however, I will positively reform. You must however allow that it is utterly impossible I can ever be half so well liked elsewhere, and I have been all my life trying to make someone love me, and never got the sort I preferred before. But positively she and I will grow good and all that, and so we are *now* and shall be these three weeks and more.

In the Middle Ages children of an incestuous union were believed to be born monsters, and the reference to the "ape" upset Lady Melbourne greatly. Nor was she the only friend who was seriously concerned. Both Tom Moore, to whom Byron had hinted his secret, and Lord Holland, who had strongly advised against the publication of *The Bride of Abydos* because of certain rumors he had heard, were extremely anxious about him. Gossip was rife. Two or three women insisted that Byron had told them he was madly in love with a woman who was now pregnant, and that if she gave birth to a girl-child it was to be called Medora. A Mrs. Villiers, a close friend of Augusta's, said that the poet had given vent to the most "extraordinary theories" at Holland House gatherings. Even schoolboys at Eton quizzed Mrs. Leigh's unfortunate nephew about the parentage of her latest child.

There was no doubt that Byron's incurable indiscretion had

led to most of the scandal. He was constitutionally incapable of keeping a secret, perhaps because of his almost pathological vanity, perhaps because he had, at times, a masochistic longing to flay himself.

But while drawing rooms buzzed with talk Byron was again writing to Lady Melbourne, this time about some expression he had used when speaking of Augusta:

> *You*—or rather *I*— have done *my* A much injustice. The expression which you recollect as objectionable meant only "loving" in the *senseless* sense of that wide word, and it must be some selfish stupidity of mine in telling my own story, but really and truly— as I hope mercy and happiness for her—by that God who made me for my own misery, and not much for the good of others, *she* was not to blame, one thousandth part in comparison. She was not aware of her own peril till it was too late, and I can only account for her subsequent *abandon* by an observation which I think is not unjust, that women are much more *attached* to men if they are treated with anything like fairness or tenderness.

In the same letter he coolly discussed Annabella Milbanke (always called "Your A" in correspondence with her aunt, to distinguish her from "My A," Augusta). Since the beginning of the year Annabella's letters had taken on a sentimental tinge which showed clearly that if Byron cared to renew his suit he would not meet with a second rebuff. For his part, while he did not "know what to make of her," he considered she would be a suitable bride and wrote candidly to her aunt:

> ...if I pursued and succeeded in that quarter, of course I must give up all other pursuits, and the fact is that my wife, if she had commonsense, would have more power over me than any other whatsoever, for my heart always alights on the nearest *perch*—if it is withdrawn it goes God knows where—but one must like something.

That was Byron's trouble—he *had* to like something and that something was uncommonly hard to find. As an affectionate small boy he had adored his mother and she had repaid his love

117

by calling him a "lame brat." He had wooed Mary Chaworth and she had spurned him. He had plunged into dissipation and found no comfort there. He had made love to Caroline Lamb and been swept into a vortex of emotion. He had sought haven with Lady Oxford and met disillusionment. He had tried to awaken the nunlike Lady Frances Webster and been bewildered by her response. Finally, he had found love beyond telling with Augusta and been forced to resign her because of the world's condemnation and his own overwhelming sense of guilt.

In his heart he knew that he never would, never could, resign Augusta—his guilt complex alone would prevent such an action. But Byron was a man unable to analyze his innermost feelings; nor did he realize, as Goethe afterwards pointed out, that he possessed "a high degree of that demonic instinct and attraction which influences others independently of reason, effort or affection, which sometimes succeeds in guiding where the understanding fails." For all his vanity he was perplexed by the strange, violent reactions his affection evoked and longed to escape from that perplexity. He was, he told himself, through with love. Marriage was his goal; in the calm of domestic bliss he would find peace.

Both Lady Melbourne and Augusta urged him to seek a bride; the former because she was terrified of what further trouble he might cause if he remained single; the latter because she had at last realized the appalling disaster which must overtake them both if something drastic were not done. There was no jealousy in Augusta, who truly loved her brother, and she suggested he should pay court to Lord Stafford's daughter, the Lady Charlotte Leveson-Gower, a "shy antelope" of a girl. A meeting was arranged but it was scarcely successful since Lady Charlotte had clearly heard the rumors about Byron and his sister. Through sheer nervousness her conversation was full of references to Mrs. Leigh, "a friend—a relation—" which so upset Byron that he developed a singular fit of shyness and went, so he told Augusta, "into one of our *glows* and stammers."

Byron himself inclined towards Lord Granard's daughter, the Lady Adelaide Forbes (principally because he thought she looked like Apollo Belvedere); but after a party at which they politely discussed "a good deal of heraldry, and mutual hatred of music; the merits of Mr. Kean, and the excellence of white soup and plovers' eggs for supper" his interest rapidly faded.

The third candidate was, of course, Annabella Milbanke, on whom Augusta frowned and Lady Melbourne smiled. (When one considers all that she knew of Byron's tempestuous career the smile may appear peculiar in the extreme, but one must remember that Lady Melbourne, then over sixty, belonged to the late eighteenth century when discretion was the highest virtue and "arranged" marriages between experienced men of the world and innocent young girls were the order of the day.) Byron himself favored Annabella, although he admitted he got hopelessly entangled in the web of correspondence she wove around him, and he was seriously thinking of proposing to her again when his most persistent inamorata turned up to exasperate him.

London was tremendously gay that spring and summer of 1814. In April the decrepit and gouty Louis XVIII paid a ceremonial visit to London, and in June the Emperor of Russia and the King of Prussia arrived with terrific pomp. The long years of war and uncertainty had ended with Bonaparte's exile to Elba and the people of England went mad with joy. In the houses of the great there were entertainments on an unprecedented scale; in the streets there were crowds of jostling, excited people who hurrahed wildly as Royalty jingled by. To begin with Byron took little part in the festivities—he preferred Bonaparte to the Bourbons—but as the gaiety mounted he too joined the round of balls, receptions, masques and routs and, despite his grumbles, enjoyed himself as much as anybody.

But Lady Caroline Lamb was also in London for this "summer of sovereigns," and as soon as her eye lit on Byron her old passion flared anew. Thereafter she haunted his rooms in Albany till the distracted man appealed to Lady Melbourne, who had promised to keep her recalcitrant daughter-in-law under control.

> It is impossible; she comes at all times, at any time, and the moment the door is open in she walks. I can't throw her out of the window; as to getting rid of her, that is rational and probable, but *I* will not receive her.

He added the ominous threat that if her persecution did not cease he would fly the country and take Augusta with him.

Lady Caroline, however, was not easily quelled. One day on his return home he discovered that she had somehow gained entrance to his library, where he had left a copy of *Vathek* on the table. Across the title page, in her handwriting, were written the words, "Remember me!" There and then he sat down and wrote the angry lines:

> Remember thee! Remember thee!
> Till Lethe quench life's burning stream,
> Remorse and shame shall cling to thee,
> And haunt thee like a feverish dream!
>
> Remember thee! Aye, doubt it not,
> Thy husband too shall think of thee:
> By neither shalt thou be forgot,
> Thou *false* to him, thou *fiend* to me!

It was not until after Byron's death that Lady Caroline read these lines; and it was fortunate indeed that she had no opportunity of studying them at the time they were written. But that they actually had an interview some time during 1814 seems certain, though her account of it (as related much later to Thomas Medwin) was probably exaggerated. He had embraced her warmly and they had had a long conversation. Then he had shown her "letters, & told me things I cannot repeat, & all my attachment went. This was our last parting scene—well I remember it. It had an effect upon me not to be conceived—3 years I had *worshipped* him."

The trouble was that Lady Caroline *did* repeat what Byron told her—presumably it was the story of his relationship with Augusta, and he related it out of a desire to wound her so cruelly that she would never trouble him again. For less than two years later, when Byron's marriage broke up, she took a leaf out of his book and hinted to all and sundry of the diabolic doings which led to his public disgrace.

✳ 8 ✳

Tired of being kept "almost a prisoner" in his rooms by Lady Caroline's importunities, Byron left London early in July to stay with Augusta at Six Mile Bottom. He then visited Cambridge, and by the 20th was on his way to Hastings, where he proposed spending a quiet three weeks with Augusta, Captain George Byron, and Hodgson. Here Byron swam a great deal, ate much turbot, and listened to Hodgson's panegyrics about the young woman to whom he was engaged. Whether these last had some effect upon him we do not know, but on August 10th he wrote to Annabella, "I did—do—and always shall love you."

She answered somewhat coyly that she was not sure he could make her happy, but as usual she surrounded this remark with so much high-flown verbiage that her suitor replied abruptly, "Very well—now we can talk of something else." One cannot help wondering if an episode he related to Moore occurred after he had penned those words:

> ...I got into a passion with an ink-bottle, which I flung out of the window one night with a vengeance;—and what then? Why, next morning I was horrified by seeing that it had struck, and split upon, the petticoat of Euterpe's graven image in the garden, and grimed her as if it were on purpose. Only think of my distress,—and the epigrams that might be engendered on the Muse and her misadventure.

Then, by the skin of his teeth, Byron managed to evade a meeting with another old love. This was Mary Chaworth Musters, who had begged him so anxiously to call upon her the previous winter. Delicate, deserted by her husband, she was intrigued by the fame which now surrounded her once-rejected swain and was determined to recapture him. Since he had not obeyed her Nottinghamshire request she had journeyed to London and called at Albany, only to be informed he was at Hastings. Nothing daunted she had pursued him to that resort and booked rooms at his hotel. It was not until she had unpacked that she found she had just missed him—the bird had flown to Newstead with Augusta.

The Abbey, as we know, always had a very special effect on Byron. In that echoing derelict house, with its outlook over the bare park to the steel-gray mere, and its atmosphere of past cruelties, he dropped all pretense of being a man of the world, a celebrity, a cynic, and became once more the boy who had gazed awestruck at the arms of "Little Sir John with the Great Beard." In his mind Newstead was linked with the Wicked Lord, with the ancestors who had swaggered their way down its long passages, and with the Byronic doom from which there was no escape save in the companionship of Augusta.

And Augusta was with him now, prattling away about the charms of Lady Charlotte Leveson-Gower, urging him to approach her, warning him against Annabella, reminding him that he "hated an *esprit* in petticoats." Half annoyed, half laughing, Byron said he would do as she thought best; so Augusta framed a formal proposal which was dispatched to Lady Charlotte, while Byron wandered off to sit among his Athenian skulls and mused on Hobhouse's description of him—a *loup garou*—a solitary hobgoblin. Well, if the lady accepted him, doubtless she would cure him of his solitary habits. If she rejected him, then he would somehow return to Greece.

The lady rejected him. Indeed she sent a letter which betrayed her fright at his proposal, and sent Augusta into a fit of weeping. Lady Charlotte was so suitable ... she had built so much on this marriage ... it was so unsettling for her dear B. Byron comforted her and said he would try the next himself, as she did not seem to be in luck, a remark which thoroughly alarmed his sister. He must not, she protested, try Miss Milbanke, for although she was doubtless a girl of great gifts and sensibility, she was definitely not the wife for a tempestuous, exacting poet.

But Byron had already made up his mind. Deaf to Augusta's pleas he sat down and composed one of the flattest, dullest letters any young woman can ever have received from a man who wished to marry her.

> ... Are the "objections" to which you alluded insuperable? or is there any line or change of conduct which could possibly remove them? I am well aware that all such changes are easier in theory than practice; but at the same time there are few things I would not attempt to obtain your good opinion. At all events I would willingly know the worst. Still I neither wish you to promise or pledge yourself to anything; but merely to learn a *possibility* which would not leave you the less a free agent.

A strangely lukewarm epistle to come from Byron's pen! But the hitherto disapproving Augusta professed herself enraptured by it. "Well," she exclaimed, "really this is a very pretty letter; it is a pity it should not go—I never read a prettier one."

"Then it *shall* go," said her brother, and go it did on September 9th.

Despite his insistence on sending the letter Byron had no hope of a favorable reply. Indeed, it seemed as if he did not particularly want one, for four days later he wrote to Hobhouse suggesting they should leave England together for an extended tour of Italy, the Mediterranean and the Near East. His money affairs, he explained, were at last satisfactory. There was £4,000 at the bank, his poem *Lara* (the first for which he accepted money) had brought £700, Claughton had forfeited his deposit of £25,000, and the Michaelmas Newstead rents would bring in a further £1,500. There was, he added, a very remote possibility that he would have to cancel the plan.

For all his observations to Lady Melbourne, Byron knew remarkably little about Annabella. It simply did not occur to him that all her sermons, her requests for classical history books, her gentle reproofs, had been carefully calculated to bring him to the point of a second avowal. He did not know that his letter was received with rapture or that the happy and relieved girl spent hours composing her answer. He admired her erudition and good breeding, laughingly alluded to her as "the Princess of Parallelograms," or "the strictest of St. Ursula's 11,000 what do you call 'ems? a wit, a moralist, and religionist," and he regarded her as a highly suitable bride.

No sooner had he written to Hobhouse than one of the gardeners brought him Mrs. Byron's wedding ring which she had lost years earlier when picking flowers. To her superstitious son the finding of the ring was an omen and there and then he declared that if Annabella accepted him he would wed her with it.

He and Augusta were at the dinner table when a servant entered with a thick envelope on a salver. Recognizing the handwriting Byron opened the missive at once, and as he read through the closely written pages he turned such a deathly white that his sister feared he was about to faint. Annabella had accepted him! When he had finished reading he handed the letter to Augusta with the dry remark, "It never rains but it pours."

But Augusta made up for his lack of enthusiasm. Now that she read in black and white that her brother's proposal had been accepted she forgot all her disapproval of Annabella and was especially delighted by one paragraph in which her future sister-in-law wrote:

> I am and have long been pledged to myself to make your happiness the first object in life. *If I can* make you happy, I have no other consideration. I will *trust* to you for all I should look up to— all I can love.

The letter was, Augusta vowed, "the best and prettiest" she had ever read and she was sure her dear B. was going to be immensely happy.

That Byron's feelings were sadly confused is shown by his answer to Miss Milbanke, a breathless effusion that betrays his agitation.

> ...I have ever regarded you as one of the first of human beings—not merely from my own observation but that of others— as one whom it was as difficult *not* to love—as scarcely possible to deserve;—I know your worth—and revere your virtues as I love yourself and if every proof in my power of my full sense of what is due to you will contribute to *your* happiness—I shall have secured my own.—It *is* in your power to render me happy—you have made me so already.—I wish to answer your letter immediately—but am at present scarcely collected enough to do it rationally—I was on the point of leaving England without hope without fear—almost without feeling—but wished to make one effort to discover—not if I could pretend to your present affection —for to those I had given over all presumption—but whether time—and my most sincere endeavour to adopt any mode of conduct that might lead you to think well of me—might not eventually in securing your approbation awaken your regard.— These hopes are now dearer to me than ever; dear as they have ever been;—from the moment I became acquainted my attachment has been increasing and the very follies—give them a harsher name—with which I was beset and bewildered the conduct to which I had recourse for forgetfulness only made recollection more lively and bitter by the comparisons it forced on me in spite of Pride—and of Passions—which might have destroyed but never deceived me....

How different that letter is from the verses concerning his feeling for Augusta which he had sent to Tom Moore a brief month or two before:

> I speak not, I trace not, I breathe not thy name,
> There is grief in the sound, there is guilt in the fame:
> But the tear which now burns on my cheek may impart
> The deep thoughts that dwell in that silence of heart.

Too brief for our passion, too long for our peace,
Were those hours—can their joy or their bitterness cease?
We repent, we abjure, we will break from our chain,—
We will part, we will fly to—unite it again!

He wrote to Lady Melbourne telling her he intended to "reform most thoroughly" and do his utmost to make her niece happy; but in a letter to Moore he said, "You need not be in a hurry to wish me joy, for one mayn't be married for months," and he confessed to Hobhouse that the character of wooer "in this regular way" did not sit easily on him. But when congratulations began to flow in, his spirits rose with a bound. It was really remarkably pleasant to have people approving his conduct instead of condemning it, to receive ardent expressions of devotion from Annabella, to listen to Augusta's lyrical descriptions of what his life was going to be. Almost, in those September weeks at Newstead, he persuaded himself that he was a normal, happy young man.

IV

The Careful Pilot of My Proper Woe

Byron's mood of contentment vanished when Augusta returned to her home near Newmarket and he returned to London. Suddenly he found himself caught up in a hustle of wedding preparations, and there was nothing he disliked more than "fuss, and bustle, and ceremony." There were long prosy letters from Sir Ralph Milbanke, Annabelle's father, concerning marriage settlements; and since Hanson was involved in serious trouble with the Portsmouth family, who were querying the validity of the marriage between his daughter and the mentally deficient Earl, he could not spare the time to journey north to County Durham and confer with Sir Ralph's lawyers. Then Annabella naturally kept pressing Byron to visit her home at Seaham—after all, he had not seen her for several months and had never met her parents—but he suddenly displayed a curiously conventional streak and replied primly that he could not think of coming until the lawyers had met and discussed financial affairs.

The truth was that he hated being prodded into making decisions. He had, moreover, the uneasy feeling that the house on the bleak Durham coast was likely to be cold and uncomfortable, and that he would not get on with Annabella's parents. But at last Hanson and the Milbankes' lawyers fixed the settlements. Left without any excuse for delaying his visit any longer and exasperated beyond measure by the goadings of Lady Melbourne and Lady Milbanke, he set out sulkily towards the end of October. In spite of the fact that Lord Wentworth, Annabella's uncle, was lingering at Seaham in order to meet the man his heiress was about to marry, Byron dallied over his journey. He spent a night or two with Augusta at Six Mile Bottom, then proceeded slowly to Newark—where he again missed Lord Wentworth, who had come south to that town—and very nearly decided that he would go to Newstead instead of traveling on north. The news that Mary Chaworth Musters had become insane deepened his gloom, and as the coach rumbled through Yorkshire he was in an exceedingly ill humor.

He arrived at Seaham on the evening of November 2nd. Annabella, who had been in a state of palpitation for days because of his lateness, heard the scrunch of the carriage wheels on the drive and went down to the drawing room to greet him. But Byron was in one of his unapproachable moods. He stood stiffly by the fireplace, made no move to come forward but waited until she was close to him before he kissed her hand. "It is a long time since we met," he said formally, then relapsed into silence. It was a greeting so unlike the one poor Annabella had envisioned that she muttered some excuse and fled to her own room, where she relapsed into tears.

The meeting with her parents passed off better than might have been expected. Sir Ralph was a bluff, red-faced man with a habit of telling incredibly long stories which seemed always to lack point—his sister, Lady Melbourne, called him "old twaddle Ralph." His wife, who had had the misfortune to lose her hair and so wore an elaborate wig, was a bustling, managing woman who ran her husband and household with marked efficiency. Both parents adored their only child who had not been born till fifteen years after their marriage. Country folk themselves, they were a little awed by the handsome and famous poet Annabella was engaged to, and they set themselves to entertain him.

Byron kept playing with the links of his watch chain all evening, a sure sign of boredom with him, but he too was anxious to create a good impression, paying very little attention to his betrothed but regaling her parents with stories of Edmund Kean, a subject on which he talked exceedingly well. At bedtime, however, he turned to Annabella and inquired courteously at what hour she came downstairs in the morning. She answered that ten o'clock was her usual time, and the following day, after a wakeful night during which she alternately imagined a touchingly sentimental scene and worried lest her strange lover should still be in the depressed state of mind he had been in on arrival, she tripped downstairs punctually. But Byron was, as usual, dawdling over his dressing, over which he liked to spend the greater part of the morning. Between each part of his toilet he read or wrote letters and he was seldom ready to face the world before one o'clock. Annabella waited about until noon then, unable to bear the commiserating glances of her mother and her old governess Mrs. Clermont, went for a lonely walk along the shore.

That Annabella loved Byron is beyond dispute. Behind her reserve hid a passionate nature, though her very considerable will power held it in check, and one feels that if her betrothed had given her the least encouragement during his fortnight's stay at Seaham she would have thrown her pride to the winds and allowed him to see the depth of her feeling for him. But Byron seemed positively to avoid being alone with her, and on the rare occasions when this did happen he was either taciturn and obviously bored, or in a mood which she learned to dread, a mood in which he talked endlessly of Augusta. Augusta was so dear, so wonderful. They had such fun when they were together, they shared so many secrets, they talked a private language nobody else could understand. When she (Annabella) was "playful"—and his tone inferred she was not playful nearly often enough—she put him somewhat in mind of Augusta, though she must realize that he could never give her as much love as he gave his sister. If she had accepted his first proposal over two years earlier then things might perhaps have been different, but her refusal had forced him into an experience which had left an indelible mark on his heart.

Against her will, for Annabella was essentially a good woman who did not allow dark or wicked thoughts to occupy her mind, she grew jealous of Augusta and one day in desperation she told Byron in a hysterical voice that she would release him from their engagement. To her alarm he turned white and "fainted entirely away." Surely she thought, as she fussed over him with brandy and burned feathers, he did truly love her after all? But the very next day he treated her with such indifferene that the poor girl, who was rapidly reaching the point of nervous collapse, retired to bed.

Byron did not love Annabella, though he made himself believe he did, and while at Seaham he began to have doubts as to whether they would be happy together or not. She was such an extraordinarily silent girl, and as he told his confidante Lady Melbourne, "I like them [women] to talk, because then they *think* less." He found her countenance pleasing, but there was a hint of sharpness about her straight nose and thin lips and she was inclined to be a shade dogmatic in her opinions. At the same time, he told Lady Melbourne, "I fear she won't govern me; and if she don't it won't do at all; but perhaps she may mend of that fault." And as the days passed he grew yet more restless and depressed. Annabella was "overrun with fine feelings, scruples about herself and her disposition." She had actually suggested he should cut his stay short. She suffered from some mysterious complaint which necessitated her retiring to bed every few days. She had made a scene (when she offered to break the engagement) which reminded him painfully of Lady Caroline Lamb and had greatly upset him.

The truth was that life at Seaham bored Byron to extinction. He quite liked Sir Ralph—"to my mind the perfect gentleman"

—but when he was forced to listen to the same anecdotes night after night when the ladies had left the dining room he had the greatest difficulty in retaining his self-control. He had disliked Lady Milbanke at sight, sensing that if he were not careful she would "manage" him as she managed her own family, and he had conceived a positive loathing of "the respectable Mrs. Clermont," who now acted as companion to Annabella's mother and poked an inquisitive nose into every household happening. Certainly the house itself was far more comfortable than he had expected, but there was very little to do and each time he glanced out of the windows at the sullen gray sea he was swept by a longing for the blue Ægean, for the carefree days in Greece, for the vanished youth which had slipped so quickly through his fingers.

He left Seaham on November 16th. Sir Ralph and Lady Milbanke sincerely regretted his departure, for despite his boredom Byron had deliberately set out to charm them, and they were quite dazzled by his looks, his conversation, and his wit. Annabella, however, saw him go with strangely mixed feelings. She loved him, but his behavior had been so difficult that she had lived in a constant state of agitation. His absence brought relief, yet she longed for him to come back. Had she resembled other girls of her day and age she would have poured out her doubts to her parents, who would most likely have insisted upon breaking the engagement. But Annabella had been brought up to regard reserve as a leading virtue, to think over things most carefully before acting; and she was also intensely proud. She could not possibly admit Byron's capricious behavior to a father and mother who had always complimented her on her self-reliance, so she bottled up her anguish and wrote him apologizing for her "troubled visage" which, she said, must have caused him pain. She was rewarded by an epistle from Cambridge, whither he had gone to vote for a friend who was a candidate for a medical professorship. It began simply "My Love" and it ended with a plea which touched her heart, "Well but—Sweet

Heart—do write and love me—and regard me as thine." Her doubts disappeared as if by magic—Byron loved her.

But Byron, although he wrote regularly and always included a few words of endearment, was by no means sure that he wanted to go on with the marriage after all. Annabella's disposition was not so serene and gentle as he had imagined; she was an exacting sort of a girl; she thought too much of her own abilities. Of course he had gone to Six Mile Bottom on his way to Cambridge, and he found Augusta's company soothing after the strain of his Seaham visit. Augusta never bothered him with demands, or lectured him about his past, or talked about mathematics. Augusta was soft and pliant, sweet and sensual, the only woman with whom he could be completely and utterly natural.

And when he eventually got back to London a host of troubles descended upon him. His period of financial ease had been short-lived. Newstead remained unsold, and although Claughton had renewed his offer to purchase, negotiations had fallen through. His debts were mountainous once more and his creditors growing impatient. Hanson was so entangled in preparations for the lawsuit which Lord Portsmouth's family were bringing against him that he had no time for his ordinary legal business, and Byron himself expected to be subpoenaed to give evidence. A new parrot he had bought had bitten him severely on the finger. His liver was out of order because he had drunk far too much at Cambridge. The lawyers had decided that he was to settle £60,000 on Annabella and £300 a year dress allowance, while Sir Ralph provided a dowry of £20,000 and a jointure of £1,000. The only bright spot was the fact that Lord Wentworth was old and sick, and that Annabella would inherit his fortune when he died.

Suddenly Byron decided that it would be unwise to marry until Newstead was sold. He wrote to Annabella pointing out that Claughton had again backed out and that he thought they should postpone the wedding. " 'To marry or not' that's the question—or will you wait?" The letter had the effect of a bomb on the Seaham household. Lady Milbanke wrote to say the wedding cake was already made. Sir Ralph wrote that he had composed an epithalamium which he was going to read aloud on the great day. Annabella wrote saying firmly that she proposed to marry him at once whatever his circumstances and would he please fix a date.

Even when it was clear there was no way of escape Byron procrastinated. The Portsmouth lawsuit might hold him in London. He had to get a special license from the Archbishop of Canterbury. He *might* be able to journey north for Christmas but he was not sure. His frequent setting back of dates gave grave concern to the Milbankes and Annabella was in a state of high tension when word came that Byron and Hobhouse, who was to be his best man, were leaving London on Christmas Eve.

"Never was lover in less haste," wrote Hobhouse afterwards, "the bridegroom more and more *less* impatient," for at the last minute Byron decided to spend Christmas Day with Augusta and rejoin Hobhouse in Cambridge on the 26th. He did not turn up until late in the afternoon, so it was not until the evening of the 30th that they arrived at Seaham where Annabella waylaid Byron in the passage, threw her arms round his neck, and burst into tears. Hobhouse, who had not met her before, found her "rather dowdy-looking," but was impressed by her quiet manner and the evening passed off pleasantly enough, as they were joined at dinner by Sir Ralph's agent, Mr. Hoar, and the Reverend Thomas Noel, an illegitimate son of Lord Wentworth, who was to officiate at the wedding.

There was a slight coolness to begin with over Byron's tardiness, but the loyal Hobhouse's lame excuses were scarcely necessary for Byron exerted his charm to such purpose that the whole company hung upon his words. Annabella ate little and sat with her eyes fixed on her lover's "bold and animated face," but Hobhouse noted that her devotion was "regulated with the utmost decorum," and felt that Byron genuinely cared for her.

The next two days passed peacefully, but in the evening of New Year's Day, 1815, "dinner was not quite so jolly" as on the

133

previous evenings and in his room Byron remarked gloomily to his friend, "Well, Hobhouse, this is our last night; tomorrow I shall be Annabella's." Had it been possible he would have fled from Seaham that night because his thoughts were again dwelling on the Byronic doom.

❋ 2 ❋

In a Memoir, which he showed to Moore and which was later destroyed, Byron——

> ... described himself as waking, on the morning of his marriage, with the most melancholy reflections, on seeing his wedding-suit spread out before him. In the same mood, he wandered about the grounds alone, till he was summoned for the ceremony. . . . He knelt down, he repeated the words after the Clergyman; but a mist was before his eyes—his thoughts were elsewhere; and he was but awakened by the congratulations of the bystanders, to find that he was—married.

According to Hobhouse, Byron was already sitting at the breakfast table resplendent in a white embroidered waistcoat, a frilled shirt, and white kid gloves when he came downstairs. "Her Ladyship could not make tea, her hand shook," and shortly after half-past ten the party proceeded to the drawing room where Thomas Noel and another clergyman awaited them. When the family and guests had seated themselves the door opened and Annabella made her entry, followed by Mrs. Clermont. "She was dressed in a muslin gown trimmed with lace at the bottom, with a white muslin curricle jacket, very plain indeed," and her face was as white as her frock.

Two ornate cushions (which Byron later complained were hard) had been placed on the floor, and on these the couple knelt while Noel began to read the marriage service. Annabella looked full at her bridegroom and made her responses in a clear voice, but Byron mumbled his and gave Hobhouse a wry smile when he repeated the words, "With all my worldly goods I thee endow." The ceremony was soon over. Lady Milbanke embraced her new son-in-law tearfully and Mrs. Clermont sobbed in the background. The bride was on the verge of weeping as she signed the register, and immediately hurried away to change as they had a long drive ahead of them to Halnaby Hall, Sir Ralph's Yorkshire estate. When she came down, dressed in a slate-colored satin pelisse trimmed with bands of white fur, Hobhouse gave her a complete collection of Byron's poems bound in yellow morocco and wished her happiness. "If I am not happy," she answered firmly, "it will be my own fault."

It was not yet noon when he handed the bride into the carriage and grasped Byron's hand. For his part Byron clung to his friend's hand so tightly that the carriage was already moving down the drive before he was at last persuaded to release his grip. Amid the bangs of a *feu de joie* and the ringing of church bells Lord and Lady Byron set off on their honeymoon.

Their wedding journey was surely the strangest and saddest ever recorded. Annabella, nervous but determined to make her husband happy, sat back in her corner and tried to make conversation. Had not the flower decorations on the improvised altar been pretty? Did he not think Lady Milbanke had kept up wonderfully well? Was not Thomas Noel an excellent young man? She met with no response from her husband, who sat wrapped in a dark cloak and scowled fiercely whenever she addressed him. The moment Noel had pronounced them man and wife he had realized what an appalling mistake he had made. He should never have married this cold, prim girl with her history books and mathematical problems. He belonged to Augusta . . . Augusta . . . Augusta . . . the name jogged through his mind to the rhythm of the wheels, and presently he burst into a wild tuneless singing which lasted until they reached Durham—a city Sir Ralph had represented in Parliament—and heard the pealing of bells. Abruptly Byron turned to his wife. "Ringing for our happiness, I suppose?" he sneered.

Having begun to speak he was in no mood to desist. Characteristically, he did not blame himself for having proposed to Annabella, he blamed her for marrying him. Back he went again to his original offer of marriage, upbraiding her for her refusal, muttering that between then and now something diabolic had occurred which had left a memory that would never be effaced. "What could induce you to marry me?" he snarled.

"Good heavens!" she answered, "because I loved you."

"No," said Byron. "You have a spice of Mother Eve; you married me because your friends wished you not to do so. You refused me twice and I will be revenged."

He then elaborated his ideas. He would make her suffer as few women had suffered. He would submit her to every kind of indignity. She would soon learn that he was possessed of a devil.

"It must come to a separation!" he cried.

But after an hour or so of this tirade, when Annabella was weeping hopelessly, his mood suddenly changed and he reached for her hand. He had not meant a word he had said, and she must put all memory of it from her mind. He would devote his life to her service and be so tender a husband that all other women would envy her. Yet no sooner had she dried her tears and summoned up a wan smile than he swung back to violent speech. He did not know how long he could keep up the trying part he had been called upon to play. She was a spoilt child but she must realize she was now to obey him in everything, put herself entirely into his power "and I shall make you feel it." She did not know that he and her aunt, Lady Melbourne, had hatched up the plot to trap her between them. On he went and on, as the coach swayed over the Yorkshire moors and the snow began to fall.

Nor did his melodramatic outbursts cease when at last they reached Halnaby Hall. Byron dismounted first and, according to the butler, did not attempt to hand his wife out but stalked off alone. She walked up the steps "with a countenance agonized and listless" and looked so tired and despairing that the man wondered if he should dare offer her his arm. At dinner Byron sat in gloomy silence and afterwards informed her coldly that he hated sharing a bed with a woman, but that if she liked she could share his. Provided a woman was young she was bound to be quite satisfactory sexually.

Annabella, brought up with a rigid sense of duty, did share his bed and a terrifying experience it must have been for her. The bed was a huge four-poster with red damask curtains and Byron, who was always afraid of the dark, insisted on a taper being lit although there was plenty of light from the fire. He was asleep long before poor Annabella but suddenly he awoke screaming out, "Good God, I am surely in Hell!"

The next morning he received a letter from Augusta and when he had scanned it he read aloud the opening words: "Dearest, first, and best of human beings." "What do you think of them?" he asked his wife. He did not, however, read her Augusta's description of the feelings which had overwhelmed her at the hour he was being married: "As the sea trembles when the earth quakes" so she had shaken with grief, but the letter induced in him "a kind of fierce and exulting transport" and led him to further cruel teasing of his wife.

Yet that same first morning of their married life he wrote to Lady Melbourne painting a scene of domestic bliss.

> You would think we had been married these fifty years. Bell is fast asleep on a corner of the sofa, and I am keeping myself awake with this epistle—she desires her love, and mine you have had ever since we were acquainted.

And when Annabella wisely encouraged him to talk openly about his lameness he responded with gratitude. "You are a good kind Pip—a good-natured Pip—the best wife in the world."

In lighter moments he called her "Pippin" because he said the

137

word suited her round face, and she called him (goodness knows why) "Duck," an appellation which seemed to please him. "If anything could make me believe in Heaven," he told her once, "it is the expression of your countenance this moment"; but half an hour later he would throw her back into her misery by relating such horrible stories of past amorous adventures that she began to wonder if he were really sane. He told her crudely how he had tried to seduce the thirteen-year-old daughter of Lady Oxford; he embellished the Caroline Lamb affair until it was distorted out of recognition; he gave her full details of his undergraduate dissipations. And, of course, ever and anon he reverted to that dread, mysterious happening of 1813 which had changed his whole life, and having delivered himself of a series of innuendoes he would talk endlessly of Augusta. "I only want a woman to laugh," he explained, "and don't care what she is besides. I can make Augusta laugh at anything. No one makes me happy but Augusta."

Their "treacle moon," as Byron called it, must have been a nightmare for Annabella. She never knew from one minute to the next what mood he would be in. Once, when reading Dryden's *Don Sebastian*, she asked him a question about incest, and he flew into an ungovernable rage, shouting at her that she must never mention the subject in his hearing again. When he found a gray hair among his thick auburn curls he spent the rest of the day mourning his vanished youth. He was obsessed by the idea that some enemy was lurking somewhere awaiting an opportunity to kill him, and even when they read together in the library he kept a brace of loaded pistols on the table beside him. At night his fears mounted and he would prowl for hours around the house carrying a pistol and a dagger, and on one occasion he came to bed in a state of such abject terror that in an effort to soothe him she put her head on his shoulder. "You should have a softer pillow than my heart," he murmured, and she answered, "I wonder which will break first, yours or mine."

Long afterwards she said they were "the only words of despair he ever heard me utter," and even when he was at his most violent she tried to treat him gently for she was convinced that he was suffering from some mental disorder which only calmness and patience could alleviate. But Byron admired neither of these virtues and the more his wife reasoned with him the angrier he became, and the deeper grew his remorse over Augusta and his resentment over his marriage.

The three weeks at Halnaby dragged to a close and the Byrons then returned to Seaham, where they were to stay for just over a month. Strangely enough Byron's spirits rose as they drove to Durham and Annabella, who had determined not to let her parents sense her unhappiness whatever happened, was vastly relieved. Byron seemed to make every effort to behave as a son-in-law should. He played draughts with Lady Milbanke, took part in the parlor games the family played with enthusiasm, and even acted in a charade wearing his dressing gown and his mother-in-law's wig.

Soon after their arrival at Seaham he was writing in his dressing room late one night and, finding the heat from the big fire unendurable, poured water on the glowing coals. As a result he was almost asphyxiated by the fumes but managed to crawl into the bedroom where Annabella revived him with *eau de Cologne*. He relapsed into a faint but when he came to he imagined he was dying and, according to his wife, "broke forth into the wildest ravings of despair, saying that he knew he was going to Hell, but that he would defy his Maker to the last, with other expressions of a revengeful nature. . . ." She managed to soothe him down and after a while he said to her gently, "I have tried everything—I will try virtue, I think. Perhaps I shall go to Heaven, holding by the hem of your garment."

This incident made a deep impression on Byron's mind and for some time afterwards he was on his very best behavior. But he found life at Seaham unconscionably dull. Gathering shells on the seashore and walking round the vegetable garden with Lady Milbanke were not pursuits which appealed to him, and in the evenings he grew so bored with Sir Ralph's prosy anecdotes that he simply got up and walked out of the dining room leaving his host still talking "over various decanters, which can neither interrupt him nor fall asleep—as might have been the case with some of his audience."

He wrote to Moore, who had been staying at Chatsworth, pleading for news of the great world.

> Pray tell me what is going on in the way of intriguery, and how the w——s and rogues of the upper Beggar's Opera go on —or rather go off—in or after marriage; or who are going to break any particular commandment. Upon this dreary coast, we have nothing but county meetings and shipwrecks: and I have this day dined upon fish, which probably dined on the crews of several colliers lost the late gales. But I saw the sea once more in all the glories of surf and foam,—almost equal to the Bay of Biscay, and the interesting white squalls and short seas of Archipelago memory.

He was heartsick for Augusta, who wrote rather cattily to Annabella: "Only think of B. playing drafts. He now has so many occupations...but I am vain enough to think he does not forget Guss."

He was very far from forgetting her and he was also more than a little annoyed with Lady Melbourne on her behalf. For that lady had got it into her head that Augusta was "very wicked and very clever," and in her letters she kept reminding Byron that "although you have no *Corbeau Noir*, actually *noir*, you may have one flying about, with *many* black feathers in her plumage." Always roused by any criticism of his sister Byron replied: "I suppose your C...*noir* is X (as he alluded to Augusta), but if X were a raven, or a griffin, I must still take omens from her flight."

By the middle of February he was clearly in a dejected frame of mind, for he suggested to Moore that they should go to Italy, adding, "If I take my wife, you can take yours; and if I leave mine, you may do the same." A few days later he had news that the Duke of Dorset, one of his Harrow adorers, had met his death in the hunting field and this depressed him even further. "There was a time in my life," he said lugubriously, "when this would have broken my heart."

Although he abhorred "the agonies of packing and parting" Byron was delighted when March 19th arrived and they drove southwards towards Six Mile Bottom, he with his "chin upon a bandbox," though he was exceedingly annoyed because Lady Milbanke had urged him to "take care of Annabella." "What on earth does your mother mean by telling me to take care of you?" he snapped. "I suppose you can take care of yourself!"

✳ 3 ✳

They stayed the night at Wandsford and that evening Byron was at his most irresistible. "You married me to make me happy, didn't you?" he demanded of Annabella. "Well, then, you do make me happy." But an hour later he was warning her of "some impending, inevitable misery" that awaited her in the near future, and the uneasiness she had felt when their visit to Augusta was first mooted returned in strength. Byron had said he wished to go alone and suggested she should stay on with her parents, an idea which quite shocked her conventional mind. Why, they had only been married just over two months and in her opinion it was not right that a bride and bridegroom should be separated. Byron had reluctantly given way, but then Augusta had sent a series of foolish, muddled letters explaining that she really had not enough room for the two of them, a maid and a valet, that the children were ailing, that she was deplorably short of staff. All these excuses had served to harden Annabella's determination to accompany her husband; but as they neared Newmarket and Byron's mood grew blacker she knew foreboding.

The house itself was an old one, with a long low frontage and large Georgian windows. It was comfortable and homely and at sight of it some of Annabella's fears disappeared; but practically at once she realized that their visit was going to be a hundred times harder to endure than she had ever imagined. The moment he set foot over the doorstep Byron behaved abominably. He seemed absolutely bent on destroying the peace, not only of the two women who loved him, but of himself. With a savagery worthy of the "Wicked Lord" he heaped humiliation after humiliation on both wife and sister, made the most vile innuendoes, and flew into such violent rages that they trembled when they heard his "terrible step." He was obviously a creature in torment, and the more agonized he became the more cruel was his tongue. The very first night he said to Annabella, "Now I have *her*, you will find I can do without *you*—in all ways"; and he made such appalling remarks to his sister that they "sometimes made Augusta ready to sink." She was frankly terrified of him, "seemed fearful of every word he uttered, and fearful of checking him," yet fluttered helplessly around him like a moth unable to keep away from a flame. The two women were naturally drawn together by their mutual fear, but Byron was determined that they should have no chance for confidences and separated them whenever he found them together. "We don't want *you*, my charmer," he would sneer at Annabella and dismiss her to her room, or he would come downstairs in the morning and taunt Augusta by reminding her of all the secret signs they had amused themselves inventing when they were snowbound at Newstead. And why did she not wear the gold brooch he had given her, he demanded, the brooch which held his hair and hers and had three crosses (their private symbol) on the back? Having reduced Augusta to pulp he would again whirl on Annabella or swear at Fletcher "with a degree of rage that seemed to threaten his life."

He was well aware that he was encompassing his own disaster and that of the two nearest to him, but he could not stop.

> I have been cunning in mine overthrow,
> The careful pilot of my proper woe.

Only with the tiny Medora did his manner change. He was most gentle with her and Annabella found "the tenderness of his expression" when he looked at her "quite lovely." Timidly she said she would like to see a painting of the two of them together but started up in alarm when he rounded on her and said in an awful voice, "You know, that is my child." He then went on to explain that Colonel Leigh had been away from home for a long period around the time she had been conceived.

Poor Annabella did not know whether she hated the nights when he deliberately recoiled from her physical nearness, and, if she moved unconsciously while asleep awakened her by shouting "Don't touch me!" more than she hated the nights when she "heard the freezing sound of heartless professions—more intolerable than his uncontrolled abhorrence." All she did know was that Halnaby had been nothing to this ghastly existence.

The terrified Augusta, who was seeing this sadistic side of her brother for the first time, was only too glad when they departed for London on March 28th. Byron had commissioned Hobhouse to find them a home and he had rented a house belonging to the Duchess of Devonshire, No. 13 Piccadilly Terrace, for £700 a year. It was a wonder that the superstitious Byron did not complain about the ominous number, but he was pleased with the house and took an interest in furnishing it.

For a little while life was more placid. Byron seemed to have left his demons at Six Mile Bottom and was both affectionate and cheerful. Annabella did everything she could to avoid upsetting him and looked after him so devotedly that it really seemed as if they might settle down to ordinary married life; and perhaps they would have done so, at any rate for a time, if Annabella had not taken the extraordinary step of inviting her sister-in-law to stay. On the face of it her action seems incredible. She was by no means a stupid woman, and from their wedding day onwards Byron had gone out of his way to convince her of the relationship existing between himself and his sister. But one has to remember her zeal for reform. Uppermost in her thoughts was the idea of turning her husband into a reasonable, God-fearing being, and she seems to have imagined that the best way to do this was to confront him with the person he had so cruelly wronged. To her mind Augusta was an innocent victim—though deplorably weak—and she regarded her as a brand to be snatched from the burning. Perhaps there was another reason too behind Annabella's invitation. Perhaps, suffering from the strain induced by the turmoil of the past three months, she felt she needed an ally if she were to hope to conquer the dark side of Byron's nature and thought that if she could impress her own stronger personality on the feckless Augusta the latter would come to her aid. Later, she wrote:

> It was hopeless to keep them apart. It was not hopeless, in my opinion, to keep them innocent. I felt myself the guardian of these two beings *indeed* "on the brink of a precipice."

These were fine words, but when Byron greeted his sister "with lowering looks of disgust and hatred," and again reverted to the subject of their sin even his wife's iron resolution was sorely tried. Several times she felt sanity deserting her and suffered a sudden impulse to kill or wound Augusta, the cause behind Byron's mad rages, but always she summoned self-control to her aid and forced herself into a mood of "romantic forgiveness."

One feels that Byron might have abandoned his role of Turkish despot had Annabella given way to her emotions. But when she answered his most bitter taunts with a resigned smile he was stung to further excesses, and when she preserved a Niobe-like attitude towards his sister his one desire was to wound her so deeply that she would cry for mercy.

But Annabella was cast in a sterner mold than he realized. Even when she was summoned to join her parents at Lord

Wentworth's deathbed in Kirkby Mallory, Leicestershire, she gave them no inkling of the wretched situation and wrote Byron a long, loving letter telling him that her dearest hopes were confirmed and she was going to bear his child. The idea of fatherhood calmed him momentarily and he replied entreating her to come home as he felt sure she should not stay in an atmosphere of grief. When she returned, however, Byron learned to his chagrin that Lord Wentworth, who had died on April 17th, had left his fortune to Lady Milbanke for her lifetime. Only on her death (and she was a remarkably healthy woman) would the money come to Annabella, and meanwhile her mother was to revert to her maiden name of Noel.

This was appalling news. He had made no secret of the fact that he was marrying an heiress and his multitude of creditors were demanding immediate settlement of their claims. Before many days had passed bailiffs arrived at Piccadilly Terrace to carry out an execution order—the first of eleven which were to occur before the following January. Annabella was unmoved; Sir Ralph's financial affairs had been liable to a series of crises. Byron felt humiliated beyond measure. The action insulted his strong sense of family pride, and the knowledge that his neighbors were observing events with curiosity so exasperated him that he flung out of the house and sought consolation with some of his old cronies. The round of dissipation into which he plunged and the amount of drink he swallowed merely accentuated his depression, but with a dogged stubbornness he persisted in his course and pretended delight when he was elected to join Lord Essex, Douglas Kinnaird, George Lamb and Peter Moore on the Drury Lane Committee which had been formed to find and cast plays for production at that theater.

In the journal of *Detached Thoughts* he kept while at Ravenna in 1821 Byron harked back with nostalgia to those hectic months of 1815.

> The scenes I had to go through!—the authors, and the authoresses, and the milliners, and the wild Irishmen, the people

from Brighton, from Blackwall, from Chatham, from Cheltenham, from Dublin, from Dundee, who came in upon me! To
all of whom it was proper to give a civil answer, and a hearing,
and a reading. Mrs. Glover's father, an Irish dancing-master of
sixty years, called upon me to request to play *"Archer,"* drest in
silk stockings on a frosty morning, to show his legs (which were
certainly good and Irish for his age, and had been still better).
Miss Emma Somebody, with a play entitled the "Bandit of
Bohemia," or some such title or production. Mr. O'Higgins,
then resident at Richmond, with an Irish tragedy, in which the
unities could not fail to be observed, for the protagonist was
chained by the leg to a pillar during the chief part of the per-
formance....

It was not to be expected that Annabella would approve of
the Drury Lane Committee and a company which included that
sharp-featured man of the world, Douglas Kinnaird, who gave
wild parties from which her husband returned in the early hours
morose and sodden with brandy. Nor did she like his more
respectable friends. She found the Holland House gatherings
most distressing, could not forget that Lady Holland had been
a divorcée, and considered that her dinner-parties had a "Varnish
of Vice." She greatly mistrusted her aunt, Lady Melbourne, that
unscrupulous, charming woman who had egged Byron on to
innumerable amorous adventures; she feared Lady Caroline
Lamb, though that lady was going through one of her douce
periods and showed no signs of renewing her attentions to
Byron; and her description of the still pursuing Mrs. Chaworth
Musters, whom she met at Melbourne House, was "such a
wicked-looking cat I never saw."

She even regarded John Cam Hobhouse with disfavor, making it plain that he was not a welcome visitor, and since Augusta
took color from her strong-minded sister-in-law the atmosphere
of Byron's home grew steadily more uncongenial to him. The
only caller approved by his womenfolk was a young American
named George Ticknor, who had come to tell the poet of the
intense admiration felt for him by his fellow countrymen, and

who left an interesting record of his interviews. "Instead of having a thin and rather sharp and anxious face as he has in his pictures, it is round, open and smiling; his eyes are light, and not black; his air easy and careless." Just as Ticknor was leaving a friend arrived and breathlessly poured out the news of Waterloo.

"But is it true?" cried Byron. "Is it true?"

"Yes, my lord, it is certainly true; an aide-de-camp arrived in town last night; he has been in Downing Street. . . . He says he thinks Bonaparte is in full retreat towards Paris."

"I am damned sorry for it," answered Byron vehemently, and added, "I didn't know but I might live to see Lord Castlereagh's head on a pole. But I suppose I shan't, now."

Ticknor found Annabella agreeable but not pretty, and was impressed by Byron's affectionate manner towards her. On a later visit, when he spoke with her alone,

> . . . she talked upon a considerable variety of subjects—America, of which she seemed to know considerable; of France, and Greece, with something of her husband's visit there—and spoke of all with a justness and a light good-humour that would have struck me even in one of whom I had heard nothing.

But behind the façade of polite good manners noted by Ticknor the violent scenes continued and Byron's intervals of gloom grew more pronounced.

> People have wondered [he wrote in his Ravenna journal] at the Melancholy which runs through my writings. Others have wondered at my personal gaiety; but I recollect once, after an hour, in which I had been sincerely and particularly gay, and rather brilliant, in company, my wife replying to me when I said (upon her remarking my high spirits) "and yet, Bell, I have been called and mis-called Melancholy—you must have seen how falsely, how frequently." "No, B.," (she answered) "it is not so; at *heart* you are the most melancholy of mankind, and often when apparently gayest."

But at the time Byron had no wish to be reminded of the gloom which lay so heavily upon him. He wanted to busy himself with worldly affairs, to escape from the reproachful faces of his wife and sister, to talk nonsense when he felt like it, to drown melancholy in wine.

The one serious encounter which made an impression on him during that troubled spring and summer was his meeting with Sir Walter Scott in John Murray's parlor at 50 Albemarle Street. Byron had long had an immense admiration for Scott's works and "the two greatest poets of the age," as Mr. Murray's son described them, took an immediate liking to each other. Scott gave Byron an engraved Turkish dagger and Byron reciprocated by presenting Scott with a Grecian urn of silver.

❋ 4 ❋

Augusta did not leave London until the end of June and for the next few weeks Byron and Annabella seemed more at peace. According to her they "shared a sort of conventional language of nonsense" and she was often to be found sitting on his knee. Only Hobhouse and Moore suspected that this halcyon calm would not last; the rest of the Byrons' friends and acquaintances (including Lady Melbourne, who was vastly relieved by Augusta's departure) nodded wisely to each other and murmured consolingly that the troubled days were over. "Since my marriage," Byron wrote to Moore in July, he had lost much of his paleness, "and—*horresco referens* (for I hate even *moderate* fat)—that happy slenderness, to which when I first knew you, I had attained."

His state of plump contentment was short-lived. In the second half of August he decided to go alone to Six Mile Bottom and during the days between decision and departure his behavior was "perfectly ferocious." From Epping, however, he sent a conciliatory letter asking Annabella to forward "*two phials* labeled drops which the learned Fletcher with his wonted accuracy" had not placed in his traveling medicine chest. The phials were sent with an epistle beginning "Darling Duck," and containing a graphic account of the orgy of house cleaning in which the servants were indulging in his absence; and a few days later Byron wrote a humorous account of catching his toe in a mousetrap in his bedroom, and added that the Leigh children looked "shockingly—quite green—& Goose being as red as ever, you have no idea what a piece of patchwork might be made of the family faces."

Apparently Byron and his sister had by no means regained their former attitude to each other, for he returned from Six Mile Bottom full of tenderness towards Annabella and hatred against Augusta—to whom he somberly referred as "Mrs. Leigh." Unfortunately, September saw the reopening of Drury Lane, and Byron immediately threw himself into theatrical affairs—to the detriment of both health and temper.

There was one particularly gay party at which Sheridan, Kinnaird, "and others of note, and notoriety" were present of which he wrote to Moore:

> ...it was first silent, then talky, then argumentative, then disputatious, then unintelligible, then altogethery, then inarticulate, then drunk. When we had reached the last step of this glorious ladder, it was difficult to get down again without stumbling.

Some time in the small hours Kinnaird and Byron assisted the hopelessly drunk Sheridan—

> ...down a damned corkscrew staircase...to which no legs, however crooked, could possibly accommodate themselves. We deposited him safely at home, where his man, evidently used to the business, waited to receive him in the hall.

At home his conduct again became deplorable. Doubtless owing to his potations he suffered a recurrence of a once-familiar nightmare in which his dead mother pursued him like an obese and vengeful fury, and was again haunted by the idea that somebody lurked waiting to attack him during the night watches.

Sweating and shivering, he cowered in his bed imploring Annabella to go in search of the intruders. She, with the birth of her child drawing nearer, endeavored to maintain a steadfast attitude of gentleness towards him, but she wrote long and agitated letters to Augusta saying:

> His misfortune is an habitual *passion for Excitement*, which is always found in ardent temperaments, where the pursuits are not in some degree organised.... The love of tormenting... drinking, gaming &c. are all of the same origin.... I am inclined to think that a vitiated stomach, particularly if arising from habits of excess, is the chief cause of the sensation of Ennui.

She hinted that she feared that Byron's mind might be deranged, and the greatly alarmed Augusta wrote back that she truly believed her brother was insane.

In her efforts to "manage" her difficult husband Annabella developed a certain archness highly irritating to a man of Byron's temperament. On putting her head round his study door she inquired in a flutelike voice, "Am I in your way?" and was mortified to receive the growled response, "Damnably!" When she tried to rouse him from his brooding by saying jocularly that his parrot had bitten her toe he leapt to his feet with an oath and threw the cage, with the bird in it, out of the window, much to the consternation of passers-by. When she indulged in playful chiding he roared at her, and when she remarked how nice it was they were going to have a peaceful domestic evening together he immediately ordered his carriage and drove off to Watier's or some other club.

About this time Byron took to laudanum-drinking in addition to his other vices and naturally enough this made him even less tractable. On an occasion when a "sad brute" of a bailiff put himself in possession of his library—which contained some exceedingly valuable books—and announced that its contents would be seized if a certain debt were not paid within a few days, he tore headlong from the house after a violent scene in which he told his wife, as she wrote to Augusta, that he would "at once abandon himself to every sort of desperation." In the same letter she informed her sister-in-law that he never spoke except to tell her she had insisted upon marrying him against his will, and that his wild behavior was entirely her fault. "...it seemed impossible to tell if his feelings towards you or me were the most completely reversed; for as I have told you, he loves or hates us together."

As autumn deepened into winter Byron spent more and more time among his Drury Lane circle of friends. The argus-eyed Rogers espied him sitting back in the corner of his private box with an actress named Miss Boyce, with whom he was having an affair; and he himself delighted to regale Annabella with highly colored accounts of his various amours with ladies of the theater. Feeling she could no longer endure life alone with him she begged Augusta to come to stay about three weeks before her child was expected, and also persuaded George Byron, his cousin's heir, to do likewise.

Meanwhile Lady Noel wrote fussing, distracted letters from Seaham concerning her daughter's well-being. She was delighted that Annabella had engaged Mr. le Mann (a male midwife who enjoyed a great reputation for skill); but she was so worried lest any mishap occur that she was sending Mrs. Clermont, who would remain with her darling daughter until she was safely delivered. Byron, of course, was furious, since he could not stand the sight of Mrs. Clermont and was quite sure she spied on his every movement.

On Sunday, December 10th, Annabella's pains began and she retired to her bedroom while (according to her) Byron sat in his study beneath throwing soda-water bottles at the ceiling. At a later period Hobhouse affirmed that his friend was not *throwing* the bottles but merely employing his usual method of opening them by smashing their necks with the poker. Whichever version was the true one he created an appalling din which could scarcely have helped his poor wife.

The child was a girl (she was to be named Augusta Ada) and a current story—angrily denied by Byron—had it that when he was summoned to Annabella's room his first remark was, "The child *was* born dead, wasn't it?"—a question not calculated to soothe the exhausted mother; and all through his wife's convalescence he talked at length about his determination to get rid of the Piccadilly Terrace house, adding that he would then either take bachelor apartments or go abroad alone. Meanwhile the bailiffs continued to sit, to be paid off with difficulty, to sit again, and on January 6th, 1816, when they had been married exactly a year and four days, Byron wrote Annabella a stilted note in which he suggested that she and the child should go to stay with her mother at Kirkby Mallory until the financial outlook was brighter.

On January 15th Annabella, with baby, Mrs. Clermont and nursemaid, set out on their journey. Byron afterwards avowed that a tender reconciliation scene had followed his apology for his abrupt note; but according to Annabella he had merely bidden her an ironic farewell on the eve of her departure with the words, "When shall we three meet again?" and had not even bothered to leave his room when he heard them descending the stairs to the waiting coach. Even so Annabella, who firmly believed their separation was only temporary, was tempted to throw herself down outside his door "and wait at all hazards."

Her indomitable will restrained her, however, and when they rested that night at Woburn she wrote a loving note in which, unfortunately, she stressed his need for reform:

> Dearest B.—The Child is quite well, and the best of Travelers. I hope you are *good*, and remember my medical prayers and injunctions. Don't give yourself up to the abominable trade of versifying—nor to brandy—nor to anything or anybody that is not *Lawful & Right....*

From Kirkby Mallory she sent him an epistle which began "Dearest Duck," extolled the merits of a new water closet which had been installed, and told him how greatly her parents longed to see him. The country air, she added, was already doing her good but she would have felt a great deal better if she had not been "always looking about for B."

But almost by the same post she wrote to Augusta, who had stayed on at Piccadilly Terrace, that she had "made the most explicit statement" to her mother and father concerning Byron's mental state, and that they were determined to do everything in their power to help him regain his senses. Several medical men she had secretly consulted before leaving London had assured her that her husband was suffering from some form of delusion and she had now written to le Mann asking him to see Byron and give a full report. Meanwhile, she trusted that "the good Goose" would dilute the contents of the laudanum bottle "with three-quarters of water" and see that some special pills were taken regularly.

Annabella had told her parents only of Byron's supposed mental sickness and had not passed on the knowledge she had so bitterly gained about the relationship between her husband and his sister. But when she received a report from le Mann stating that although Byron was eccentric and violent at times he was indubitably sane her whole attitude of mind towards her husband underwent a sudden change. So long as she had been able to persuade herself that all his diabolic hints sprang from a disordered mind she had not fully believed that he and Augusta had committed a ghastly sin, and she had been convinced that with careful treatment he would become a normal, lovable man. Now, with le Mann's coldly technical letter before her, she saw how wrong she had been. Byron was not mad; he was *bad*, bad all through, a monster who positively gloried in the doing of evil and for that reason incurable. She loved him, but for the sake of her innocent babe she must flee from him— it was unthinkable to expose the child to such contamination— and it was her painful duty to acquaint her parents with the whole horrible truth.

As may be imagined the worthy Sir Ralph and his wife were completely shattered by her revelations. Lady Noel departed post-haste for London, where she upbraided Augusta for her brother's "unmanliness" and spent hours in anxious consultation with an ecclesiastical lawyer named Dr. Lushington, who was inexpressibly shocked but felt there might be some chance of bringing about a reconciliation. Annabella stayed on at Kirkby Mallory alternately rolling about on her bedroom floor in hysterics and galloping wildly across country with the local hunt.

> Disease or not [she wrote to Augusta], all my recollections and reflections tend to convince me that the irritability is inseparably connected with me in a greater degree than with any other object, that my presence has been uniformly oppressive to him from the hour we married ... and had we continued together he *would* have gone mad. Le Mann don't know all, or he would think so ... I have done nothing except on the strictest principle of Duty, yet I feel as if I were going to receive sentence from the Judge with his black cap on. ...

For one tragic moment when she scribbled the words, "O that I were in London, if in the coal-hole!" Annabella's love for her husband nearly outweighed her determination to leave him. But the next instant, with that almost inhuman control over her emotions characteristic of her, she was assuring Lady Noel —who had returned from London with all manner of legal advice—that nothing would induce her to resume her married life.

Sir Ralph then wrote to Byron suggesting a friendly separation, but the well-meaning Augusta, nearly distraught by her sister-in-law's ominous letters, by her uncomfortable interview with Lady Noel, and by her brother's behavior, foolishly intercepted the letter and returned it with a flurry of useless explanation. Now thoroughly aroused Sir Ralph traveled up to town and on February 2nd sent a missive marked *Private* round to Piccadilly Terrace by hand. There was nothing conciliatory about this second letter. In the coldest terms it requested that Lord

Byron name a legal representative to discuss a separation and said that under no circumstances could Lady Byron's parents consider allowing her to return to her husband.

✳ 5 ✳

This letter came as a terrific shock to Byron. True, he had scoffed to Augusta, who had stupidly withheld some of the more poignant passages in Annabella's epistles, that nothing would induce him to play the role of invalid at Kirkby Mallory with his prosy in-laws hovering around him. He might visit his wife for a few days and try to beget a son and heir before giving up his London house and going abroad for a long period, but if he chose to leave his wife and child for an indefinite period it was entirely his own affair and nothing to do with anybody else—least of all a sister who had shown herself unloving and disloyal. But to Byron, who was always author, producer and chief actor in his own drama, it was his prerogative to decide how each act should be played and the sudden knowledge that Annabella had usurped his particular privilege completely overwhelmed him.

He wrote at once to Sir Ralph, pointing out that there was no reason for a separation. He and his wife, he asserted, had parted in harmony and she had only gone to Kirkby Mallory because of certain financial embarrassments. He hinted that he suffered some physical infirmity which induced "a morbid irritability of temper," but that Lady Byron had never had cause to complain of ill-treatment; and he paid Annabella some handsome compliments before informing his father-in-law that until he had received her express sanction of these proceedings he would take leave to doubt the propriety of Sir Ralph's interference.

155

To Annabella herself he wrote three days later in very different strain:

DEAREST BELL. No answer from you yet; but perhaps it is as well; only do recollect that all is at stake, the present, the future, and even the colouring of the past. My errors, or whatever harsher name you choose to call them, you know; but I loved you, and will not part from you without your express and expressed refusal to return to, or receive me. Only say the word that you are still mine in your heart, and

"Kate, I will buckler thee against a million."

Annabella did not reply direct but to Augusta:

I will only recall to Lord Byron's mind his avowed and insurmountable aversion to the married state, and the desire and determination he has expressed ever since the commencement to free himself from that bondage as finding it quite insupportable. . . .

Again Augusta was guilty of hiding the letter, so when Hobhouse came to see Byron he said no word had yet been received from Kirkby Mallory. On his friend's advice Byron wrote again, this time sending the letter under cover to her personal maid, and in two days' time received an answer which stunned him. Annabella told him she had already sent a reply to his first epistle to Augusta, and that she had suffered such misery since the very day of her marriage that she considered a separation the only possible course. She added that it was his unfortunate habit "to consider what you *have* as worthless—what you have lost as invaluable. But remember that you declared yourself most miserable when I was yours."

That letter wounded Byron in his most vulnerable spot, his pride, and he replied on February 8th:

All I can say seems useless—and all I could say might be no less unavailing, yet I still cling to the wreck of my hopes, before they sink for ever. Were you, then, *never* happy with me? Did you never at any time or times express yourself so? Have no marks of affection of the warmest and most reciprocal attach-

ment passed between us? or did in fact hardly a day go down
without some such on one side, and generally on both? Do not
mistake me: I have not denied my state of mind—but you know
its causes—and were those deviations from calmness never followed by acknowledgments and repentance? ...You say it is my
disposition to deem what I have worthless. Did I deem *you* so?
Did I ever so express myself to you, or of you to others? You
are much changed within these twenty days or you would never
have thus poisoned your own better feelings and trampled on
mine.

To this and other letters Annabella replied reminding him
that

> ...it can be fully and clearly proved that I left your house under
> the persuasion of your having a complaint of so dangerous a
> nature that any agitation might bring on a fatal crisis....I should
> have acted inconsistently with my unchanged affection for you...
> by urging my wrongs at that moment.

Long epistles from Hobhouse and Francis Hodgson were
coolly acknowledged and as coolly dismissed, and on February
2nd Annabella left her baby in Lady Noel's charge and came to
London with her father. They stayed at Mivart's Hotel and the
very day of her arrival she had a long private interview with
Dr. Lushington and gave him a far more explicit account of
Byron's misdemeanors than ever she had given her parents. She
explained, with that cold logic that so seldom deserted her, that
she had no doubt that there had been an incestuous relationship
between Byron and Augusta before his marriage, but that in
her opinion a woman had no right to leave her husband because
of his pre-nuptial torts—even deeds "deepest in the catalogue of
human law." She did not believe (and very possibly she was
right) that anything had occurred between the two since her
marriage: she did believe that Byron had "the will to go on
sinning" and that nothing could arrest his downward progress.
On hearing the whole story the horrified Dr. Lushington quite

changed his mind and averred that any thought of reconciliation was out of the question.

Meanwhile all was hubbub at Piccadilly Terrace. Poor Augusta darted hither and thither after her brother, terrified one moment that he would shoot himself and the next that he would swallow an overdose of laudanum. Byron talked endlessly and darkly of suicide, interviewed lawyers and wrote frantic letters to Annabella and to friends he thought might intervene on his behalf.

And all around London rumors buzzed. Hobhouse was seriously exercised when Lady Melbourne sent for him, demanded to know if the separation was yet official, and asked him to ensure that all the letters she had written Byron should be burned. He was even more exercised when he heard from Augusta and George Byron of his friend's "very great tyranny, menaces, furies, neglects and even real injuries," or when he was obliged to listen to the former's muddled half-confessions— "Ah, you don't know *what* a fool I have been about him."... "He can never respect *me*." There was a brief meeting between Annabella and Augusta, at which the latter implored her sister-in-law to return because Byron was bent on self-destruction, and the former answered resolutely that "she could not help it, she must do her duty." To Lord Holland, who at the beginning of March volunteered to act as intermediary, Byron vowed that the whole affair had been engineered by Lady Noel and her spy Mrs. Clermont and insisted that if he could have a private interview with his wife all would be well. But Lord Holland's efforts were no more effective than those of Hobhouse and Hodgson, and although Byron actually offered to take him to Mivart's Hotel one evening his courage failed him at the last minute and he sat down and wrote instead. Back came a terse answer that any interview was out of the question.

On every side the stories which had been bandied around London drawing rooms at the time of Medora Leigh's birth burst forth anew; and belief in their truth became more pronounced when Annabella, in a mistaken effort to protect Augusta's good name, wrote to the sharp-tongued Mrs. George Villiers that "*not one* of the many reports now current have been sanctioned by me, my family, or my friends." It was surely peculiar, said people slyly, that Lady Byron had not definitely denied the truth of the reports. There was no smoke without fire, they added portentously, and proceeded to embellish the stories by every means in their power.

In point of fact, although nobody was aware of it, Annabella had yielded to advice and had a legal document drawn up in which she stated her suspicions about Byron and his sister and explained why, despite these, she had treated Mrs. Leigh in such a friendly fashion. The document was to be used if Byron ever attempted to seize the small Augusta Ada and hand her into the care of her aunt.

But ignorance of the existence of this document did not deter the scandalmongers. The Tory press exulted over the downfall of the "Whig and atheist" they had so long detested. Smudgy lampoons were hawked through the streets. The mass of the people—who had no idea of the meaning of the word incest—decided that an actress called Mrs. Mardyn was Byron's mistress and said they would boo her off the stage if she appeared at Drury Lane. The Duchess of Devonshire, who had never forgotten Annabella's refusal of her son Augustus Foster, declared that Lady Byron "*would* marry a poet and *reform* a rake," and on March 16th friends prevailed upon Augusta to leave Piccadilly Terrace and take up residence in the rooms in St. James's Palace to which she was entitled as a Woman of the Bedchamber to the Queen.

❋ 6 ❋

The following day Byron penned a formal agreement to the drawing up of a deed of separation, and began to busy himself with preparations—for he had determined to go abroad. With typical extravagance he ordered a huge new carriage which was to be an exact replica of one owned by Napoleon and started negotiations with a "J. Tournier" to purchase "the Coronation Robes of Buonaparte."

He also, to his lasting regret, allowed himself to become involved in correspondence with a young woman who, signing herself "E. Trefusis," confessed in an ardent letter that she had loved him for many years. She stressed the fact that she was of unsullied reputation and asked cunningly what he would do if she threw herself upon his mercy. "Could you betray her, or would you be silent as the grave?" In no mood for dalliance Byron did not answer, and a second letter in the same hand—but this time signed "G.C.B."—came asking if the writer would find it convenient to receive that evening at seven o'clock "a lady to communicate with him on business of peculiar importance."

Byron agreed half-heartedly, and promptly at the time appointed a good-looking, dark-haired girl arrived and introduced herself as Clara Mary Jane Clairmont, the daughter of the philosopher William Godwin's second wife. Her stepsister, Mary Godwin, she explained, had run away to the Continent nearly two years earlier with the poet Percy Bysshe Shelley and she—Claire, as she liked to be called—had accompanied them on a pilgrimage across France. She insisted upon telling him all about Shelley's strange enthusiasms and asked if he could give her an introduction to somebody at Drury Lane.

Her real object soon became clear—she wanted to be Byron's

mistress and he, his puritanical side affronted by this direct approach, delivered her a long lecture on Shelley, a young man of whom at that time he disapproved. But no sooner did he get rid of Miss Clairmont than she appeared again on his doorstep with some fresh suggestion. She had given up the idea of the stage and had started a novel she wished advice on. She thought it would be wonderful if they could drive out of London one evening "by some stage or mail about the distance of ten or twelve miles. There we shall be free and unknown; we can return early the following morning."

Byron told her she was a "little fiend" and scolded her about the ideas of feminism and free love she had picked up from Shelley and her sister, but there was something about the girl which aroused his desire so he at last proposed they should meet at a house in Dover Street. Very soon, however, he was cursing himself for a fool, because Miss Clairmont took to haunting Piccadilly Terrace, made it plain that she wished to go abroad with him, and brought her sister Mary to see him. Mary was unaware of their relationship but thought Byron was mild and gentle, very different to what she had imagined. Claire was full of airs and graces—obviously proud of being able to exhibit so famous a personage as a friend—and Byron got rid of his visitors as soon as he decently could. The importunate Claire, however, was back in a day or two's time and though he besought her to leave him alone she persisted in her attentions.

Forsaken by Annabella, hurt beyond measure by her treatment of him, he could not resist Claire's wiles. But he did not yield to all her importunities and many times when she called he gave orders to say that he was out.

Nevertheless he was exceedingly lonely those last few weeks in London. Hobhouse and Hodgson remained faithful but he feared to go to the theater lest the mob hiss him, and he hesitated to visit the houses of the great lest an inquisitive acquaintance allude to his broken marriage. He wrote a poem to Annabella which was not of his best, and a vitriolic sketch of

Mrs. Clermont, and had them privately printed, knowing full well that somebody would ensure they reached a wider public. Sure enough, the poem to Annabella appeared in a Sunday newspaper on April 14th and was not, on the whole, favorably received. J. P. Curran protested that he did not understand its whimpering tone—"Here is a man who first weeps over his wife, and then wipes his eyes with the public"; and Wordsworth complained that the stuff was "wretched doggerel, disgusting in sentiment, and in execution contemptible."

It seems more than likely that Annabella read the verses, either then or later, but her reaction to them was not recorded. Perhaps she too felt that the opening stanza was too melodramatic, too far removed from the truth:

> Fare thee well! and if for ever,
> Still for ever, fare thee well:
> Even though unforgiving, never
> 'Gainst thee will my heart rebel.

Not until April 8th did Byron realize how great was his social downfall. With misguided but real kindness Lady Jersey and Madame de Lieven invited Augusta and himself to a huge and fashionable party they were giving at Almack's. Lady Jersey was an acknowledged leader of fashion and was supremely confident that if the brother and sister were seen at one of her gatherings slanderous tongues would be stilled on the instant. She was woefully mistaken. The room was crowded and lively with talk when Augusta and Byron made their entry, but as soon as the guests realized who had come among them they stopped chattering abruptly and fell back to make a pathway for the pair. In complete silence they walked towards their hostesses, Augusta with flaming cheeks and head held high, Byron with his countenance dark with anger and his limp more pronounced than usual. Many of the women deliberately cut the sister, and when the brother reached a fireplace at the far end of the room and stood resting an arm on the mantel, people left the room "in crowds." Only little, red-haired Miss Mercer Elphinstone, a quick-witted heiress who later became Comtesse de Flahaut, ventured to approach him. "You had better have married me," she said, flirting her eyelashes at him. "I would have managed you better."

Byron had been alone when he first came to London as an obscure young peer: he had never been so alone as he was this night at Almack's, when the very people who fawned on him in the days of *Childe Harold*'s fame turned their backs and jostled one another in an effort to get away from his revolting presence. All he had ever wanted, celebrity, position, affection, vanished in the space of a breath.

A week later, on Easter Sunday, he parted from Augusta, who was returning to her family at Six Mile Bottom. The quarrels and recriminations of the past year were erased from both their minds and while Augusta wept and clung to her dear B., he promised her his undying love. Slowly he walked homeward and sat down to write a final letter to Annabella:

> More last words—not many—and such as you will attend to; answer I do not expect, nor does it import; but you will at least hear me.—I have just parted from Augusta, almost the last being whom you have left me to part with.
>
> Wherever I may go—and I am going far—you and I can never meet again in this world, nor in the next. Let this content or atone.—If any accident occurs to me, be kind to Augusta; if she is then also nothing—to her children. You know that some time ago I made my will in her favour and her children, because any child of ours was provided for by other and better means. This could not be prejudice to you, for we had not then differed, and even now is useless during your life by the terms of our settlements. Therefore,—be kind to her, for never has she acted or spoken towards you but as your friend. And recollect, that, though it may be an advantage to you to have lost a husband, it is sorrow to her to have the waters now, or the earth hereafter, between her and her brother. It may occur to your memory that you formerly promised me this much. I repeat it—

for deep resentments have but *half* recollections. Do not deem this promise cancell'd, for it was not a vow....

The following Sunday Byron signed the deed of separation, and the next evening he was visited by Samuel Rogers, Isaac Nathan, the Jewish composer, Hanson and Douglas Kinnaird. They ate a cake and drank two bottles of champagne brought by Kinnaird, but the atmosphere was one of melancholy and soon Byron and Hobhouse, who had been staying at Piccadilly Terrace for some time, retired to bed.

On Tuesday the 23rd, Hobhouse was up and about by six o'clock, extremely worried lest the bailiffs arrive before he could get his friend out of the house; but Byron, dilatory as usual, did not appear until half-past nine. Scrope Davies had come with his chaise which set off first carrying Hobhouse, Fletcher, Robert Rushton, a Swiss servant named Berger, and a foolish young doctor called John William Polidori, whom Byron had engaged as his private physician. The poet himself and Davies entered the Napoleonic carriage which had just been delivered and a large crowd which had gathered on the pavement laughed and groaned as the vehicles moved off.

Hobhouse's fears were justified. Exactly ten minutes after Byron's carriage turned into Piccadilly the bailiffs came panting up, declaring that they wanted to seize the new coach. Disappointed in this aim they ranged through the house removing not only furniture but the occupants of the aviary and a tame squirrel as well, while an agent from the Duchess of Devonshire arrived to claim arrears of rent.

At eight o'clock that evening the party reached Dover to find the inn packed to the doors with inquisitive folk who had come to see the last of the "disgraceful" Lord Byron. He wisely retired at once to his room, where he stayed for most of the next day because the wind was unfavorable and the boat could not sail. After dinner, however, his devoted friends smuggled him out of the hotel by a back entrance and he and Hobhouse walked up to see the grave of the great Churchill. Distressed to note that it needed returfing Byron gave the old sexton five shillings for this purpose and later wrote a poem on its neglected condition.

Early on the morning of April 25th the captain told Hob· house he was anxious to be off. But the hours passed and still, despite a great deal of running to and fro, Byron lingered over his dressing. At last he appeared, linked arms with Hobhouse, and limped down to the jetty gazing disdainfully ahead of him and paying no heed to the muttering crowds who watched his every step. As the boat glided out of the harbor he pulled off his much-decorated traveling cap and waved it at Hobhouse, who responded by running to the end of the pier. "I gazed until I could not distinguish him any longer. God bless him for a gallant spirit and a kind one."

But Byron remained on deck until the chalk cliffs were but a shadowy blur. He was leaving his home, his country, everything he counted dear. He was twenty-eight years old and it seemed his life was already over.

V

✻✻✻✻✻✻✻✻✻✻✻✻✻✻✻✻✻✻✻✻✻✻✻✻✻✻✻✻✻✻

And I Am Going Far

O<small>N</small> the morning of April 27th, 1816, Byron stepped ashore
at Ostend in a state of profound gloom. Through the past
year of excursions and alarums he had often reiterated his longing to leave England and trouble far behind; now that he had
actually satisfied that longing he had abruptly lost interest in all
idea of travel, lost interest even in the prospect of a return to
Greece, the only land in which he had found true happiness. He
did not wish to look to the future—in his opinion there was none.
All he wanted to do was to gaze backwards at the tragic events
which had led up to his departure, and although deep in his heart
he knew that he had willfully, deliberately destroyed the fabric
of his own life he defended himself to himself by blaming others
for the débâcle. He had told Annabella that he still loved her,
but during his slow progress through the Low Countries he
thought of her as the instigator of his downfall. She had married
him and she had betrayed him. She had displayed a cold, im-
placable will utterly at variance with her early protests of affection; she had taken his child from him; she had told heaven
knew what exaggerated stories to her interfering parents and the
snakelike Mrs. Clermont; she had persuaded her personal maid

to sign an affidavit that Lady Byron had left Piccadilly Terrace against her own wish. For these things he could not, would not forgive her.

The hurt to his pride was so grievous that it distorted his vision. Hour after hour, as he paced his hotel rooms, or sat hunched in a corner of the Napoleonic coach, he dwelt on the past, reliving every incident up to that appalling culminating scene at Lady Jersey's party when his whole world fell about him like a tumbling house of cards. Hobhouse had argued with him, insisting that his ostracism by society was merely temporary and that there was absolutely no need for him to leave England; but Hobhouse, dear loyal friend though he was, had no conception of the feelings which racked him.

And above and beyond all other torments was the remorse he felt over that "dear bright being" who had always been closer to him than anyone in the world:

> She was like me in lineaments; her eyes,
> Her hair, her features, all, to the very tone
> Even of her voice, they said were like to mine;
> But soften'd all, and temper'd into beauty:
> She had the same lone thoughts and wanderings...
> Pity and smiles, and tears—which I had not;
> And tenderness—but that I had for her;
> Humility—and that I never had.
> Her faults were mine—her virtues were her own—
> I loved her, and destroy'd her!

It was small wonder that the anxious young Dr. Polidori, who had been tremendously elated by being appointed personal physician to England's greatest poet, was bewildered by his patron's melancholy. Moreover, Mr. John Murray had promised him five hundred guineas (a great sum to an impecunious doctor) if he would write a detailed record of their travels; but how could he write anything lively or amusing about a man who only broke silence to remark that he thought Rubens was "a very great dauber," and who (here the poor doctor blushed for shame) "fell like a thunderbolt upon the chambermaid" the moment they reached their Ostend hotel?

Only when they rode on horseback across the field of Waterloo did Byron rouse himself. Here his boyhood idol, Napoleon, had suffered final defeat—and had not many of his admirers long confirmed his own impression that there was an extraordinary resemblance between him and Bonaparte? Riding slowly over the smooth turf which had so lately been the scene of havoc, Byron began to compose verses on the battle, and when vociferous peasants pushed forward to show him their collections of war trophies he bought several for his English friends.

But once they had left Waterloo behind, Byron lost interest in their journey and was by turns irritable and taciturn. He hated sightseeing and was bored by the Low Countries where "a mole-hill would make the inhabitants think that the Alps had come here on a visit." He fretted when they were held up by a series of minor repairs to the coach, brooded over the perilous condition of his finances (for the second time the reserve price on Newstead had not ben reached at an auction sale and his debts were mountainous), and raged at the "child and childish Dr. Polly-dolly" because a bottle of the "strongest *Pot Ash*" had got broken.

Finally they crossed the frontier from the Rhineland into Switzerland and on May 25th reached Sécheron on Lake Geneva where Byron, while signing the register in the Hôtel d'Angleterre, savagely wrote his age down as one hundred years.

He was tired of hotel life, of Polidori's constant requests that he inspect some church or picture, of being gaped at by tourists. He was also half afraid that the remarkably persistent Miss Clairmont might pursue him, so two days after his arrival he crossed the lake to Diodati where he had heard there was a house to let. As he stepped from the rowboat on his return three people came forward to greet him—Claire Clairmont, her sister Mary Wollstonecraft Godwin, and Percy Bysshe Shelley.

Byron had never met Shelley, but what he had heard of him

he did not like. He could not approve of a young man who got himself expelled from Oxford, played outrageous pranks on everybody, ran away with a philosopher's virgin daughter, and gave vent to amazing theories on atheism, free love and social reform. "All green tea and fine feelings and high-flown radicalism" had been Byron's comment, and he had already warned Claire Clairmont against any association with him. Now, confronted by an extraordinary-looking creature whose rounded shoulders semed quite out of keeping with the rest of his large body, and whose shrill voice reverberated against the eardrums, he recoiled instinctively. Byron, the dandy with the carefully tended auburn curls, could not tolerate a man whose brown hair straggled untidily over the collar of a suit which its owner had long outgrown.

Yet within an hour or two Byron had succumbed to Shelley's faunlike charm and asked him to dine with him that evening. Shelley's wild enthusiasms, his infectious high laugh, his eager bright eyes and intellectual brilliance combined to efface any first impression and Byron, whose snobbism was never far below the surface, observed with pleasure that although his fellow poet dressed in deplorable clothes and paid no heed to the finer points of his toilet, he yet retained delightful manners and was "as perfect a gentleman as ever crossed a drawing room."

It is doubtful whether Shelley would have appreciated such a compliment. Brought up by an aristocratic and rigid father who had been so scandalized by his son's behavior that he had tried to clap him into an asylum, he had no manner of use for the "vulgar and noisy *éclat*" of the great world Byron loved. For his part he was entirely won over by the charm of one he had long regarded as the leader of the Romantic movement, and when they parted that first evening he invited him to continue their conversation the following day.

The Shelleys were also staying at the Hôtel d'Angleterre, so it was natural that they should spend most of their time with their new-found friend. In the daytime they hired a boat and were rowed on the lake; in the evenings they indulged in endless talk which so stimulated Byron that he began work on a third canto to *Childe Harold*. Disarmed by Shelley's vibrant eagerness he found that almost against his will the sharp poignant pain of the past months was fading into a dull ache. He wished, however, that Shelley had been alone and not accompanied by the two women. Ever suspicious of women with brains he did not take to the earnest, fair-haired Mary, while Claire was a constant nuisance. From the moment of their meeting by the lakeside she inundated him with notes about his unkind neglect and whispered requests that he visit her room on the top floor. Perhaps out of sheer exasperation but more probably out of indolent habit Byron renewed the affair which had started in London, but it was an unsatisfactory business altogether and he was relieved when the Shelleys, with Claire, their child and a nursemaid, moved to a villa called Campagne Chapuis. True, it was only five minutes away from the Villa Diodati, to which he himself was going in a fortnight's time, but so long as they were not living under the same roof he felt he could evade his possessive mistress.

By the middle of June Byron had settled into Diodati and renewed his intimacy with the Shelleys, though he very carefully surrounded himself with so many members of his entourage that Claire found it increasingly difficult to see him alone. He did, however, employ her to copy out his poems—always with Polidori or Fletcher within reach—and long afterwards she related an incident which bears a curious resemblance to the one related by Lady Caroline Lamb. According to Claire, Byron asked her one afternoon if she did not consider him "a terrible person." She answered that she could not believe such a thing about him, whereupon he unlocked a drawer, drew out Augusta's letters, and told her to read them. This she was unable to do as they contained

> ...long spaces written in cyphers which he said only he and she had the key of—and unintelligible to all other people.... I mentioned the cyphers to Mary and Shelley but the latter said they

most likely were used to convey news of his illegitimate children—
I supposed so too and thought no more of Mrs. Leigh.

Whether one believes this ingenuous statement or not, it is
apparently true that Byron flew into a temper and accused Claire
of stealing one of the letters. It was found after an agitated search
and he apologized for his suspicions.

Meanwhile poor Polidori, who had complained of his patron's
taciturnity such a short time before, found himself caught up in
such a web of talk that he was spellbound, bewildered, miserable
all at once. He had immense literary ambitions of his own, but
often he failed to remember all the conversations he listened to,
and when he did he seemed unable to set them down in his
journal. The five hundred guineas promised by Mr. Murray
receded into the middle distance and this agitated him so much
that he demanded furiously of Byron, "What can *you* do, that
is beyond my power?"

"Why," his employer replied, "since you force me to say so,
I think there are three things."

"Name them!" cried the doctor.

Byron smiled and pointed first out of the window at the river,
then at a candle which burned at the far end of the room. "I can
swim across that river—I can snuff out that candle with a pistol
shot at a distance of twenty paces—and I have written a poem
[*The Corsair*] of which fourteen thousand copies were sold in
one day."

It was this last achievement which stung Polidori, who forthwith began to write a tragedy and dramatically presented his
work to the Shelleys and Byron when they met for their usual
evening talk. "Ah," said Byron, after reading it aloud in his low,
musical voice, "I assure you, when I was in the Drury Lane
Committee, much worse things were offered to us."

But worse was to follow. A temporary break in the weather
kept the party indoors and throughout a whole day they regaled
each other by telling ghost stories. Like Byron, Shelley was a

mass of superstitions and imagined himself at times the victim of persecution. Unlike Byron, he actually suffered hallucinations, and on this particular day the ghostly tales completely unnerved him. By midnight he was in a distraught condition and Byron was emphasizing the eerie atmosphere by reciting Coleridge's *Christabel.* He had reached the lines:

> Her silken robe, and inner vest
> Dropt to her feet, and full in view
> Behold! Her bosom and half her side—
> A sight to dream of. . . .

when Shelley swayed to his feet with an unearthly scream. Catching up a candlestick he shambled through the door leading to the garden moaning like a banshee. Mary rushed after him and revived him by throwing cold water over his head and giving him a whiff of ether. Presently he was led back, shaken but calm, and explained to the company that he had suddenly remembered a dreadful story of a woman who "had eyes instead of nipples, which taking hold of his mind horrified him. . . ."

It was not surprising that such scenes also unnerved Polidori, or that on one occasion he fled to his room, snatched a bottle of poison from the medicine chest, and vowed he was going to kill himself. Fortunately, he decided to write a dramatic farewell letter first, and as he was doing so Byron walked in with outstretched hand. His kindness, Polidori wrote later, quite restored his composure; but at the time the poor young man was so overwhelmed by Shelley's wild speech, Byron's moods, Mary's solemn insistence that he should teach her Italian, and Claire's fierce pursuit of her lover, that he developed a morbid sense of his own inferiority which led him into extremely stupid words and actions.

Rowing Byron on the lake one day Polidori missed his grip on the oar, which caught Byron full on the knee-cap. The injury was most painful, but Byron said merely that he hoped the doctor would exercise more care in future. Instead of saying he was sorry for his clumsiness Polidori burst out viciously, "I am glad of it. I am glad to see you can suffer pain." Incensed by his rudeness Byron replied coldly: "Let me advise you, Polidori, when you, another time, hurt anyone, not to express your satisfaction. People don't like to be told that those who give them pain are glad of it; and they cannot always command their anger. It was with some difficulty that I refrained from throwing you into the water and, but for Mrs. Shelley's presence, I should probably have done some such rash thing."

But Polidori was beyond snubs or lectures or sympathetic treatment. He conceived a violent jealousy of Shelley and challenged him to a duel, a suggestion which that pacifist merely laughed at. He made impudent remarks in an endeavor to draw attention to himself. He continued to mutter darkly of suicide, and he spent hours in his room confiding his unhappiness to his journal. Finally, he managed to sprain his ankle, but even this accident happened in a ridiculous way. The Villa Diodati had a low balcony and one morning when he and Byron were standing on it Byron suggested he should jump down and help Mary, who could be seen toiling up the steep hill. Though the distance was but a foot Polidori tripped and fell. Complaining that he was seriously, if not fatally, injured he was carried indoors by Byron and Fletcher and the poet himself limped around attending to the injury. By way of gratitude the doctor said in a surprised tone, "Well, I did not believe you had so much feeling!"

Polidori's enforced seclusion was a relief to the whole company, and on June 23rd Byron and Shelley set out by boat on a romantic pilgrimage around Lake Geneva. To Hobhouse Byron wrote:

> Tomorrow we go to Meillerei, and Clarens, and Vevey, with Rousseau in hand, to see his scenery, according to his delineation in his Héloïse, now before me; the views have hitherto been very fine, but, I should conceive, less so than those of the remainder of the lake.

It was after leaving Meillerei that they ran into a sudden storm and feared their boat was about to sink. Byron immediately divested himself of his coat and prepared to plunge into the lake but Shelley, who had reluctantly followed his friend's example, suddenly changed his mind, sat down on a locker, and said firmly that he would "sink without a struggle." He was not, he added, afraid—although he could not swim. Water had a tremendous attraction for him and when he was in danger from it he suffered a "mixture of sensations" not wholly unpleasant. Fortunately, while he was expressing these sentiments the storm had abated and the boat was brought under control again.

The following day they sailed to the source of the Rhône and afterwards visited the Castle of Chillon. From Ouchy, where they spent two rainy days, they went to the now deserted house and garden where Edward Gibbon had lived and worked. Here Byron plucked a sprig of acacia and gathered a handful of rose leaves to send to John Murray, and on June 30th they returned to Diodati, well content with their pilgrimage and on excellent terms with each other.

Though Byron still spent most of his time with the Shelleys he paid several visits to Coppet, where his old acquaintance, Madame de Staël, was now installed. Voluble as ever (though she had not many months to live), she greeted Byron with delight—forgetting that she had once called him a demon—and lectured him on his attitude towards his wife. Strangely enough he listened to her politely and even went so far as to put forward a hint about reconciliation in a letter to England; but while he enjoyed Germaine de Staël's company he did not relish that of the guests who thronged her drawing room in order to stare at him "as at some outlandish beast," and when the elderly Mrs. Hervey, a sister of Beckford of Fonthill, fainted dead away on being introduced to him he withdrew from the Coppet circle.

Byron had courted celebrity as assiduously as any man; but the kind which had followed him since his departure from England was definitely not to his liking. Everywhere he went people nudged each other, peered at him out of the corners of their eyes, called at the Villa Diodati on some trumpery excuse in the hope of seeing him, crowded around the gates when he drove out in his carriage. They even went so far as to take up a strategic position at a distance and scan his windows through spy-glasses—an occupation which led to the alarming rumor that some innocent tablecloths being aired on the balcony were articles of feminine apparel belonging to the large selection of mistresses he kept in the villa for his delight. And lately he had heard from England a most disquieting rumor that he and the disgraceful Mr. Shelley had formed a "league of incest" and were enjoying "promiscuous intercourse" with two sisters.

Wrapped up as he had been in his English fame Byron had not fully realized that through *Childe Harold* and his other poems he had become a figure of legend all over Europe. To writers all over the Continent he was the Great Romantic, the leader *par excellence*, and to do them justice many of those who haunted the Villa Diodati were impelled to do so by admiration rather than by curiosity. Hypersensitive as he was, still haunted by a sense of guilt, he shrank from their scrutiny and avoided meeting strangers.

This meant that he was limited to the Shelleys' company, and while he had grown remarkably fond of Shelley he was heartily sick of Claire, that restless, demanding young woman who never gave him a moment's peace. He was therefore glad to welcome Mathew Gregory Lewis, when that odd, bulbous-eyed little man arrived in August fresh from a visit to the plantations he had inherited in Jamaica. Byron had not been particularly impressed by Lewis when he first met him at Holland House and had rudely described his famous best seller, *The Monk,* as being "all the sour cream of cantharides"; but now Lewis appeared as a friend from the past.

But soon Lewis had come and gone and Byron, who was expecting Hobhouse and Scrope Davies to join him, was relieved when Shelley announced that legal business called him back to

England. Good John Cam, he felt, might not appreciate the vagaries of Shelley's mind; besides, he had no wish for his friends to meet Claire, who had just given him the unpalatable information that she was pregnant. Fortunately, Shelley's theories on free love and the inherent goodness of mankind came to the rescue and he generously offered to take her back with Mary and himself and look after her until the birth of her child. Byron thought this an excellent idea. He did not consider he was under any obligation to Claire (though it is doubtful whether he told Shelley so) and when they departed at the end of August he sat back relievedly to await the coming of Hobhouse and Davies.

❋ 2 ❋

What joy it was to have the two dear fellows beside him once more! Talking and laughing with them he was transported back to London, to Almack's and Watier's, to the convivial gatherings at Tom Cribb's, to "The line of lights, too, up to Charing Cross," to the mad, carefree days when he and they had rampaged around the town. He made a determined effort to hide his own discontent with his exiled existence and succeeded so well that Hobhouse wrote to Augusta that her

> ...excellent relative is living with the strictest attention to decorum.... A considerable change has taken place in his health; no brandy, no very late hours, no quarts of magnesia, nor deluges of soda-water. Neither passion nor perverseness....

Augusta, however, alarmed by rumors and considerably harassed by Lady Byron and Mrs. Villiers, had already written to her brother and on September 8th Byron gave her a flippant account of his affair with Claire:

> As to all these "mistresses," Lord help me—I have had but one. Now don't scold; but what could I do?—a foolish girl, in spite

of all I could say or do, would come after me, or rather went before—for I found her here—and I have had all the plague possible to persuade her to go back again; but at last she went. Now dearest, I do most truly tell thee, that I could not help this, that I did all I could to prevent it, and have at last put an end to it. I was not in love, nor have any love left for any; but I could not exactly play the Stoic with a woman, who had scrambled eight hundred miles to unphilosophize me....

Davies could only spare a few days but the three friends managed an expedition to Chamonix; after which Byron told Polidori he feared they did not suit each other well and gave him £70 as a parting gift. Left to themselves he and Hobhouse made a fortnight's tour of the Bernese Alps which undoubtedly did a great deal to soothe the troubled state of his nerves. For despite his appearance of calm Byron had lately been suffering an even darker mood than before. From regarding his wife as the instigator of his woes he had passed to a passion of remorse for the sin he had committed against the being he loved best; now he had reached a stage when he realized that he could never expiate his crime:

> There is a power upon me which withholds,
> And makes it my fatality to live,—
> If it be life to wear within myself
> This barrenness of spirit...
>   For I have ceased
> To justify my deeds unto myself—
> The last infirmity of evil.

During their mountain tour Byron kept a fragmentary journal —which he later sent to Augusta—and although he told her that "neither the music of the shepherd, the crashing of the avalanche, nor the torrent, the mountain, the glacier, the forest, nor the cloud, have for one moment lightened the weight upon my heart, nor enabled me to lose my own wretched identity," one senses, through reading of the journal, that the lonely mountain passes of the Jura did in truth bring him a measure of relief.

Early in October Byron and Hobhouse crossed the Simplon and made their way through Lombardy to Milan, where they were delighted to find Lord and Lady Jersey. Byron greatly enjoyed visits to the Scala, where he was vastly intrigued by the behavior of Italian society, but his favorite haunt in the city was the Ambrosian museum. Here were lodged the love letters of Lucrezia Borgia and Cardinal Pietro Bembo, and beside them, encased in a crystal block, was a lock of Lucrezia's glittering golden hair. These relics so fascinated Byron that, rather to the consternation of the librarian, he returned day after day to pore over them.

> ... a lock of her hair [he wrote to Augusta], so long—and fair and beautiful—and the letters so pretty and so loving that it makes one wretched not to have been born sooner to have at least seen her. And pray what do you think is one of her *signatures?*—why this + a Cross—which she says "is to stand for her name etc." Is not this amusing? I suppose you know that she was a famous beauty, and famous for the use she made of it; and that she was the love of this same Cardinal Bembo (besides a story about her papa Pope Alexander and her brother Caesar Borgia—which some people don't believe—and others do), and that after all she ended with being Duchess of Ferrara, and an excellent wife and mother also; so good as to be quite an example. All this may or may not be, but the hair and letters are so beautiful that I have done nothing but pore over them ... and I mean to get some of the hair if I can....

Byron asked for permission to copy some of the letters, but this was refused. He then employed subterfuge, waiting until the watchful librarian's back was turned and trying to filch the lock from its crystal casing. All he managed to steal was a single shining hair which he kept until his death.

In Milan at the time was Stendhal, otherwise Henri Beyle, who had been with Napoleon through the Russian campaign. Beyle was tremendously impressed with Byron, of whom he wrote afterwards in his letters:

J'ai dîné avec un joli et charmant jeune homme, figure de dix-huit ans, quoiqu'il en ait 28, profil d'un ange, l'air le plus doux. C'est l'original de Lovelace, ou plutôt mille fois mieux que le bavard Lovelace. . . . C'est le plus grand poète vivant, Lord Byron.

Finding that, although an Englishman, the poet was a great admirer of Napoleon, Beyle had long and highly interesting discussions with him.

But Milan did not hold Byron for long. By November he was on the road again and on the 11th he reached Venice, that lovely, decaying, watery city which was to capture and hold his heart for three long years. He did not regret the passing of her days of grandeur; he took little interest in her architectural beauties; he felt inexpressibly soothed by her quietude, by the soft speech of her people, by the Eastern atmosphere which still clung about her.

He took lodgings in the Frezzaria at the house of a draper called Segati and within five days of his arrival fell in love with his landlord's wife, Marianna. She was twenty-two years old and, he told Moore, "like an antelope . . . with large, black, oriental eyes." Her features were regular and inclined to be aquiline, her skin clear and soft, and her hair "of the dark gloss, curl and color of Lady Jersey's." Even Hobhouse approved of the lady and Byron wrote ecstatically to Douglas Kinnaird, "I meant to have given up gallivanting altogether . . . but, I know not how it is, my health growing better, and my spirits not worse, the 'besoin d'aimer' came back upon my heart again, and, after all, there is nothing like it."

Marianna was lively, unexacting, and altogether a welcome change from Claire Clairmont, who still pestered him with letters either twitting him about his drinking habits or imploring him to write her without delay. Her society banished the last shreds of his melancholy and when Hobhouse departed to spend two months in Rome with relations Byron decided to employ his days in taking lessons in Armenian from Father Pasquale of the Armenian Convent (*sic*) on the island of St. Lazzaro. Every

morning he went there by gondola and studied either in the great
library which looked out over the lagoon, or in the walled garden, or in the private rooms the grateful monks had said he might
regard as his own. They looked upon him as a benefactor because,
in payment for his lessons, he had contributed a thousand francs
towards publication of the Armenian-English grammar their
Librarian was preparing, and for his part he found the company
of these tranquil, simple men strangely satisfying even if he did
not get very far with the learning of their language.

At twilight he drifted back to Venice across the still water
and spent a happy evening with Marianna or even, occasionally,
visited the *salons* of Countess Albrizzi and Countess Benzoni,
two noted hostesses who were only too glad to welcome such a
famous guest. "If I could but remain as I now am," Byron told
Kinnaird, "I should not merely be happy, but *contented*, which
in my mind is the strangest, and most difficult attainment of the
two—for any one who will hazard enough may have moments of
happiness."

Sometimes he thought vaguely of returning to England when
the spring came, not to stay but to visit his excellent dentist Mr.
Waite, and his barber Mr. Blake, and to give his support to the
reform party in the Lords; but as the days slipped by and he
grew more and more enamored of Venice he put the idea out of
his head till two pieces of news came to upset his drowsy contentment. The first was a letter from John Murray informing
him that at a booksellers' dinner he had taken orders for no
fewer than seven thousand copies each of the Third Canto of
Childe Harold and *The Prisoner of Chillon and Other Poems*,
which Shelley had taken back with him the previous summer
and which were now published. The second was a letter from
Shelley himself stating that Claire had given birth in Bath on
January 12th, 1817, to a "beautiful girl . . . a creature of the most
exquisite symmetry," who was to be named Clara Allegra.
Shelley then went on to tell Byron of the recent suicide of his
wife Harriet Westbrook, and launched out into a tirade against

her aged father and her sister Elizabeth which had precious little truth in it.

Byron was delighted with the news from Murray, felt quite pleased that he had fathered a second daughter (though he did not propose to do anything about her or her mother), and was indifferent to the fate of poor Harriet. But these reminders of the world outside proved unsettling and when Carnival began at the end of January he threw himself into all the excitements of "fiddling, masquerading and singing." As a result he got into a scrape which very nearly lost him his Marianna. A gondolier brought him an unsigned note in which the writer asked him to meet her at one of three suggested rendezvous. He replied that she might either see him at his home alone at ten in the evening (Marianna and her husband being at a conversazione) or at the ridotto at midnight. At ten precisely his door opened and in walked a pretty Italian girl of nineteen who confessed she was Segati's sister. According to Byron they made innocent conversation for a few minutes only to be interrupted by Marianna, who entered like a whirlwind, seized her sister-in-law by the hair, and bestowed on her sixteen violent slaps. The girl screamed and fled; Marianna collapsed in Byron's arms and the combined efforts of Fletcher and himself failed to revive her. Climax was provided by the arrival of Signor Segati, who found his wife fainting on the sofa with "all the apparatus of confusion, dishevelled hair, hats, handkerchiefs, salts, smelling-bottles—and the lady pale as ashes, without sense or motion." The Signor demanded to know what was wrong, a question skillfully parried by Byron, who suggested the first thing to be done was to help the lady regain her senses. The next day he kept out of the way and Marianna evidently gave her husband some sort of explanation, for everything went on as before—but the episode had taught Byron that Marianna was not the sweet, easy-going young woman he had imagined.

The strenuous gaieties of Carnival took their toll and by the time Lent began, towards the end of February, he was physically exhausted. It was then that he sent Moore the finest lyric he was ever to write:

> So we'll go no more a-roving
>   So late into the night,
> Though the heart be still as loving,
>   And the moon be still as bright.
>
> For the sword outwears its sheath,
>   And the soul wears out the breast,
> And the heart must pause to breathe,
>   And love itself have rest.
>
> Though the night was made for loving,
>   And the day returns too soon,
> Yet we'll go no more a-roving
>   By the light of the moon.

"For the sword outwears its sheath" was a phrase peculiarly applicable to Byron. His demonic energy drove him to live at a pace with which his never robust body could not keep up, and even during his periods of abstinence he further weakened his physique by purges, starvation and violent exercise. The riotous weeks of the Venice Carnival left him in such a low condition that he succumbed to a fever, not, he assured Hobhouse, "the low, vulgar typhus, which is at present decimating Venice, and has half unpeopled Milan; but a sharp, gentlemanly fever that went away in a few days." He refused to see a doctor, but the illness shook him more than he cared to admit although he declared stoutly he was perfectly well again and had a "monstrous appetite." He had lately been suffering from attacks of giddiness and twinges of rheumatism, his auburn hair was turning gray, and he fancied that his firm white teeth were becoming loose. The danger signals alarmed him—did he not have a loathing for old age?—and he decided in April that he would join Hobhouse in Rome.

In his cumbersome Napoleonic coach, which held among other things a bed, a chest of silver, and "every apparatus for dining," he left Venice, his route taking him through Ferrara, Padua, Bologna and Florence. This journey gave him the material for the Fourth Canto of *Childe Harold*, which was dedicated to Hobhouse. But although Byron recorded the deep emotion he felt upon seeing cities, tombs and statues which recalled an earlier, fairer world, it was Rome herself that moved him most:

> The Niobe of nations! there she stands,
> Childless and crownless, in her voiceless woe;
> An empty urn within her withered hands,
> Whose holy dust was scatter'd long ago;
> The Scipios' tomb contains no ashes now;
> The very sepulchres lie tenantless
> Of their heroic dwellers: dost thou flow,
> Old Tiber! through a marble wilderness?
> Rise with thy yellow waves, and mantle her distress.

Hobhouse, who uneasily remembered the occasion in Athens when Byron had described the Parthenon as being "rather like the Mansion House," was relieved by his friend's reaction to the Holy City. In truth, it was the "Chaos of ruins" in Rome which appealed to Byron:

> ...Rome is as the desert, where we steer
> Stumbling o'er recollections; now we clap
> Our hands, and cry "Eureka!" it is clear—
> When but some false mirage of ruin rises near.

The friends rode together all around the city and often made their way across the Campagna to the Alban hills. Alone, Byron wandered through the Palatine and the Colosseum, where the rough undergrowth sprouted unchecked amid the crumbling man-made walls. Always preoccupied with thoughts of death he ruminated as he walked on the heroism of the men who, given but a short time to live, had yet built such monuments to human endeavor.

But not all his days were spent in this melancholy yet pleasing fashion. The famous sculptor Bertel Thorwaldson was in Rome,

183

and Hobhouse persuaded Byron to sit to him. When Thorwald-son asked him to sit in a chair and then posed him to his liking, Byron put on a petulant expression and began to fidget, moving his head this way and that like a spoiled child. "Will you not sit still?" demanded the exasperated sculptor. "You need not assume that look." Byron gave him a glance of extreme hauteur and said that his expression was the one he habitually wore, whereupon Thorwaldson set to work grimly and portrayed him as he wished to look. The result was Byron at his most arrogant, and while his friends praised the bust he himself detested it because, he asserted, his usual expression was far more unhappy.

Then there were enjoyable diversions with Lord Lansdowne and the Jerseys, who were spending the spring in Rome, and less enjoyable encounters with other of his fellow countrymen who ostentatiously ignored him. As usual too there were the hordes of gaping tourists and on one occasion, we are told, an English lady who was escorting her daughters around the roof of St. Peter's loudly ordered her girls to look the other way till the ineffably wicked Lord Byron had passed by. These incidents annoyed Byron to such a degree that he began to yearn for the privacy of Venice—and possibly for the arms of Marianna.

But the day before he left he felt drawn to attend a macabre spectacle, the guillotining of three robbers, and afterwards de-scribed the scene to John Murray.

> The ceremony—including the *masqued* priests; the half-naked executioners; the bandaged criminals; the black Christ and his banner; the scaffold; the soldiery; the slow procession; and the quick rattle and heavy fall of the axe; the splash of the blood, and the ghastliness of the exposed heads—is altogether more im-pressive than the vulgar and ungentlemanly dirty "new drop," and dog-like agony of infliction upon the sufferers of the English sentence.... The pain seems little; and yet the effect to the spectator, and the preparation to the criminal, are very striking and chilling. The first turned me quite hot and thirsty, and made me shake so that I could hardly hold the opera-glass (I was close, but determined to see every thing, once, with attention); the

184

second and third (which shows how dreadfully soon things grow indifferent), I am ashamed to say, had no effect on me as a horror, though I would have saved them if I could.

❋ 3 ❋

On his return to Venice in the beginning of June Byron found the heat and smells of the Frezzeria overpowering, so after a little search he took the Palazzo Foscarini at La Mira on the Brento, and to this pleasant if neglected old house he transferred his belongings—including Marianna, whose complacent husband apparently made no objection. Here his first guest was Monk Lewis, and towards the end of July Hobhouse arrived. Byron had greatly benefited by his stay in Rome and seemed, so his friend noted, to be making every effort to keep in good health. He drank but little, ate reasonably well, and went riding each evening with Hobhouse.

Byron's generosity was already a legend among the impoverished peasants of the district and one evening, when they passed a group of people, two very pretty girls ran up to them. The taller, a handsome girl whose black eyes and hair were well set off by the white veil then worn by peasant women, addressed Byron by name and demanded to know why, since he was so free with his money to others, he did not help her and her friend. He answered jokingly that she looked much too beautiful to need aid, and she retorted that if he saw her poor home he would not think so. An evening or two later the girls appeared in their path, and this time Byron proffered financial help to the tall one if she really required it. No ulterior motive was in his mind, but the young woman quickly replied that she had a very "ferocious" husband, a baker. It was the sort of remark calculated to put Byron on his mettle. In a very short time the black-eyed beauty had managed to curb her husband's ferocity and transported herself bag and baggage to La Mira.

185

Her name was Margarita Cogni and she was an extraordinary character. Brought up in the back alleys of Venice she was known as La Fornarina and feared throughout the city for her temper, her greed, and her amazing physical strength. Marianna, not realizing how formidable this new rival was, lay in wait for her with a group of friends, and advised her to take her departure; but La Fornarina advanced on her with eyes flashing and arms flailing, screaming that Marianna was not the English Milord's wife and nor was she. "*You* are his *Donna*, and *I* am his *Donna*; *your* husband is a cuckold, and *mine* is another. For the rest, what *right* have you to reproach me? If he prefers what is mine to what is yours, is it my fault . . .?" Before this attack poor Marianna meekly retreated, and although La Fornarina graciously permitted her to continue visiting La Mira she had to content herself with a much smaller share of Byron's attention than formerly.

But La Fornarina possessed a high degree of cunning. For so long as Hobhouse was in Italy—and he remained in that country until the beginning of 1818—she kept in the background, reserving her wild protests of love, her furious tempers, and her coarse jokes for the moments when she was alone with Byron. Consequently the pompous John Cam had little idea of her true character, and even less of the ascendancy she was gaining over his friend.

When Monk Lewis went back to England in August the Fourth (and last) Canto of *Childe Harold* was already completed, and for a time Byron gave himself up to the society of his friends. He and Hobhouse visited Arqua and Padua, Douglas Kinnaird and his brother appeared for a stay in Venice, there were several convivial but comparatively harmless evenings, social calls on the Countess Benzoni, dinners with Richard Belgrave Hoppner, the British Consul. On the surface it was an innocuous existence, and Hobhouse reported that Byron was "well, and merry and happy, more charming every day." Until mid-November they remained at La Mira, often spending their afternoons out at the Lido, where Byron kept his horses, and here they would gallop for miles along the sands. Byron was toying with the idea of writing a long verse-novel (which later became the famous *Don Juan*), and he was greatly heartened by news from Hanson that a Colonel Wildman, whom he had known slightly at Harrow, had bought Newstead for a sum approaching £95,000.

The Newstead sale meant that Byron could at last pay his debts and have enough left to lead an exceedingly comfortable life in Italy, where expenses were much less than in England. He discussed his business affairs most sensibly with Hobhouse, wrote explicit instructions to Hanson, and, when he moved back for the winter months to the Frezzeria, continued his new and decorous way of life.

❄ 4 ❄

Hobhouse left Italy early in January, 1818, and so soon as he had gone Byron took the Palazzo Mocenigo, a huge, frowning building on a curve of the Grand Canal. The ground floor, which was very damp and haunted by evil odors, housed Byron's carriages and the variety of "dogs, birds, monkeys..." he had collected. A marble staircase led to the living apartments, a series of large echoing rooms which were—and remained—almost devoid of furniture, and somewhere around the place were about fourteen servants, mostly Italian. The house was dominated by La Fornarina who, while she did not actually live there, walked in and out as she pleased.

The events of the past two years had taught Byron self-control, a quality he had not hitherto possessed. In Switzerland he had given no inkling to Hobhouse of the devils which beset him: in Venice he had not betrayed the new and awful fear which was growing with him, the fear that Augusta was turning away from him. Filled with the overwhelming knowledge of his sin, aware that he could not hope for salvation in this world or the next, he had clung all the more tenaciously to her love, for it was the only thing which could assuage his suffering. But since the summer of 1816 her letters had become increasingly hurried and evasive—full of that "damned crinkum-crankum" of hers—and on his return from Rome he had dashed off an indignant complaint:

> I have received all your letters I believe, which are full of woes, as usual, megrims and mysteries; but my sympathies remain in suspense, for, for the life of me I can't make out whether your disorder is a broken heart or the earache—or whether it is *you* that have been ill or the children—or what your melancholy and mysterious apprehensions tend to, or refer to, whether to Caroline Lamb's novels—Mrs. Clermont's evidence—Lady Byron's magnanimity—or any other piece of imposture; I know nothing of what you are in the doldrums about at present. . . .

But Byron had a pretty shrewd idea of the cause behind his sister's "doldrums"; he was convinced that she was being influenced by his wife.

His conviction was right. Having failed to reform her husband Annabella had directed her attention to his sister, an innocent victim perhaps, but nevertheless his partner in an unforgivable crime. When Augusta had retired from Piccadilly Terrace to her rooms in St. James's Palace she had been visited by her friend Mrs. Villiers, who was all agog to learn the inside truth of the scandal which was reverberating round London. To this supposedly sympathetic listener Augusta had poured out her troubles. The dear Queen was so strict . . . she was terrified lest she heard the awful rumors . . . she had to think of her husband and the future of her children . . . she did hope Annabella did not think too badly of her . . . Annabella's continued friendship was all-important. . . .

Intrigued, but unable to piece the story together from Augusta's mumblings, Mrs. Villiers bustled off to see Annabella and plead with her to do all she could for her poor sister-in-law. Solemnly Annabella assured the lady that while she had been most grateful to Augusta for her support in many unhappy incidents, there were certain dreadful reasons why she should no longer continue to be friends with her. She went on to say that her legal advisers had told her that she should get Augusta to confess her guilt. On the grounds of sentiment she was reluctant to do this—but this was no time for sentiment and she had to think of her child. If dear Mrs. Villiers would help her, and if Augusta could be persuaded to admit her terrible sin, then they would see what could be done to rehabilitate her in the eyes of the world.

There seems little doubt that Annabella was, at least in part, actuated by jealousy. During her brief marriage she had kept that horrid emotion under control: now that she had dismissed Byron from her life she allowed it to control her. The one thing she dared not envisage—and the one thing her lawyers hoped would happen—was that Augusta should flee the country and rejoin her brother. To prevent that Annabella was prepared to do far more than merely extract a confession from her wretched sister-in-law. She told herself virtuously that she was taking action merely to save Augusta from herself, and in May, 1816, she wrote to Mrs. Villiers (who was only too eager to join the crusade) that, "My great object, next to the Security of my Child, is ... the restoration of her mind to that state which is religiously desirable."

At that moment Augusta was in process of giving birth to one of her numerous children, so her kind-hearted reformers waited until June to open the attack. Annabella then wrote hoping her "dearest Augusta" was fully recovered, and hinting subtly that certain reasons for terminating their friendship could no longer be kept in the background. Disturbed and bewildered, Augusta replied with one of her usual flustered epistles. She wasn't "wholly surprised" ... she was desperately wounded ...

she had always considered Annabella's happiness "above everything in this world."

This stupid communication was of no use to Annabella, who then subjected her victim to a bombardment by letter which would have defeated a far stronger character, and soon she had the satisfaction of informing Mrs. Villiers that Augusta had "confessed" to her guilt before Byron's marriage but protested her innocence since.

But the more Annabella thought of Augusta's letter the less she liked it—she wanted proof that the guilty relationship had continued after her marriage. Consequently, when Augusta came up to London to attend the Queen at the Regent's Fête (looking, according to Mrs. Villiers, "quite stout and well . . . perfectly cool and easy," and prattling of "Gauzes and Sattins") she was summoned to an interview with Annabella at which, although she sobbed bitterly, she reiterated that nothing had passed between Byron and herself since his marriage.

Something drastic had to be done, so Mrs. Villiers was deputed to tell Augusta that Byron himself, "through an authority she could not doubt," had given away their guilty secret. To Augusta, who had believed implicitly in her brother, this story was the last straw. Broken and humiliated she trailed back to Six Mile Bottom, whence she wrote to Annabella calling her a Guardian Angel and imploring her for advice as to how she could answer Byron's letters and how she could stop him from sending them. From that moment on every letter Byron wrote to Augusta was passed on to Annabella for perusal and comment. They were, she said, *absolute love letters,* and very likely it was the reading of them—with their references to herself as "my moral Clytemnestra"—that led her to make Augusta Ada a Ward in Chancery the following year.

Far away in Venice Byron was unaware of the whole sorry story. He did not know that his sister had been warned by his wife never to encourage "his criminal *desires,* I think I may add *designs,*" nor that Augusta, harassed beyond endurance, had turned for comfort to the piety taught her by her grandmother, nor that Annabella had enlisted the aid of Francis Hodgson, now a clergyman, in Augusta's moral reform. All he knew was that Augusta's letters grew more and more disjointed and infrequent, and that any suggestion that he should visit her in England or she visit him in Italy met with a flurry of excuses.

He had not lost faith in Augusta—he was never to do that— but he was alarmed because she, who had always been so close to him, now seemed bent on eluding him. Did she not realize his loneliness, his despair? Did she not know he loved her "better than any earthly existence"? Did not he and she share the same heritage, live under the shadow of the same Byronic doom?

Such were the thoughts that ran through Byron's mind as he galloped along the Lido sands with Hobhouse, or drank with Kinnaird, or made love to Marianna. He would not admit even to himself that the image of Augusta had faded a little, that he had grown accustomed to living without her, that she was now little more than the memory of a past and perfect love. If she was no longer his then he cared not what happened to him. Without her he must resign himself utterly to that fate which had so long pursued him.

* 5 *

Byron's thirtieth birthday on January 22nd, 1818, marked the real beginning of his career of debauchery in Venice. Bereft of Augusta, haunted by the approach of middle age, he flung himself into the pursuit of new sensations. Again he was whirled into the joys of Carnival, and by the end of the month he was sending Mr. Murray an account of a new affair:

> I am in the *estrum* and agonies of a new intrigue with I don't know exactly whom or what, except that she is insatiate of love,

and won't take money, and has light hair, and blue eyes, which are not common here, and that I met her at the Masque, and that when her mask is off, I am as wise as ever.

La Fornarina was still his favorite, but she had no objection to sharing his favors with others, so soon the Palazzo Mocenigo saw a procession of women, most of them from the lowest quarters of Venice, who fought on the marble staircase, shrieked at the servants, and delighted Byron by their free speech and their abandon. With them came their pimps—and a host of other queer characters from gondoliers to tramps who camped out on the ground floor between the pens housing Byron's menagerie. The place was Bedlam, and in the servants' quarters an unhappy Fletcher struggled to keep the greedy, dishonest Italian footmen in some sort of order while his master, apparently unperturbed by the din going on above and below him, sat in his first-floor rooms writing *Don Juan* and sipping gin and water.

In the afternoons Byron often went out to the Lido to ride, taking Richard Hoppner as a companion, and sometimes he attended Countess Benzoni's receptions, but most of his spare time was spent either with his various concubines or with the riffraff of Venice, whose conversation amused him. His chief consolation, however, was La Fornarina, because she could always make him laugh, and as the days passed she became more importunate in her demands. As the mistress of an English Milord she should, she insisted, dress like a lady, and to this end she discarded her *fazziolo* (veil) in which she looked beautiful, and bought an expensive ostrich-plumed hat in which she looked frightful. Byron burned the hat, but she promptly rushed off to buy another—also a dress with a long train in which she trailed happily around the huge rooms.

But La Fornarina had a quality more useful than her ability to make Byron laugh. Somewhere in her career she had picked up quite a knowledge of housekeeping and presently, having quarreled with her husband and called him a "consumptive cuckold," she took up her abode in the Palazzo and assumed the role of housekeeper. At first highly indignant at her intrusion into his domain, Fletcher at length admitted that she got far more work out of the servants than he had managed to do, and according to Byron, "the expenses were reduced to less than half, and everybody did their duty better." He, who had always been the most extravagant of men, was beginning to exhibit the care over pounds, shillings and pence which characterized his later years. Although for the first time for many years he was living well within his income, he scrutinized each item of expenditure and wrote long letters to John Murray on the subject of literary payments.

For some time Byron had been receiving occasional letters from Shelley about the future of little Allegra, a subject which her father had managed to evade. He did not mind supporting the child but he would have no more to do with Claire Clairmont. "I shall acknowledge and breed her [Allegra] myself," he wrote to Douglas Kinnaird, "giving her the name of Biron (to distinguish her from little Legitimacy)." Claire's letters he had stubbornly refused to answer, but recently Shelley had written again, pointing out as tactfully as he could that something must be done, and warning his friend that although Claire was an exceedingly difficult creature, ill-treatment of her might lead to a further condemnation of his behavior on the part of his friends in England. Byron was determined to guard his Venetian independence, but after much argument it was agreed that Allegra should be handed over to him and that Claire should refrain from coming to Venice. Shelley and Mary, who had been married the previous December, brought their own two children, with Claire and her child, to Milan in early April, and towards the end of that month Allegra, in the charge of a Swiss nursemaid called Elise Foggi, was sent off to her father.

The Palazzo Mocenigo was scarcely a suitable home for a small English child a little over a year old. Byron was pleased to find she gave signs of beauty and encouraged her to display temper—even at that early age Allegra was self-willed. La

Fornarina took a great fancy to the child and stuffed her with sticky sweetmeats which upset her stomach. The servants alternately spoiled and ignored her, and it was left to Mrs. Hoppner, Swiss wife to the Consul, to keep an eye on her well-being.

But Byron had not much time to devote to Allegra. The news of Lady Melbourne's death in the spring of 1818 had greatly upset him, although he assured his publisher that the time was past in which he could feel for the dead. She had, he reflected, been the best friend he had ever had—and friendship meant a very great deal to Byron. Moreover, her passing meant that yet another of the few remaining links connecting him with England had snapped. Everybody, everywhere, he reflected morosely, was lost to him. Hobhouse was engrossed in his political career, Kinnaird was involved in a quarrel with his mistress, Scrope Davies was gallivanting off somewhere. Nobody even bothered to write to him, or to send him the variety of articles, from books to tooth powder, which he had asked them to order. And now Hanson, the lawyer, had the effrontery to suggest that he, Byron, should journey all the way to Geneva in order to sign the necessary papers for the Newstead sale! In a fury he dashed off an addition to a letter he was writing to Murray.

> Tell Mr. Hobhouse and Mr. Hanson that they may as well expect Geneva to come to me, as that I should go to Geneva. The messenger may go on or return, as he pleases; I won't stir: and I look upon it as a piece of singular absurdity in those who know me imagining that I should;—not to say *Malice*, in attempting unnecessary torture. If, on the occasion, my interests should suffer, it is their neglect that is to blame; and they may all be damned together....

Solitary, touchy, liverish with dissipation, Byron turned his back on the world which was so sadly neglectful of him, and resumed his riotous life at the Palazzo Mocenigo. He also went on with *Don Juan* and in a spirit of defiance continued to send lurid details of his love affairs to Hobhouse, Kinnaird, Moore and Murray.

Partly owing to these letters, partly owing to accounts given by visitors to Venice, the wildest tales of his behavior sprang into circulation. When Shelley first heard these he assured the weeping Claire that they were all lies, but when Elise Foggi wrote a series of hysterical letters saying that she and Allegra were surrounded by dreadful Italian men with no morals, and Mrs. Hoppner wrote her misgivings about the Palazzo Mocenigo, he felt it was time to take action. Claire kept insisting that she must go at once to snatch her child from that dreadful household, but Shelley wrote to Byron, asking if he might see him and making no mention of Allegra's mother.

Byron raised no objection to the meeting and fixed a date. Shelley, accompanied by Claire, arrived on a pouring wet August night, and while they sat shivering in a gondola on the way to their hotel the gondolier regaled them with startling accounts of a rich English nobleman who kept all the prostitutes and pimps in Venice. At the hotel it was even worse, for their waiter, seeing they were English, added a variety of spicy details the gondolier apparently had not heard. By next morning, when they went to the Consul's house, Claire was in a hysterical state, and when Allegra, for whom Mrs. Hoppner had sent, was produced she declared the child had lost all her liveliness.

There was a long and anxious discussion betwen the Hoppners and Shelley. Hoppner's report on Byron confirmed the awful stories they had already heard, but he strongly advised Shelley to go to the Palazzo alone and not to mention Claire's presence in Venice, since his Lordship had frequently said that if she appeared in the city he would leave it immediately.

Rather apprehensively, Shelley approached the Palazzo Mocenigo at three o'clock that afternoon but, to his amazement, Byron greeted him in the warmest fashion and listened to his proposition with the greatest good temper. Shelley explained that Claire was anxious to take Allegra to Florence for a time. Byron replied that while he did not object to a week's reunion between mother and child he did not wish to lose her for longer, firstly because the Venetians would imagine he had grown tired of her, secondly because he felt that if Claire regained control she would not readily part with the little girl again. "If Claire likes to take it," he ended, "let her take it. I do not say what most people would in that situation, that I will refuse to provide for it, or abandon it. . . ." But he added that "she must surely be aware herself how very imprudent such a measure would be."

The relieved Shelley accompanied Byron to the Lido, where they "rode along the sands of the sea" and Byron, overjoyed to have a friend to confide in again, poured out (according to Shelley) "histories of his wounded feelings, and questions of my affairs, and great professions of friendship and regard for me." By next morning, when Shelley again called at the Palazzo, he was again under Byron's spell. As he wrote later in the foreword to his poem *Julian and Maddalo* (Maddalo being Byron):

> His passions and his powers are incomparably greater than those of other men; and, instead of the latter having been employed in curbing the former, they have mutually lent each other strength. . . . His serious conversation is a sort of intoxication. . . . There is an inexpressible charm in his relation of his adventures in different countries.

Byron was at his most affable and offered the Shelleys the use of a villa at Este, in the Euganean Hills, which he had rented from Hoppner but never occupied. Shelley accepted the offer with gratitude and it was arranged that at a later date Allegra should join her mother at Este for a month. Unfortunately, the Shelleys' second child, Clara, developed dysentery just after they arrived at the villa, and they brought her at once to Venice, where she died. Soon, however, they returned to Este and Byron congratulated himself on having got rid of Claire until one September day (as he wrote to Augusta), she

> . . . came prancing over the Apennines—to see her child; which threw my Venetian loves (who are none of the quietest) into great combustion; and I was in a pucker till I got her to the Euganean Hills, where she & the child now are. . . .

By the end of October the restless Shelleys were on their way to southern Italy, and Byron had agreed to hand Allegra into the care of Mrs. Hoppner; but in the interim he and Shelley had had several further long talks which had somewhat lessened the latter's hero worship of his friend. Most likely Byron, out of a desire to shock, had enlarged on details of his Venetian life, and Shelley said severely that the women with whom he consorted were "perhaps the most contemptible of all who exist under the moon—the most ignorant, the most disgusting, the most bigoted; Countesses smell so strongly of garlic that an ordinary Englishman cannot approach them. Well, L.B. is familiar with the lowest sort of these women, the people his gondolieri pick up in the streets." He added an even more ominous hint about Byron's male acquaintances:

> ...wretches who seem almost to have lost the gait and physiognomy of man, and who do not scruple to avow practices, which are not only not named, but I believe even conceived in England.... He says he disapproves, but he endures. He is heartily and deeply discontented with himself; and contemplating in the distorted mirror of his own thoughts the nature and habits of man, what can he behold but objects of contempt and despair?

It was true that Byron was thoroughly discontented. He kept assuring himself that his free, independent life in Italy had cured him of any desire to return to England, yet there were moments when he would have given everything he possessed to go back. He was out of temper with his English friends and could not forgive them for "the atrocity of their late neglect and silence," yet he yearned for their company. He took new mistresses and mingled with the dregs of Venice, yet he was bored with dissipation.

At last, in the middle of November, Hanson and his son arrived with the Newstead papers. They were supposed to have brought with them three large packages of goods which Byron had ordered through John Murray. For some reason they only brought one parcel, and this Hanson immediately sent to Byron by messenger on the night of their arrival. When Byron opened it he flew into a rage. He had particularly wanted some books and the package contained nothing except a "few different-sized kaleidoscopes, tooth-brushes, tooth-powder, etc., etc." So angry was he that he sulked all next day and did not send his gondola to fetch the Hansons until seven in the evening.

The feelings of John Hanson and his son Charles as they stumbled through the ground floor of the Palazzo can well be imagined. On either side of them monkeys chattered, dogs growled, parrots squawked and they started apprehensively when they caught sight of a wolf and a fox, recent additions to the menagerie. In the shadows they glimpsed the humped shapes of the coaches, and past them flitted the sinister figures of the gondoliers and others who inhabited this curious underworld. They were ushered up the marble staircase, through a great deserted billiard room and a bedroom to the apartment where Byron stood awaiting them. He appeared to be extremely nervous and when he saw John Hanson, the man who had once welcomed him to Newstead as a boy, the man who had stood by him through all the tragic events of 1816, his eyes filled with tears. For a moment or two he was unable to speak; then with an effort at cheerfulness he said, "Well, Hanson! I never thought you would have ventured so far. I rather expected you would have sent Charles."

Both father and son were shocked by Byron's appearance. His face was puffy, his body corpulent, his hair long and graying. In dress he was still dandified, but his clothes seemed flashy and ill-cut, and he wore far too many rings and brooches. His manner, however, was as charming as ever and he applied himself alertly to business, of which there was much to be transacted. It was concluded by November 17th, when Byron signed, and Fletcher witnessed, a fresh codicil to his will. The Hansons were making their farewells when they happened to mention that a young Mr. Townsend, whom Colonel Wildman had sent with them as his representative, had been at Harrow. Byron at once sent Fletcher to his hotel to invite him to join them, and when he came Byron immediately inundated him with questions about the school and the Drury family. Mr. Townsend answered as best he could, but he was sadly disappointed with the appearance of the poet of whom he had heard so much. ". . . He looked 40. His face had become pale, bloated, and sallow. . . . The knuckles of his hands were lost in fat."

Whether one of the Hansons or young Townsend passed on their impressions, or whether she received information from another quarter is not known, but a month later Augusta was giving a very similar account of her brother in one of her half-feline, half-pious letters to Francis Hodgson.

> Of our poor dear B. I have received 2 letters within this last year:—the last dated Septr. This is all I can tell you *from* him, and that he wrote (*as usual to me*) on the old subject very uncomfortably, and on his present pursuits, which are what one would dread and expect; a string of low attachments. *Of* him,— I hear he looks *very well*, but *fat*, immensely large, and his hair long.

Annabella had evidently done her work all too well.

❊ 6 ❊

While excess had left its mark on Byron's features, it certainly had not impaired his creative genius, for the first two Cantos of *Don Juan*, composed while he was at the Palazzo Mocenigo, are among his finest work. He had completed the first Canto by November, 1818, and sent it to Murray under the care of Lord Lauderdale, who had been in Venice, and he wrote the second between December 13th and January 20th. He had also, during the summer of 1818, written "above forty-four sheets of very long paper"—his memoirs, he told Murray, which he proposed should be kept among his documents to be used as "a kind of

Guidepost in case of death." This manuscript was afterwards burned and its destruction was greatly criticized.

Byron might have expected opposition to *Don Juan*, in which he had not only pilloried Sir Samuel Romilly, Lord Castlereagh, Southey, Coleridge and Wordsworth among others, but also ridiculed Lady Byron, whom he introduced as Don Juan's mother, Donna Inez:

> In short, she was a walking calculation,
>   Miss Edgeworth's novels stepping from their covers,
> Or Mrs. Trimmer's books on education,
>   Or "Coeleb's Wife" set out in quest of lovers,
> Morality's prim personification,
>   In which not Envy's self a flaw discover;
> To others' share let "female errors fall,"
> For she had not even one—the worst of all.

An even more virulent stanza ran:

> For Inez call'd some druggists and physicians,
>   And tried to prove her loving lord was *mad*,
> But as he had some lucid intermissions,
>   She next decided he was only *bad*;
> Yet when they asked her for her depositions,
>   No sort of explanations could be had,
> Save that her duty both to man and god,
> Required this conduct—which seem'd very odd.

When John Murray received the first Canto he read it with growing dismay and called Hobhouse, Moore, Kinnaird and Scrope Davies into consultation. They too read the poem and were "unanimous in advising its suppression." They pointed out with one accord "the inexpediency of renewing his domestic troubles by sarcasms on his wife ... the indecency of parts ... the attacks on religion ... the abuse of other writers. ..."

Byron was in high dudgeon. He had expected *Don Juan* to shock the public, indeed he had hoped it would do so, but for his old friends to offer such stern criticism was intolerable. He straightaway wrote a joint letter to Hobhouse and Kinnaird refusing to make any cuts except in the Castlereagh stanzas and in the dedication.

> I appeal not to "Philip fasting," but to Alexander drunk; I appeal to Murray at his ledger, to the people, in short. Don Juan shall be an entire horse, or none. If the objection be to the indecency, the Age which applauds the "Bath Guide," and Little's poems, and reads Fielding and Smollett still, may bear with that. ... I will not give way to all the cant of Christendom. I have been cloyed with applause, and sickened with abuse; at present I care for little but the copyright; I have imbibed a great love for money, let me have it; if Murray loses this time, he won't the next; he will be cautious, and I shall learn the decline of his customers by his epistolary indications. But in no case will I submit to have the poem mutilated. ...

"Give me the money!" That was the burden of Byron's song at this period—and a telling indication of the change two years of Venice had wrought in him. In the same letter he besought his friends to try and put off the payments of certain of his debts "till after Lady Noel's death ... if till *after* her damnation, better, for that will last for ever; yet I hope not; for her sake as well as the creditors I am willing to believe in purgatory."

The tenacious Hobhouse wrote again and again begging him to agree to a privately printed edition of fifty copies only. In a fit of irritation with the whole affair Byron gave way—but within a week or two he wrote autocratically to Kinnaird: "Tell Hobhouse that Don Juan must be published—the loss of the copyright would break my heart." Then, like an angry child smarting under an undeserved scolding, he flung himself back into the delights of Carnival.

But the savor had departed. He could not forget the strange defection of Augusta or the faint-heartedness of Hobhouse, Murray and company. He felt exceedingly unwell, so queasy that he could not "eat anything with relish but a kind of Adriatic fish called *Scampi*, which happens to be the most indigestible of marine viands." La Fornarina had shown herself as the virago that she was and had staged a number of impossible scenes. On the last night of the Carnival, when Byron was in attendance on the high-born Madame Contarini, she rushed forward and snatched off the lady's mask, and on another occasion, when a sudden storm blew up and Byron's gondoliers had a "tight struggle" to bring him back safely from the Lido, he found her standing on the steps of the Palazzo, drenched to the skin and looking like "Medea alighted from her chariot." By way of greeting she yelled at him, "Ah! Dog of the Virgin, is this a time to go to the Lido?" and tore up the marble stairs. "Her joy at seeing me," wrote Byron to John Murray, "was moderately mixed with ferocity, and gave me the idea of a tigress over her recovered cubs."

Hitherto amused by her scenes Byron now found them unendurable, and when he was besieged by complaints about her conduct he told her quietly that she must go. This she refused to do, "threatening knives and vengeance." The following day, while Byron was at dinner, she forced an entry by breaking a glass door, snatched a knife from his hand, and cut his thumb. Fletcher held her by the arms until the gondoliers arrived to escort her away, while Byron—doubtless remembering Caroline Lamb's escapade at Lady Heathcote's ball—had his thumb bandaged and resumed his dinner. As she was being led downstairs, however, La Fornarina thrust aside her captors and threw herself headlong into the Canal and, when rescued, had to be revived by a doctor. The servants implored Byron to send for the police, but sensibly enough he ignored this request and sent the now frightened woman home. At the same time he dismissed the more disreputable of his hangers-on and a sudden peace descended on the Palazzo Mocenigo.

La Fornarina was not the only one to fall into the Canal. Having suffered a surfeit of debauchery Byron had lately turned his attentions to a girl named Angelina, the eighteen-year-old daughter of a Venetian nobleman. A German neighbor had informed the father of Byron's presence by his daughter's window late at night. The infuriated parent had sent a priest and a commissary of police to interview the poet, locked Angelina in her room, and kept her on a diet of bread and water. There the affair apparently ended, but it had a brief recrudescence in the spring when, as Byron told Murray, "the father hath lately been laid up, and the brother is at Milan, and the mother falls asleep, and the servants are naturally on the wrong side of the question, and there is no Moon at Midnight just now. . . ." But one night when setting out for his beloved's home he tumbled into the Canal.

> My foot slipped in getting into my Gondola . . . and in I flounced like a Carp, and went dripping like a Triton to my Sea nymph and had to scramble up to a grated window:—
>> Fenced with iron within and without
>> Lest the lover get in or the Lady get out.

But even before this accident Byron had been growing tired of Angelina. She wanted to marry him, she could not understand why he did not divorce his wife, the bars on her window precluded any real attempt at love-making. He was weary of Venice and he was thirty-one years old. Once again he thought yearningly of a quiet domestic life and in April (three weeks before the Carp episode) Countess Benzoni had presented him to the Countess Teresa Guiccioli, a lady who promised him the quietude for which he longed.

VI

❋❋❋❋❋❋❋❋❋❋❋❋❋❋❋❋❋❋❋❋❋❋❋❋❋❋❋❋❋❋

For We'll Go No More A-Roving

TERESA GUICCIOLI had been born Teresa Gamba, second of the five pretty daughters of Count Ruggiero Gamba, a Ravenna nobleman. At the age of eighteen, having finished her education at S. Chiaro—a new-fashioned convent school upon which the Church later frowned—she was inspected (there seems no other word) by Count Alessandro Guiccioli, who then announced graciously that he would take her as his third wife. Fifty-seven years old, Guiccioli had been a libertine and a political turncoat in his time and enjoyed an unenviable reputation in the Romagna. Cold, rapacious, subtle, with an immense sense of his own importance, he was scarcely the husband for a girl just out of the schoolroom, but the docile Teresa had little say in the matter and the first few months of her marriage appeared to be happy enough.

On her wedding journey early in 1818 Teresa had gone with her husband to one of Countess Albrizzi's receptions and expressed a wish to see Canova's bust of Helen. It was Byron who offered her his arm and escorted her to view the treasure, but he hardly glanced at the bride and she was far too shy to look at him.

Very different was their second meeting at Countess Benzoni's at the beginning of April, 1819. Tired out by travel, Teresa had not wanted to attend the conversazione at all and had begged Guiccioli that they should stay but a few moments. But the moment she entered the doorway she saw, sitting on a sofa opposite, a "celestial apparition" whose beauty took her breath away. Her hostess introduced him as *"Pair d'Angleterre et son plus grand poète,"* and presently Teresa was so enthralled by talk of Venice and Ravenna, of Dante and Petrarch, that she was startled when Guiccioli came up and reminded her they had been at the reception hours instead of minutes. She rose obediently and walked out of the room as if in a trance. Already she knew she loved this fascinating, handsome English poet whose name was a byword in Venetian society.

Remembering the descriptions of Byron's appearance given by the Hansons and Mr. Townsend only a few months earlier, one feels it likely that Teresa's account of a "celestial apparition" was somewhat exaggerated. But Teresa was a young, romantic girl out of love with an elderly husband who would have no objection to her taking a lover always provided the affair was conducted according to the rules laid down by Italian society. Most married women of her station had a *cavaliere servente* who danced discreet attendance in public and received certain favors in the strictest privacy. Without any real knowledge of the world it never occurred to Teresa that Byron was singularly unsuited for the role she intended him to play.

For his part he was attracted by her youth, her liveliness, her red-gold ringlets, and during their first conversation he asked her to meet him alone the following day. This she agreed to do, and while Teresa said afterwards that she "was strong enough to resist at that first encounter" she succumbed at the second and thereafter the lovers kept a daily secret rendezvous, aided and abetted by Fanny Silvestrini, who had formerly been Teresa's governess and was now her companion.

Guiccioli was anxious to visit his estate on the Po on the way back to his Ravenna home, so Teresa had little more than a week in which to persuade her lover to follow them to Ravenna, a proposition which rather startled Byron. His conquest of Teresa had been almost too easy; he disliked being hustled; in the past three years he had (or rather, he thought he had), given up any idea of a sentimental attachment, and his state of mind was partially revealed in a letter to Hobhouse.

> ...but she wants me to come to Ravenna, and then to Bologna. Now this would be all very well for certainties; but for mere hopes; if she should plant me and I should make a "fiasco," never could I show my face on the Piazza....
>
> She is pretty, but has no tact; answers aloud, when she should whisper—talks of age to old ladies who want to pass for young; and this blessed night horrified a correct company at the Benzoni's, by calling out to me *"mio Byron"* in an audible key, during a dead silence of pause in the other prattlers, who stared and whispered their respective *serventi*. One of her preliminaries is that I must never leave Italy. I have no desire to leave it, but I should not like to be frittered down into a regular Cicisbeo. What shall I do? I am in love, and tired of promiscuous concubinage, and have now an opportunity of settling for life.

Hobhouse answered in alarm:

> ...Don't you go after that terra firma lady; they are very vixens, in those parts especially, and I recollect when I was at Ferrara seeing or hearing of two women in the hospital who had stabbed one another...and all *per gelosia*! Take a fool's advice for once, and be content with your Naiads, your amphibious fry; you make a very pretty splashing with them in the lagune, and I recommend constancy to the neighbourhood. Go to Romagna indeed! Go to old Nick, you'll never be heard of afterwards, except your ghost should be seen racing with Guido Cavalcanti in the wood.

Not only Hobhouse but Douglas Kinnaird as well warned Byron against following Teresa; and he had many arguments with Hoppner and other friends in Venice about the matter. Meanwhile, through the agency of Fanny Silvestrini, such ardent letters came from the lady that he thought several times of backing out of the whole project. And yet—there was something about Teresa that drew him irresistibly; she reminded him of Augusta, reminded him so strongly that he wrote to his sister on May 17th:

> But I have never ceased nor can cease to feel for a moment that perfect and boundless attachment which bound and binds me to you—which renders me utterly incapable of *real* love for any other human being—for what could they be to me after *you*? My own xxxx we may have been very wrong—but I repent of nothing except that cursed marriage—and your refusing to continue to love me as you had loved me—I can never forget nor *quite forgive* you for that precious piece of reformation —but I can never be other than I have been—and whenever I love anything it is because it reminds me in some way or other of yourself....

After her usual deplorable custom Augusta forwarded the entire letter straight to Annabella with a flustered note:

> He is surely to be considered a *Maniac*—I do not believe any feelings expressed are by any means permanent—only occasioned by the passing and present reflection and occupation of writing to the unfortunate Being to whom they are addressed....

But Byron, unaware of the full extent of his wife's influence over her sister-in-law, waited restlessly for a loving reply which did not arrive, and at this point he received an urgent summons from Teresa, who had fallen ill in Ravenna. She was, she declared, in a consumptive decline; but although there was a tendency to consumption in the Guiccioli family the truth was rather more prosaic—Teresa had had a miscarriage. However, her letter had the desired effect. Having procrastinated all through May, Byron finally set off from Venice on June 1. The weather was hot, the roads were dusty, and as he sat in his cumbersome coach he conned over the *Stanzas to the Po* he was composing for his mistress:

A stranger loves the Lady of the land,
  Born far beyond the mountains, but his blood
Is all meridian, as if never fanned
  By the black wind that chills the polar flood.

My blood is all meridian; were it not,
  I had not left my clime, nor should I be,
In spite of tortures, ne'er to be forgot,
  A slave again of love,—at least of thee.

But by the time he reached Padua his mood had darkened and he was already regretting his departure from Venice and writing crossly to Hoppner that

> ...to go to Cuckold a Papal Count, who, like Candide, has already been "the death of two men, one of whom was a priest," in his own house, is rather too much for my modesty when there are several other places at least as good for the purpose. She says they must go to Bologna in the middle of June, and why the devil then drag me to Ravenna? ... The Charmer forgets that a man may be whistled anywhere *before*, but that *after*— a Journey in an Italian June is a Conscription, and therefore she should have been less liberal in Venice, or less *exigent* in Ravenna.

There was no further instruction from Teresa and in a thoroughly bad temper he proceeded to Bologna, where he announced he was settled like a sausage and would be broiled like one if the hot weather continued. From there he wrote to tell Hoppner he was giving up the whole expedition, but during the night he suffered yet another change of heart and scribbled on the envelope, "I am just setting off for Ravenna, June 8th, 1819. I changed my mind this morning, and decided to go on."

❋ 2 ❋

Byron arrived in Ravenna on June 10th and was deeply shocked to learn from Count Guiseppe Alborghetti, the Secretary General of the province, that the Countess Guiccioli was "at death's door." Horrified, he protested that if the lady died he had no wish to survive her, but his fears were allayed by a visit from Count Guiccioli, who assured him his wife was slowly recovering and invited him to visit her at their Palazzo. Quite apart from his determination that the affair should be conducted in the accepted conventional manner, the Count had reasons of his own for encouraging Byron as a guest; but to begin with visits to Teresa were extremely unsatisfactory, because doctors and relatives thronged the room and there was no opportunity for private conversation.

Fearing that Teresa really was "going into a consumption," Byron asked the Count for permission to call in the famous Professor Aglietti, a request to which that wily gentleman affably agreed. Within a short time Teresa had so much recovered that the lovers were again able to meet secretly "by the aid of a Priest, a Chambermaid, a young Negro-boy, and a female friend"; and although Byron was irritated by the fact that there were no bolts on the doors and mistrusted the over-friendly attitude of the Count, who often called at the inn for him and took him out "like Whittington, the Lord Mayor" in a coach with six horses, he wrote to Hoppner asking him to send on his English letters and his horses, and soon he had settled down to a lazy, pleasant existence. He rose late, wrote letters or worked on *Don Juan,* spent the early evening riding along the sandy tracks in the great pine forest accompanied by Teresa in "a high hat and sky-blue riding habit," attended her to the theater or some other function, made love, and returned to his writing until the early hours.

At Venice he had feared that Teresa might turn out "a sort of Italian Caroline Lamb" with "the same red-hot head, the same noble disdain of public opinion," but in the drowsy air of Ravenna he found her a sweet, pliable creature who made few exacting demands upon him and had a most soothing effect. She was indeed the very antidote he needed after his hectic years at the Palazzo Mocenigo and for a month or two he was content.

In August the Guicciolis left for Bologna, whither Byron followed them, and it was then that the Count made the first move in a long and subtle campaign. Outwardly an important and blameless nobleman he was secretly backing the Liberals, a risky game in a province ruled by the Austrian police. Aware that his every movement was under suspicion, he conceived the brilliant idea of asking Byron to use his influence with friends in England and get him appointed honorary British Consul at Ravenna. At the same time he offered Byron some ground-floor rooms in his Bologna home, the Palazzo Savioli, into which he gladly moved. Byron also wrote to John Murray, who had excellent connections with the Tory party, to approach Croker, Canning, or Peel, and "ask them to appoint (*without salary or emolument*) a noble Italian (whom I will name afterwards) Consul or Vice-Consul for Ravenna. He is a man of very large property,—noble too; but he wishes to have a British protection, in case of changes."

But no sooner had Byron settled into his new quarters than the Count took Teresa on a tour of his estates elsewhere. Bored by solitude and angered by several letters from Hoppner and Alexander Scott urging him to give up Teresa, he sent for the three-year-old Allegra, amused himself by watching her play in the gardens, and wandered disconsolately around his mistress's sitting room—where he picked up her copy of *Corinne* and wrote on the index page the melancholy lines which were to be a comfort to her in the future:

> You will not understand these English words, and *others* will not understand them, which is the reason I have not scrawled them in Italian. But you will recognise the handwriting of him who passionately loved you, and you will divine that, over a book which was yours, he could only think of love. In that word—beautiful in all languages, but most so in yours—*Amor mio*—is comprised my existence here and hereafter. I feel I exist here, and I fear that I shall exist hereafter,—to *what* purpose you will decide; my destiny rests with you, and you are a woman, eighteen

years of age, and two out of a convent. I wish that you had staid there, with all my heart,—or, at least, that I had never met you in your married state.

But all this is too late. I love you, and you love me,—at least you *say so* and act as if you *did* so, which last is a great consolation in all events. But *I* more than love you, and cannot cease to love you.

Think of me, sometimes, when the Alps and the ocean divide us, but they never will, unless *you* wish it.

Once again he grew restless, unhappy, out of tune with life. With Teresa by his side it had been easy enough to drift through the summer days playing the *cavaliere servente*, professing a great interest in opera, holding his *Dama*'s fan or fetching her shawl; now, in her absence, he felt he could not endure this mode of life any longer. He toyed vaguely with the idea of returning to England, but believed that country to be on the verge of revolution, and through a newspaper mention of a colonization scheme for Venezuela his thoughts turned to South America. Why should he not go there to settle in a new virile land with "fellows as fresh as their world, and fierce as their earthquakes"? A life of action had always appealed to him; now, at thirty-one, he was acutely conscious of the need for haste if he were to make any move at all. He would embark, he told Hobhouse, "(with Fletcher as a breeding beast of burthen) and possess myself of the pinnacle of the Andes, or a spacious plain of unbounded extent in an eligible earthquake situation."

The South American idea was temporarily shelved when the Guicciolis returned from their expedition and the Count, still as charming as ever, announced his intention of leaving his wife in Byron's care while he went on to Ravenna. The Bolognese raised incredulous eyebrows when they learned that the husband had left his spouse unchaperoned and alone with her lover; but worse was to follow, for in September the two abruptly left for Venice. According to Teresa the reason for the journey was that she was again suffering from ill-health and wished to consult Professor

Aglietti, but it was unfortunate that when they drew up at a Padua inn on the third and last night of their journey two fellow guests proved to be those inveterate Venetian gossips, the Countess Benzoni and her *cavaliere servente*, the aged Count Rangoni.

These two immediately spread the news all round Venice and drawing rooms buzzed with rumor. It was one thing for Byron to indulge in sordid affairs in the Palazzo Mocenigo: it was quite another for him to career halfway across Italy with the married lady to whom he was seriously attached. Such behavior was unforgivable, and when it became known that Teresa had not gone to the town apartment prepared for her by her husband's steward, Lega Zambelli, but was instead staying at her lover's house at La Mira, tongues wagged harder than ever.

Whether the real intention of the pair had been to elope together is not clear; but certainly Teresa, who had an eye for dramatic effect, had already thought of the idea, while a month or two later Byron wrote to Kinnaird:

> We were very nearly going off together from Padua, for France and America, but as I had more prudence, and more experience, and I knew that the time might come when both might repent, I paused and prevailed upon her to pause also.

With a naïveté which is hardly credible Teresa wrote to her husband telling him that Aglietti had examined her and prescribed "another journey and change of air." This being the case Byron had suggested that he should take her to Garda and Como, a tour which would be of the greatest benefit to her health, so she asked her dear Alessandro's permission and awaited a speedy reply "with the greatest anxiety." Surprisingly enough the Count answered that he saw no objection to the proposed excursion if it was going to improve her health, but by the time his letter arrived Teresa and Byron were so happily ensconced at La Mira that they no longer wished to move. Once more it was her shadowy resemblance to Augusta that enchanted her lover. Her laughter, her love of silly baby-talk, her patent adoration for himself all combined to make him remember another blissful interlude spent apart from the world. Venice and its gossip seemed very far away from the villa on the Brenta, where they lived a remote, peaceful existence.

It was an interlude which could not endure, as Byron at least must have known. In the beginning of October Tom Moore arrived, as satisfying and witty a friend as ever, and Byron insisted he should stay at the Palazzo Mocenigo. He himself always returned to La Mira late at night, but they spent the days and evenings together, talking about their work, about the glittering years spent in London, about a thousand subjects they had in common. Moore noticed that his friend's growing stoutness had marred "the picturesqueness of his head," and found it in him to wish that Byron would avoid "much curious conversation about his wife." He was also a shade concerned at the scandal occasioned by the La Mira ménage, but he admitted after he had met Teresa that she seemed both charming and devoted. All too soon Moore left for Rome, taking with him the manuscript of Byron's Memoirs, and with his going the idyllic calm of La Mira was ruffled. Teresa was worried by letters from her father, who was horrified to learn that she was living openly with her lover, and from her young brother Pietro, who wrote at length about the disgraceful stories which circulated round Lord Byron's name. In the case of Byron himself, the reunion with Moore had stirred up all his longing for action, while a letter from Hoppner concerning a rumor that he had abducted some young girl from a convent in Ferrara roused his ire.

> The Ferrara story is of a piece with all the rest of the Venetian manufacture [he wrote savagely]. "*Convent*"—and "*carry off*" quotha!—and "*girl*"—I should like to know *who* has been carried off—except poor dear *me*. I have been more ravished myself than any body since the Trojan war....

And now Count Guiccioli made the second move in his elaborately thought-out campaign. While still at Bologna he had asked Byron to lend him a thousand pounds. This Byron had promised to do, but when his banker warned him that he did not think the Count was acting in good faith he hastily made the excuse that on investigation he had found his funds were insufficient. Then had come the news that there was no hope of a Consular appointment, so Guiccioli had renewed his request for a thousand, which was flatly refused. Furious at such a snub from the man who had had the effrontery to spirit his wife away to Venice the Count suddenly appeared in that city one November day and demanded that Teresa choose between her lover and himself. Naturally, Teresa wept that she would stay with Byron, whereupon the Count staged a succession of scenes, alternately threatening revenge and sobbing that the elopement had ruined his life. Byron, who saw far more clearly than either of them that Teresa's life would be unbearable if she persisted in breaking up her marriage in such a way, eventually persuaded her "with the greatest difficulty" to return to Ravenna with her husband, and gave her a half-promise that he might perhaps rejoin her there later on.

But once the Guicciolis had departed he gave way to gloom. Teresa had become a habit and without her, in the damp, echoing Palazzo Mocenigo to which he had moved for the winter months, he was desperately lonely. Again he thought of going to South America and taking Allegra with him; but almost at once he discarded the notion and decided to return to England. There at least he could escape from this Venetian life-in-death and embroil himself in politics—besides, England held Augusta, and if he saw her he was convinced that he could induce her to leave Colonel Leigh and share some quiet country home with him. Much as he hated uprooting himself, he gave orders for packing to be started, and busied himself in settling up his Venetian affairs; but when his arrangements were nearly completed Professor Aglietti called to tell him that poor small Allegra had gone down with tertian fever. All his plans were abandoned, and by the time the child was convalescent he was again possessed by inertia. Still, something had to be done and for the second time he lashed himself into the making of preparations until there came a morning when he had "his gloves and cap on, and even his little cane in his hand," and was merely waiting for a servant to pack the pistols and other weapons with which he always traveled. Suddenly he declared that if the clock struck one before everything was in order he would not leave that day. The clock did strike, and the servants were told to unpack.

But at the end of the year Count Gamba wrote frantically from Ravenna that Teresa had suffered such a serious breakdown in health that he was ready to waive all opposition to the liaison if Byron would return to his daughter's side. Furthermore, Count Guiccioli added his pleas to those of his father-in-law, and almost before he realized the possible effects of his action Byron was again climbing the staircase of the gloomy Palazzo Guiccioli to renew his role of *cicisbeo*.

❋ 3 ❋

The moment she saw Byron Teresa recovered in miraculous fashion and the evening following his arrival she insisted upon his accompanying her to a reception given by her uncle, the Marchese Cavalli, a leader of Ravenna society. Byron wrote to Hoppner that

> The G.'s object appeared to be to parade her foreign lover as much as possible, and, faith, if she seemed to glory in the scandal, it was not for me to be ashamed of it. Nobody seemed surprised;—all the women, on the contrary, were, as it were, delighted by the excellent example. The Vice-legate, and all the other Vices, were as polite as could be....

The Gamba family radiated kindness and the strange Guiccioli, who seemed to have erased the scenes of last November from his memory, not only welcomed Byron warmly but pressed him to occupy rooms in his Palazzo.

As at Bologna Byron acquiesced and within a few weeks was installed with his own servants—including Fletcher and Tita Falcieri, the huge gondolier he had brought from Venice—and the menagerie of birds and beasts which he took everywhere. At first uncertain whether he would "stay a day, a week, or all my life," he soon drifted into the comfortable if slightly boring routine of provincial life, escorting Teresa to rather dull con- verazioni where the women sat primly in a circle while the men played at "dreary *Faro* or *Lotto Reale* for small sums," driving on the *Corso* or riding through the pine forest, attending the theater or making love. He looked back on his period in Venice, that "Sea-Sodom," as on a revolting nightmare, and not even the news that Hobhouse was enduring nominal confinement in New- gate for having written a Radical pamphlet roused him from his lethargy. Poor old George III had died and been succeeded by a son who was hated by Tories and Whigs alike, there had been that shocking affair the Peterloo Massacre, Arthur Thistle- wood had plotted to execute the entire cabinet and declare a republic; but only when he heard from Kinnaird that Scrope Davies had fled the country and his creditors because of gambling debts did Byron write to Hobhouse:

> So Scrope is gone. . . . Gone to Bruges where he will get tipsy with Dutch beer and shoot himself the first foggy morning. Brum- mell at Calais; Scrope at Bruges; Buonaparte at St. Helena, you in your new apartments, and I at Ravenna, only think! so many great men! There has been nothing like it since Themistocles at Magnesia, and Marius at Carthage.

The Byron of 1816 would have flown to the defense of his friends: The Byron of 1820 was content to linger in a quiet Italian city where only the churches and tombs reminded one of its ancient and stormy history. He was, so he told his friends, "drilling very hard to learn how to double a shawl"; he had

Allegra with him; he occupied himself with buying furniture for his rooms, a new landau, horses, saddles.

It all sounded very innocuous, very unlike Byron. But in truth he was busying himself with much more dangerous affairs. Count Gamba and his young son Pietro were fierce patriots, members of the *Carbonari*, a secret society pledged to overthrow the dominion of Metternich and his spies. Byron, who had strong Liberal sympathies although he regarded the English industrial reformers as "low, designing, dirty levellers, who would pioneer their way to a democratical tyranny," was attracted by the ardent aristocrats who were prepared to fight for Italy's freedom, and it needed little persuasion on the part of the Gambas to enlist him as a member of the *Carbonari*. The organization appealed to the dramatic side of Byron's nature. There were secret meetings in the pine forest, and great exchanges of passwords, and much chalking of slogans on the walls of houses. There was a vast amount of talk, a deal of complicated plotting and very little action.

Ever since his arrival in Milan nearly three and a half years earlier Byron had been suspected by the Austrian police of being a revolutionary. After all, they argued, he was rich, he wrote wild and indecent verse, he was reputed to be an atheist so what else could he be? Unaware of this the Gambas assured their friend that the police would never suspect an Englishman, and suggested that their members should use his apartments as their headquarters. He agreed eagerly—it was a notion after his own heart. Within a week or two his bureaux were crammed with secret papers, his chairs and tables littered with the appurtenances of war, his stairway a meeting place for mysterious figures who were obviously disguised.

It was not to be expected that that astute man, the Count Guiccioli, would approve of such goings-on in his own house. He possessed Liberal sympathies himself, but it suited him to run with the hare and hunt with the hounds, and the last thing he wished was to draw the attention of the police to the Palazzo

Guiccioli. He therefore announced for the second time that Teresa must choose between him and her lover; and for the second time Byron strongly advised her to remain with her husband. Teresa, however, swore that she would not live with her husband again unless he allowed her to stay with *"mio caro Byron."* Why, she cried passionately, should she be "the only woman in Romagna who is not to have her *Amico?"* The exasperated Guiccioli retorted that he would divorce her, whereupon the angry Count Gamba sprang to his daughter's defense and demanded a separation, with the return of Teresa's dowry of 4,500 scudi. Unable to bear the thought of parting with such a sum Guiccioli dropped the idea of divorce and agreed that the business should be placed before the Papal Vice-Legate, who would ask for the Pope's arbitration on it.

From March until July the affair dragged on, and in the meantime the three main characters in the drama continued to occupy the same house. Byron, quite exhilarated by the thought that he might receive a stiletto in the back (for it was common talk that Guiccioli had already "arranged" one or more assassinations), carried a formidable array of pistols when he rode to and from the *Carbonari* meetings.

But there was no attempt on his life, the revolt promised so volubly by the *Carbonari* failed to materialize, and he was beset by minor irritations which upset his never equable temper. When he relinquished his tenancy of the Palazzo Mocenigo its owner had taken on a scoundrely servant who Byron swore had cheated him. He therefore refused to pay the rent still owing until the man was dismissed, and a long and undignified quarrel ensued. Even more trying was the fact that Claire Clairmont was again writing to him about Allegra's future. She and the Shelleys were then living at Pisa but were going for the summer to Lucca and wished the child to go with them. If she were not allowed to do so then Claire threatened to descend on Ravenna and create a scene.

It was not altogether unnatural that the Shelley family should have been disturbed by the meager items of news they had been able to gather about the child. Mrs. Hoppner, who had rather heartlessly handed the care of the little girl to whoever happened to present themselves, had given the Shelleys grim accounts of Byron's life in Venice and hinted that his Ravenna existence was just as profligate. Letters to Byron had brought terse, unsatisfactory answers or been ignored. The impulsive Shelley, haunted by persecution mania and hypochondria, was convinced that Allegra was unhappy, or ill, or both, and added to the general confusion by writing Byron what he imagined were tactful letters.

When actually with Shelley Byron was moved by his spell; but when away from him he forgot his charm and remembered the "green tea and fine feelings and high-flown radicalism," the fetishes about everything from food to religion, the squalid disorder of his household. So now, instead of writing direct, Byron chose to deal through Hoppner:

> About Allegra, I can only say to Claire—that I so totally disapprove of the mode of Children's treatment in their family, that I should look upon the Child as going into a hospital. Is it not so? Have they *reared* one? Her health hitherto has been *excellent*, and her temper not bad; she is sometimes vain and obstinate, but always clean and cheerful, and as, in a year or two, I shall either send her to England, or put her in a Convent for education, these defects will be remedied as far as they can in human nature. But the Child shall not quit me again to perish of Starvation, and green fruit, or be taught to believe that there is no Deity....

For the moment the Puritan in Byron was uppermost, but while one cannot blame him for his disapproval of the Shelleys' ideas on diet for the young, one must deplore his cutting reference to the deaths of their two children. However, Allegra stayed on with her father, who took a house in the country for her, and, temporarily at least, the Shelleys receded into the background.

In July the Pope issued a Papal decree declaring a formal

separation between the Guicciolis. The Count was to pay Teresa the sum of two hundred pounds a year, and she was to return to her father's villa not far from Ravenna. This adroitly diplomatic arrangement satisfied everybody. Teresa retired to the villa while Byron, who visited her daily, remained in the Palazzo with her husband. Fortunately, the place was so vast that there was no need for them to see each other, and while Guiccioli attended to his many affairs Byron closeted himself with his fellow conspirators.

But the trouble with the *Carbonari* was that they possessed no real leaders. The countless plots they made were always so loosely constructed that they fell to pieces, and as the year wore on Byron grew increasingly petulant about the endless muddles and petty squabbles which constantly occurred between the members. Then the priests annoyed him because, as he wrote to Kinnaird, they were doing their best to persuade the local government to banish him from the city.

> They try to fix squabbles upon my servants, to involve me in scrapes, and lastly they [the governing party] menace to shut Madame Guiccioli up in a *convent*. The last piece of policy springs from two motives; the one because her *family* are suspected of liberal principles, and the second because mine (although I do not preach them) are known, and were known when it was far less reputable to be a friend to liberty than it is now.

By December he was thoroughly out of patience with both friends and enemies, but on the evening of the 9th, as he was preparing to visit Teresa, he heard a shot followed by a tremendous commotion from his servants who were shouting that someone had been murdered. "As it is the custom here to let people fight it through," he wrote to Murray, "they wanted to hinder me from going out; but I ran down the Street." Here he found the Military Commandant of Ravenna lying on his back with five wounds, one of which was in the heart.

> There were about him Diego, his Adjutant, crying like a Child; a priest howling; a surgeon who dared not touch him; two

or three confused and frightened soldiers; one or two of the boldest of the mob; and the Street dark as pitch, with the people flying in all directions.

Very sensibly Byron sent Diego for the Cardinal, and instructed Tita and another servant to take the Commandant upstairs and lay him on Fletcher's bed. The poor man groaned "*O Dio!*" and "*O Gesu!*" several times, but expired before a surgeon could be found. Within a short time soldiers and police swarmed into the house, showed their surprise at the Englishman's action in harboring the Commandant, and asked a great many questions which failed to pin any guilt on Byron or his household. "I shall never be deterred from a duty of humanity," he told Murray grandly, "by all the assassins of Italy, and that is a wide word."

Privately, he hoped that the killing of the Commandant, who had had liberal views, would be the signal for a real revolt. He was doomed to disappointment. The *Carbonari* stayed silent, the snow fell so thickly that it was impossible to go out riding, the Palazzo became a place of imprisonment where all he could do was read, write, reflect on his ennui, and play with his menagerie. Perhaps as a New Year resolution, perhaps merely as an antidote to boredom, he again started to keep a journal on January 4th, 1821, and in it, on his thirty-third birthday, he wrote the lines:

> Through life's road, so dim and dirty,
> I have dragged to three-and-thirty.
> What have these years left to me?
> Nothing—except thirty-three.

All through his diary (one of the most revealing things he ever wrote) runs a strain of melancholy, a yearning for the past. Reading about Milton's Sabrina Fair reminded him of the distant, carefree days when he and Edward Long had gone diving in the Cam.

> Though Cam's is not a very translucent wave, it was fourteen
> feet deep, where we used to dive for, and pick up—having

thrown them in on purpose—plates, eggs, and even shillings.
I remember, in particular, there was the stump of a tree (at least
ten or twelve feet deep) in the bed of the river, in a spot where
we bathed most commonly, round which I used to cling and
"wonder how the devil I came there."

The sound of a barrel organ playing in the street recalled the
years of his London triumph:

> Oh! there is an organ playing in the street—a waltz, too! I
> must leave off to listen. They are playing a waltz which I have
> heard ten thousand times at the balls in London, between 1812
> and 1815. Music is a strange thing.

When he was induced by Teresa to eat boiled cockles and drink
Imola wine for supper, and in consequence suffered an atrocious
bilious attack, he remarked

> ...the complete inertion, inaction, and destruction of my chief
> mental faculties. I tried to rouse them, and yet could not—and
> this is the *Soul!!!* I should believe that it was married to the
> body, if they did not sympathise so much with each other. If the
> one rose, when the other fell, it would be a sign that they longed
> for the natural state of divorce. But as it is, they seem to draw
> together like post-horses.

His sense of loneliness mounted, yet he could not summon
the energy to break free from Teresa and Ravenna. Irritable and
depressed, his letters to his English friends developed a waspish
tone, and when Kinnaird told him of his mother-in-law's serious
condition he snapped back:

> As to Lady Noel, what you say of her declining health would
> be very well to any one else; but the way to the immortal (I
> mean *not* to die at all) is to have me for your heir. I recommend
> you to put me in your will; and you will see that (as long as *I*
> live at least) you will never even catch cold.

In a way it was a relief when the Austrian army inflicted
crushing defeats upon Italian patriot forces at Rieti and Novara
and the hopes of the *Carbonari* were dashed for good and all.

There was no need any longer to sit up half the night, a musket across one's knees, listening hopefully for shots that never came; no need to have the house thronged with quarrelsome conspirators; no need to goad the Gambas on to more active behavior for they, together with many of their friends, were told in July that they must leave the Romagna immediately. After agitated discussion, during which Teresa and her father shed an immoderate number of tears, it was decided that the family should move to Florence; but consternation broke out afresh when Byron calmly announced that he did not propose to accompany them but would follow them later.

His exact reasons for remaining in Ravenna are not clear. He may have wanted to finish the fifth Canto of *Don Juan* in peace (for it was a work of which his mistress strongly disapproved); he may have been determined to show the authorities that while they could exile his friends they could not shift him; he may have had an idea of slipping out of Teresa's life altogether; he may merely have been too selfishly lazy to face the upheaval. Whatever the reason, he bade farewell to the weeping and disconsolate Gambas and—probably because he knew an overwhelming longing for intellectual conversation with one of his own kind—invited Shelley to come and discuss Allegra's future.

From the grief-stricken Teresa came passionate letters imploring him to hurry to her side, to take great care of himself, to beware of danger, to remember the love that lay between them. Poor Teresa! who could not forget the stanzas Byron had written for her when they were at La Mira:

> Could love for ever
> Run like a river,
> And Time's endeavour
>   Be tried in vain—
> No other pleasure
> With this could measure;
> And like a treasure
>   We'd hug the chain.

But since our sighing
Ends not in dying,
And, form'd for flying,
Love plumes his wing;
Then for this reason
Let's love a season;
But let that season be only Spring.

"Let's love a season...." The words echoed and re-echoed through her mind as she and her dejected parent rumbled along the Tuscan roads. Byron was everything to her, she could not imagine life without him, he must join her at once else she would die. At every stop she wrote yet another tear-stained epistle, but her entreaties were unavailing. Her lover was determined to remain in the Romagna until such time as it suited him to leave it.

It is a curious fact that while Shelley's company stimulated Byron, Byron's company had the reverse effect on Shelley. No sooner had the latter arrived at Ravenna than he became convinced that his writing days were over and that his friend's work was infinitely better than his own had ever been. "I despair of rivalling Lord Byron, as well I may...," he wrote, but at the same time he enjoyed their long talks on poetry and politics, and was enchanted by the menagerie which consisted of "ten horses, eight enormous dogs, three monkeys, five cats, an eagle, a crow, and a falcon." With the exception of the horses, all these creatures had the run of the house, and one day on the great staircase Shelley met "five peacocks, two guinea-hens, and an Egyptian crane." "I wonder," he wrote pensively to Mary, "who all these animals were, before they were changed into these shapes."

He found Byron "greatly improved in every respect," and put this reformation down (rightly) to Teresa's influence. He was also immensely relieved by the news that Allegra seemed happy at her new Capucine convent school at Bagnacavallo, some twelve miles from Ravenna, and when Byron suggested he should visit the child he set off with alacrity. He found Allegra "prettily dressed in white muslin, and an apron of black silk, with trousers" in the highest possible spirits, and she insisted upon his running all over the convent with her while she talked incessantly. Even when she rang the bell which summoned the the nuns to their devotions nobody scolded her, but Shelley wrote sadly to Mary:

> Her intellect is not much cultivated. She knows certain *orazioni* by heart, and *dreams* of Paradise and angels and all sorts of things, and has a prodigious list of saints, and is always talking of the Bambino. This will do her no harm, but the idea of bringing up so sweet a creature in the midst of such trash till sixteen!

On the whole, however, he professed himself satisfied with the child's surroundings and, with his usual enthusiasm for helping others, agreed to Byron's suggestion that he should write to Teresa (whom he had not met) asking her to give up the idea of going to Switzerland with her father and brother and settle in Pisa, where Byron could take a house. Overjoyed at any concrete proposal, Teresa wrote that Pisa would suit admirably but begged Shelley to promise not to leave Ravenna without *Milord*. Byron, however, was not to be hustled and once he learned that the Gambas had left Florence for Pisa he urged Shelley also to return there and look out for a suitable house.

Before the friends parted in the end of August Shelley proposed to Byron that he should invite Leigh Hunt to Italy. Since his imprisonment Hunt had been running the *Examiner*, a leading Liberal paper, with the aid of his brother, and Shelley's idea was that he and Byron should assume joint control of the journal. Byron was delighted—he had liked Hunt when he visited him in gaol, the notion of running a journal appealed to him, and he looked forward with glee to the hubbub such a departure would cause among his friends. Fired as always by Shelley's shrill enthusiasm, he declared he would be financially responsible for all arrangements and urged that Hunt should be advised to sail without delay.

Left to himself Byron still dallied in Ravenna. He had to

finish *Cain*.... He had to wait for a letter from John Murray.
... He had to visit Allegra.... But at last even he ran out of
excuses and on September 19th he wrote lugubriously to Moore:

> I am in all the sweat, dust, and blasphemy of an universal
> packing of all my things, furniture, etc., for Pisa, whither I go
> for the winter. The cause has been the exile of all my fellow
> Carbonics, and, amongst them, of the whole family of Madame
> G; who, you know, was divorced from her husband last week,
> "on account of P.P. clerk of this parish." ... As I could not say
> with Hamlet, "Get thee to a nunnery," I am preparing to follow
> them.
>
> It is awful work, this love, and prevents all a man's projects
> of good or glory. I wanted to go to Greece lately (as every-
> thing seems up here) with her brother, who is a very fine, brave
> fellow (I have seen him put to the proof), and wild about liberty.
> But the tears of a woman who has left her husband for a man,
> and the weakness of one's own heart, are paramount to these
> projects, and I can hardly indulge them.

But it was not until mid-October that Byron's cavalcade
—complete with birds, monkeys, dogs, cats and horses—took
the road for Bologna, where he had arranged to meet his old
friend Samuel Rogers. Together they traversed the Apeninnes
to Florence, but their reunion was scarcely successful. Rogers
was fresh from London, and made Byron feel acutely conscious
of his own ignorance of worldly affairs. He knew too that a
meticulous report of the meeting would be repeated to numerous
eager audiences, so he sat rigidly in his corner of the coach and
returned monosyllabic replies to questions. "If there was any
scenery worth seeing," wailed Rogers, who had a great liking
for the beauties of nature, "he generally contrived that we should
pass through it in the dark"; but he recorded with gusto that
"on October 31st, every window of the hotel in Florence was
flung open to see Byron and his attendants leave for Pisa..."

But Byron was not concerned with sightseers: his mind was
busy with thoughts of the Greek War of Independence.

❊ 4 ❊

At Pisa Byron moved into the Palazzo Lanfranchi, a huge Renaissance building which stood on the banks of the Arno and was reputedly haunted. Here he was joined by Teresa, and by the time all the tedious business of unpacking was finished he was in an uncommonly bad temper which was not improved by constant visits from the Shelleys and their circle of friends. Shelley by himself was a delightful companion; Mary Shelley a tolerable one. But their friends. . . .! There was a brawny giantess with bad teeth called Lady Mountcashel, who had eloped with a dreary, bookish little man named Mr. Tighe. There were the Williams, he a half-pay cavalry officer desperately anxious to write, and she the pretty and deserted wife of another officer. There was the Irish Count Taafe, who had written a ponderous tome entitled a *Commentary on Dante;* and there was Shelley's cousin, Tom Medwin, who composed long tragedies in verse.

Apart from Count Taafe, whom he described as "a very good man, with a great desire to see himself in print," Byron had no manner of use for this collection of people whom the gregarious and ever generous Shelley had gathered around him. He was downright rude to Lady Mountcashel and her escort (who insisted on calling themselves "Mr. and Mrs. Mason"), and studiously indifferent to Jane and Edward Williams. Tom Medwin he put up with, but to his mind all the members of the Shelley circle were second-rate folk with absurd literary pretensions. As for poor Teresa, she was thoroughly unhappy in their company. Brought up within the narrow bounds of Italian provincial society, she had never met people who spoke, acted or thought as the Shelleys and their friends did, and she was utterly bewildered by their behavior.

Byron was particularly incensed when the Shelleys reproached him for not bringing Allegra to Pisa. Surely, they said, the child's place was with her father and she should not have been left alone in distant Bagnacavallo. Besides, Mary added with that air of conscious superiority which always maddened him, Mr. Tighe had been there and reported that the convent was very damp. The more they argued the more aloof and stern Byron became. He considered that he had treated his natural daughter very well indeed and he was perfectly sure that it was Claire Clairmont who was behind all this unwarrantable interference. After a day when Shelley reported to his wife that he had only just stopped himself from knocking Byron down, the arguments about Allegra dwindled and she remained at her convent.

More satisfying were conversations with Mary about Alexander Mavrocordato, the "real Greek Prince" who had given her lessons when he was in Pisa the previous spring. Mavrocordato was no prince but Byron was intensely interested in him for other reasons. For he was one of the leaders of the Greek Independents and at that very moment was Prime Minister of Western Greece, and Byron had by no means forgotten the hint he had given Tom Moore—sooner or later, no matter what it cost, he would go to the aid of the country he loved. So far his plans were amorphous and he showed unusual restraint in keeping them entirely to himself, but with the idea of getting in some preliminary training for a military life he told his steward, Lega Zambelli (whom he had taken on from Guiccioli), to ask the authorities for a permit to practice pistol shooting in the garden.

The request threw Pisa's governor, the Marchese Niccolo Viviani, into a tremendous state of agitation. Metternich's spies in Florence had assured him that Lord Byron had come to Pisa merely to be with "the beautiful daughter of Count Gamba"; but already this mad, rich English artistocrat had insulted the Grand Duke Ferdinand by sending Count Taafe to wait upon him and explain that he must be excused from paying his respects since it would be wrong to do so as he had not been presented to any other Italian ruling prince. Furthermore, his household servants were dangerous, uncouth fellows who stalked through Pisa streets elbowing honest citizens out of their way, and the large number of letters he received from England was distinctly ominous. A cautious reply was sent in which the Marchese pointed out that since nobody in the town was allowed to carry arms, pistol practice in the garden could not be permitted.

Thereafter the police were on the alert, but for some little time they found no evidence of revolutionary activities. Byron was preoccupied with his writing, with avoiding the Shelley clan, with soothing Teresa, with brooding over the horrible notion that his poems were losing their immense popularity. And then in January 1822, there came upon the scene that adventurer and archliar, Edward John Trelawny.

It is doubtful whether Byron ever liked Trelawny—he certainly never wholly trusted him—but for a time he made him a boon companion. The tall, dark, swaggering Cornishman with the beetling brows and sweeping mustache, who told such fantastic tales of his past life in various parts of the world, was just the sort of character Byron had created in *The Corsair*, and there was a virility about him that was strangely appealing. A friend of the Williams, he had come to Pisa especially to meet Shelley, for whose *Queen Mab* he had an immense admiration. Taken aback at first by the poet's youthful appearance he soon conceived a fondness for him which almost amounted to hero worship.

Towards Byron Trelawny's attitude was very different. Always an opportunist, he realized at once that the rich, eccentric nobleman of whose doings he had heard so much could be a most useful patron, so he set out deliberately to gain his friendship. The very day after his arrival in Pisa Shelley took him to call on Byron and his sharp eyes immediately noted the grandeur with which the poet surrounded himself. He was impressed too by his appearance (for Byron's Ravenna sojourn had greatly improved his health and figure). His clear skin was without "stain or furrow," his "small highly finished head and curly hair" surmounted an athletic and beautifully proportioned body which was clad in a braided jacket of Gordon tartan and a pair of nankeen trousers strapped down to his feet. The lameness of which Trelawny had heard was scarcely perceptible and his manner was gracious, although he seemed extremely shy.

Presently, however, he challenged Trelawny to a game of billiards, and once they were alone together he burst into a spate of talk. Within an hour Trelawny had heard all about his travels in Greece, his swimming of the Hellespont, his years of fame in Regency London, his disastrous marriage, and his life in Venice; and as he listened he shrewdly surmised that Byron was bored with his present mode of living and preferred to dwell on the past. This was a situation, he felt, which held great possibilities. If he could give Byron some fresh interest what might not Byron do for him?

For the next few weeks Trelawny danced assiduous attendance upon his new friend. He praised his poems, went riding with him, persuaded him (as he had already persuaded Shelley) to commission a friend of his, a Captain Roberts of the Royal Navy, to build him a yacht in the Genoa shipyards; and even gave him advice on social etiquette, for Byron was sadly conscious that his manners were out of date and, according to Trelawny, would ask anxiously before attending any English function: "Does rank lead the way or does the ambassadress pair us off into the dining-room? Do they ask people to wine? Do we exit with the women, or stick to our claret?"

Throughout the early spring Trelawny's company did much to lighten Byron's mood, but on a March evening something happened which led to the Gambas being exiled from Pisa. Byron, accompanied by Shelley, Pietro Gamba, Trelawny, Count Taafe and a Captain Hay, and followed by Teresa in her carriage, was returning from a country ride. The large party completely blocked the road and a Sergeant Major Masi, who was hurrying back to duty, endeavored to edge his horse past them. Unfortunately, Count Taafe's horse shied with fright and the Irishman, who was no horseman, cried out that he had been insulted.

Byron, doubtless egged on by Pietro and Trelawny, galloped after Masi and heatedly demanded an apology. This the indignant sergeant major refused to give, and when they reached the city gates he signaled to the guards to arrest the quarrelsome English. In the ensuing brawl Captain Hay was wounded in the nose and Shelley struck with the flat of a sword. Byron galloped on to the Palazzo for help and was followed by Masi, who was stopped at the gates by Tita Falcieri. The Gamba servants, always ready for a fight, joined in the fray and one of them succeeded in stabbing the sergeant major. The wound did not prove fatal but naturally enough the authorities arrested Tita and the Gamba servant, and informed Count Ruggiero that the sooner he and his son left Pisa the better.

"Lord Byron," wrote a secret agent to the Austrian Chancellor, "with his company of assassins, gave us a taste of the temper he had shown in other places." In his report he added that Tita had been sent to a gaol in Florence. "There he was ordered to shave off his long Asiatic beard. At first he thought it was to be given to his master, Lord Byron. But when he found that this was not the case, he wrapped up the hair very carefully in a sheet of paper."

The whole affair was ludicrous rather than serious but Byron, with one of his rare flashes of common sense, realized that the secret police would henceforth do everything they could to get the Gambas into trouble, so he took a villa at Montenero near Leghorn and persuaded father and son to move there. He himself remained in Pisa, for now that he had congenial company he had no wish to leave the city. He enjoyed the long rides with his friends into the country, where they would dismount at a small inn, partake of wine and cakes, and indulge in forbidden pistol practice in a secluded vineyard at the back. He enjoyed the stimulus of long literary talks with Shelley, and for relaxation there was always the company of Trelawny, who listened avidly to stories of the great figures of the theatrical and sporting worlds whom he had known in London. And more than anything he liked the even rhythm of his Pisa days—the late rising, the strict dieting, the leisurely game of billiards, the quiet nights when he sat writing, a glass of gin and water at his elbow. At last, it seemed, he had attained the peaceful domesticity of which he had dreamed so often.

But with Byron nothing was ever peaceful for long. In April a fever epidemic swept the cold damp Capuchin Convent at Bagnacavallo and on the 20th of the month Allegra died. Byron, who had known nothing of her illness, was stricken with grief. During her short life of five years he had paid all too little attention to her, treating her as an amiable little plaything: with her death he knew again his old sense of the Byronic doom. Everyone he loved, everyone belonging to him, was fated. Slowly, heavily, he gave instructions for the embalming of the child's body and wrote to John Murray:

> You will regret to hear that I have received intelligence of the death of my daughter Allegra of a fever in the Convent of Bagnacavallo, where she was placed for the last year, to commence her education. It is a heavy blow for many reasons, but must be borne,—with time. It is my present intention to send her remains to England for sepulture in Harrow Church (where I once hoped to have laid my own), and this is my reason for troubling you with this notice. The body is embalmed, and in lead. It will be embarked from Leghorn. Would you have any objection to give the proper directions on its arrival?

* 5 *

The death of Allegra marked the break-up of the Pisa circle. The Shelleys, in order to tell Claire of her daughter's death, moved with Jane and Edward Williams to a remote, uncomfortable little house called Casa Magni near Lerici on the gulf of Spezia. For a few weeks Byron remained at the Palazzo Lanfranchi in such a gloomy frame of mind that he actually

welcomed a visit from Samuel Rogers, but early in June he moved
to Montenero and for a brief space was transported into ecstatic
happiness by the presence of Lord Clare, that dearly loved friend
of his Harrow days. "I never hear the word *'Clare'* without
a beating of the heart even *now*," Byron had written in his
Detached Thoughts at Ravenna, and when they had unexpectedly met on the road between Bologna and Imola he noted that

> ...it was a new and inexplicable feeling, like rising from the
> grave, to me. Clare, too, was much agitated—*more* in appearance
> than even myself; for I could feel his heart beat to his fingers'
> ends, unless, indeed, it was the pulse of my own which made me
> think so.

And now Clare was at Montenero, as gay, as lovable as he
had been in 1804. But his visit was all too short—he was on his
way home to England—and the parting moved Byron to tears.

> The day on which they separated was a melancholy one for
> Lord Byron [wrote Teresa Guiccioli in her memoirs]. "I have
> a presentiment that I shall never see him more," he said, and his
> eyes filled with tears. The same melancholy came over him during
> the first weeks that succeeded to Lord Clare's departure when-
> ever his conversation happened to fall upon this friend.

With Clare's departure life at Montenero suddenly seemed
intolerable. The house itself, which Trelawny had described as
a "new, flimsily-built villa—not unlike the suburban verandahed
cockney boxes on the Thames"—was stiflingly hot after the
perpetual coolness of the huge Palazzo Lanfranchi, and as substi-
tutes for the exhilarating Clare the two Gambas were exceedingly
unsatisfactory. They were impulsive, overemotional, temperamental to a degree. Totally unable to manage their own lives,
they had grown to look upon Byron as their guide, mentor, and
benefactor, and nagged at him eternally to settle their difficulties.
Moreover, they had no idea of how to manage their quarrelsome
and greedy servants, so the peace of the household was disturbed
by a series of violent scenes that drew the attention of the ever-
watchful secret police.

It was into one such scene that Leigh Hunt stumbled on his arrival from England on June 29th. Since Shelley's enthusiastic invitation, accompanied by a draft on Byron's bankers, had reached him the previous autumn poor Hunt had had a shocking time. Shelley had told him airily to come by sea. "Put your music and your books aboard a vessel and you will have no more trouble," he had written, so on November 16th, Hunt, his sick wife Marianne, their six children and a nanny goat embarked at London. They all shared a damp, miserable cabin, they were all atrociously seasick, and the weather was so vile that the ship had to put into Ramsgate and remain there for three weeks. When the voyage recommenced they met so many storms that, after lunging wildly up and down the Channel for ten hideous days, they were obliged to return to the haven of Dartmouth. There they remained, shaken and wretched, for five weary months. Byron supplied them with more funds and they set sail again on May 13th. This time the voyage was an agreeable one, but Marianne was so desperately ill that when she reached Leghorn she was on the point of collapse.

It was not an auspicious beginning to their new, colorful life on the shores of the Mediterranean and Hunt, harassed by the demands of his sick wife and noisy children, thought Leghorn looked like a "polite Wapping, with a square and a theatre." Nor was he impressed by Trelawny, who greeted them on the deck of Byron's new yacht, the *Bolivar*, and as soon as he had settled his family into a hotel he sallied forth to see his patron. He reached Montenero hot, dusty and tired, to find one of the Gambas' noisiest and most alarming quarrels in progress. The previous day, it appeared, the Gambas' cook and Byron's coachman had attacked each other with knives. The rest of the household hurled themselves joyfully into the fray and despite Byron threatening to shoot the lot of them a terrific fight had developed in the courtyard. Young Pietro, with his usual impetuosity, had rushed into the battle and been wounded by one of his servants. The police had been sent for and the disturbance quelled, but just as Hunt toiled up to the house the servant who had knifed Pietro reappeared at the gates threatening vengeance.

Indoor the two Gambas were yelling that the house was in a state of siege while the tearful Teresa, her red-gold hair in wild disorder, was clinging to Byron and beseeching him not to go out for his usual afternoon ride. He was perfectly calm, welcomed his visitor warmly, and made a joke of the whole incident; but Hunt could only gaze at him in stupefaction for instead of seeing the "compact, energetic, and curly-headed person" who had visited him in gaol, he found himself facing a stoutish man whose thin graying hair touched his collar and whose outlandish clothing consisted of white trousers, a nankeen jacket, and an open-necked shirt. Byron succeeded in soothing Teresa and, putting on his gold-braided cap and a "loose riding-coat of mazarin blue," courteously asked Hunt to ride with him. Once outside, however, they were confronted by the erring servant, who immediately burst into sobs and implored the noble lord to kiss him. Byron, who had sent Fletcher for the police, told the man gently that he was forgiven, then turned and mounted his horse.

It was small wonder that Hunt was disturbed by such a welcome, but the next day, when Shelley tumbled in from Lerici full of exciting plans, his spirits rose. Byron had offered the Hunts the ground floor of the Palazzo Lanfranchi, so Shelley escorted the family to Pisa—talking volubly all the way about the wonderful Liberal paper they were going to run—and insisted upon calling in Dr. Vaccà to examine Marianne. His report was by no means good but Hunt felt decidedly more cheerful when he saw his new home and learned of the funds which Byron was prepared to place at his disposal. To his chagrin, however, Shelley could not stay to discuss the many business matters connected with their joint venture since he had already arranged to meet Williams in Leghorn and sail with him to Lerici in his new thirty-foot yacht, the *Ariel*.

It was the last time he was to see his friend. On July 8th he and Williams went aboard the *Ariel* with Charles Vivian, an English seaman found by Trelawny. The *Bolivar*, with Trelawny in command, was to escort them out to sea, but unfortunately he had omitted to obtain port clearance papers and the guard boat refused to let him leave harbor without them. So the *Ariel* sailed alone, with Trelawny watching rather uneasily from the *Bolivar's* deck, and soon she disappeared into the heat haze which hung over the horizon. The day was sultry and humid, so Trelawny went below for a sleep and awakened several hours later to find that although it was only half-past six the light had gone from the sky.

> The sea was of the colour, and looked as solid and smooth as a sheet of lead, and covered with an oily scum. Gusts of wind swept over without ruffling it, and big drops of rain fell on its surface, rebounding, as if they could not penetrate it.

The unnatural calm was followed by a short and violent thunderstorm. When it was over, Trelawny again scanned the horizon but could see no signs of the *Ariel's* high sails, and he retired to the *Bolivar's* cabin an intensely worried man. For all Shelley's adoration of the sea he was no seaman and although he and Williams had had Vivian with them the storm must have played havoc with so light a craft as the *Ariel*. Byron and Teresa had lately returned to Pisa, so Trelawny decided that the only thing to do was to wait hopefully for news that the *Ariel* had reached Lerici in safety.

No news came, and on the third day he rode to Pisa and told Byron of his fears. "When I told him his lip quivered, and his voice faltered as he spoke to me." Then he rode back to Leghorn where he waited for over a week before it was reported that a punt and some other gear belonging to *Ariel* had been washed ashore along the coast. After another ten days Shelley's body was found near Viareggio and Williams's at Bocca Lericcio and Trelawny went to identify them—a horrible task since Shelley's face and hands were devoid of flesh and Williams's body showed ghastly mutilations.

The bodies were given temporary burial in the sands where they were found, but while Byron and Hunt sat and mourned in Pisa the energetic Trelawny dashed around Leghorn persuading the authorities to grant permission for their cremation. Having obtained this he had a large iron furnace made and sent to Viareggio. He, Byron and Hunt then sailed in the *Bolivar* to Bocca Lericcio where, on August 14th, they exhumed the body of Williams, aided by Italian officials and soldiers and watched by a large crowd. The remains were so decomposed that the limbs fell from the trunk when the men touched them and Byron, who always took a morbid interest in death, horrified his companions by demanding if the body was really a human one. "Why," he exclaimed, "it's more like the carcase of a sheep. ...Let me see the jaw. I can recognize any one by the teeth, with whom I have talked. I always watch the lips and mouth: they tell what the tongue and eyes try to conceal." When the grisly task was over he suggested to Trelawny, with almost ghoulish delight, that they should go swimming in the water in which their friends had drowned but much to his disgust he was attacked by cramp when they were about a mile from shore and had to be assisted back by Trelawny.

The next morning they reached Viareggio, where the furnace was set up on the beach. It was clear, brilliant weather, and the sun beat down on the sweating workmen as they dug for Shelley in the golden sand. When the corpse was revealed the friends were startled to observe that what remnants of flesh there were had turned an inky blue. As the wood in the furnace blazed up the body was lifted onto the flames, Trelawny having first anointed it with oil and wine, and the fascinated Hunt, who was crouching fearfully in Byron's carriage, noted the "inconceivable beauty" of the funeral fire as it "bore away towards heaven in vigorous amplitude." So fierce was the heat that the body fell apart, and when the frontal bone of the skull disintegrated

Shelley's brains were revealed. According to Byron they "literally seethed, bubbled, and boiled as in a cauldron for a very long time," but although he was to describe Shelley's burning many times in the future, at the time the scene upset him so much that he swam off by himself to the *Bolivar*. He remembered Shelley's curious behavior in the squall they had experienced on Lake Geneva and wondered if, as he had then suggested, he had let the cruel waves suck him down without a struggle. He remembered too Shelley's strange passion for water—a passion he himself shared to a certain extent—and felt glad that if death had to come to him so soon it should have come in the deeps of the sea he loved so much. But on the instant he felt sorrowful again. Another being he loved had gone, "the *best* and least selfish man I ever knew," and he whom the dead poet had called The Pilgrim of Eternity had to resume his solitary way towards a doom he could not escape.

VII

✳✳✳✳✳✳✳✳✳✳✳✳✳✳✳✳✳✳✳✳✳✳✳✳✳✳✳✳✳✳

The Thorn Is in My Couch

AFTER the rumpus between the servants the Gambas had fled to Genoa but in their stead Byron had to suffer the close proximity of the Hunts and their children. In the days immediately following Shelley's death he assured Hunt that he would take his friend's place and told him that all the plans they had made would go ahead as before. But he then discovered, to his great annoyance, that Hunt had by no means told the whole truth when he accepted Shelley's invitation to Italy. Both Byron and Shelley had understood that Hunt and his brother John owned the *Examiner*, the paper which they proposed to reissue as *The Liberal:* now, with a great amount of rather garbled explanation, Hunt revealed that not only had they been forced to sell the paper in 1821, but that he himself had absolutely no money and that John was heavily in debt. Indeed, a day or two after his arrival Hunt had asked Byron for a loan to send to John and Byron, who was either short of ready cash or imagined he was, had given him his *Vision of Judgment* to publish in the *Examiner*. The sudden knowledge that this paper was no longer in Hunt's hand therefore came as a bitter blow. It meant that he would have to produce a great deal more money than he

239

had intended to launch *The Liberal,* and at the same time he would have to support Hunt and his family.

Hunt had a very real knowledge of and appreciation for literature but unfortunately, as Keats observed, he had a faculty for making "fine things petty and beautiful things hateful." Perky, ebullient, with a face like a pug dog, he was an incurable optimist, and although he had been considerably shaken by Shelley's death he was convinced that he could turn *The Liberal* into a huge success—always provided that Byron provided sufficient cash. After all, so Hunt argued, he was a man of wealth and position. It was his *duty* to support his lesser literary brethren.

This attitude was not one which appealed to Byron at all. He had promised to back the new paper and he would keep his word, but he strongly objected to being regarded as an inexhaustible fount of riches by one who had already deceived him. He found too that at close quarters Hunt was not nearly so charming or able as he had seemed at their brief London meetings. He had a tremendous idea of his own importance, he was facetious, his manner veered between the gushing and the sulky, and his conversation was so liberally besprinkled with "Dear Lord Byron" that the exasperated poet began to call him "Dear Lord Hunt."

Byron had known, of course, that Hunt had a large family, but he had never expected that they would all turn up at the Palazzo Lanfranchi. Accustomed to quietude when he wished it he detested the noisy little Hunts, whom he called variously "a kraal of Hottentots" and "a pack of Yahoos" and he even went so far as to have his bulldog, Moretto, tied up on the grand staircase lest the revolting children attempt to swarm up it to his apartments. This action infuriated the acid-tongued Marianne who declared that his fame and title counted for nothing beside his rudeness, and when he tried to make polite conversation with her she astounded him by her waspish replies. She was indeed a most difficult woman. She was determined not to like Italy, she refused to learn the language, she yearned for her cosy suburban home in Hapstead, she disapproved violently of the liaison between Byron and Teresa, and she made herself as disagreeable as possible on every occasion. Climax came when Moretto attacked her nanny goat and chewed off one of its ears. Thereafter she treated Byron with cold disdain. He, puzzled by her attitude, continued to speak courteously whenever they met, but when he learned from her husband that she had made a witty remark to the Shelleys about the portrait which George Henry Harlow had done of him, saying it "resembled a great school-boy, who had had a plain bun given him, instead of a plum one" his patience expired and if he came across her in the garden he ostentatiously turned aside.

For his part, Hunt hated living at the Palazzo Lanfranchi. He was an early riser and as he sat in his ground-floor study trying to work he was irritated beyond endurance by the sounds that floated down from the floor above. Byron's limping footfall as he wandered through the leisurely process of dressing.... Byron gossiping to Fletcher.... Byron singing snatches from Rossini's operas. The noise, Hunt fretfully averred, was enough to drive a man mad; and the situation was even worse when the poet at last came downstairs, for then he would call "Leontius" through the window and insist that his friend join him in the garden. It was a sheer waste of time, in Hunt's opinion, to lounge in a long chair under the trees and converse in bad Italian with Teresa, whom he described as "a kind of buxom parlour-border, compressing herself artificially into dignity and elegance, and fancying she walked in the eyes of the whole world, a heroine by the side of a poet." Certainly he admired her red-gold head and white shoulders, but he thought her legs were far too short for her body and he greatly disliked her air of faint patronage.

In truth, Hunt was intensely jealous of Byron. Why should this man sit "in health and wealth, with rings on his fingers and baby-work to his shirt ... just issued, like a sultan, out of his bath," when he had to comfort the ailing Marianne, tend the children, work like a beaver over the preparations for *The Liberal*, and battle with financial cares? What right had he to speak so disparagingly of the things the Hunts held dear, to call their beloved children "little Cockneys," to make him and Marianne feel like pensioners? The more he brooded over these grievances the bigger they became, and in addition he had the uncomfortable feeling that Byron's first fine enthusiasm for *The Liberal* was waning.

In this last idea he was right. But Byron was not the man to withdraw from any project he had promised to back, and while several weeks of close association with Hunt had sadly disillusioned him he was still determined to produce the paper. The violent opposition of his English friends, who had implored him to give up the notion on the grounds that it would ruin his poetical reputation, merely served to make him more stubborn, and when Hobhouse (in Hunt's words) "rushed over the Alps, not knowing which was the more awful, the mountains or the Magazine" and descended on the Palazzo Lanfranchi, Byron made it perfectly plain that he intended to go through with the scheme. Hunt, however, did not know this, for Byron only told him that Hobhouse was extremely anxious for him to sever their literary connection, so he continued to worry and sulk while his patron strolled indolently through the days as if he had not a care in the world.

Yet inwardly Byron too was a prey to doubts and fears. He was in the midst of an acrimonious correspondence with Murray, for he had fully convinced himself that that gentleman's dilatoriness in publishing his recent poems was due to the fact that there was no longer any public demand for them, and while he had once scorned literary fame he now clung to it with might and main. It was, he felt, the only thing left to cling to for had he not, through death or disaster, lost everything he held dear? His mother, Charles Matthews, Edward Long, John Edelston, Augusta Annabella, Ada, Lady Melbourne, Allegra, Shelley— the list was endless. It had been a fearful year lightened only, he reflected grimly, by the long-awaited death of his detested mother-in-law; and the condition of his own health, which had deteriorated ever since the day before Shelley's cremation when he had undertaken that exhausting swim with Trelawny, was causing him much anxiety. Then there was Teresa, whose charm was beginning to cloy, and there were the Hunts, who were a constant source of irritation, and the two Count Gambas, who were probably committing heaven knew what indiscretions in Genoa. Never, thought Byron fretfully, had a man been so beset by troubles as himself. He could not go on shouldering all these burdens; he could not go on being a *cavaliere servente*. Suddenly he remembered a boy of ten who had limped homeward through the Aberdeen streets, his head filled with dreams of greatness— was it too late to recapture the spirit of that boy?

✳ 2 ✳

In one of his rare bursts of energy Byron set about disbanding the Palazzo Lanfranchi household and took the Casa Saluzzo at Albaro, a hill village overlooking Genoa. He then made arrangements for the Hunts to share a small house in the same village with Mary Shelley (who was fast developing into. another of his responsibilities) and set out from Pisa towards the end of September with an overjoyed Teresa, who fondly imagined that her lover was making the move out of concern for her father and brother. In point of fact, Byron's main reason for going to Genoa was to enlist the aid of Pietro, that hot-headed young lover of freedom, in planning an expedition to Greece. In a letter to Moore he said:

> I had, and still have, thoughts of South America, but am fluctuating between it and Greece. I should have gone, long ago, to one of them, but for my liaison with the Countess G; for love, in these days, is little compatible with glory. *She* would be delighted to go too; but I do not choose to expose her to a long voyage, and a residence in an unsettled country, where I shall probably take a part of some sort.

243

It was true that Byron still thought vaguely of emigrating to the Americas. While living at Leghorn he had met several North Americans and been flattered by their lyrical praise of his work. He had sat for his portrait to a painter commissioned by the "Academy of Fine Arts at New York," and had come to the pleasant conclusion that the inhabitants of the New World were far more appreciative of his poetry than the dullards of England. But America was not Greece. It held none of the extraordinary appeal of the land where he had known all youthful happiness. Besides, Greece was fighting for an ideal very close to his heart. He too desired liberty more than anything else.

But there was a harder, more cautious streak in the Byron of 1822 than there had been in the Byron of ten years earlier. He had developed an inordinate love of money, and while he realized that if he went to the aid of the Greeks he would have to supply them with funds, he was particularly anxious to ascertain exactly how *much* money would be required before he finally committed himself in any way. He had studied with interest Lord Erskine's "Letter to the Earl of Liverpool," attacking the British attitude towards the Grecian war; and he had heard from Hobhouse that the cause of Philhellenism was being championed by Sir Francis Burdett, Jeremy Bentham, and other leading Whigs. With Hobhouse, these gentlemen planned to form a Greek Committee in London, but unfortunately the suicide of Lord Castlereagh on August 12 had delayed the formation of such a body. As for the situation in Greece itself, there were so many conflicting rumors that it was impossible, in Pisa at least, to gain any accurate picture of what was happening. In the busy seaport of Genoa he hoped to collect the information he sought.

The result of Byron's Genoese inquiries was disappointing. Certainly the Turkish campaign to quell the insurgents seemed to have been a dead failure, and the massacre of 23,000 Chians had roused the ire of many Europeans against the Ottoman Empire; but although the whole of the Grecian peninsula, with the exception of certain fortresses, was in the hands of the rebels, their leaders were now indulging in the most deplorable quarrels among themselves. Some were high dignitaries of the Orthodox Church; some were lawless chieftains; some were astute politicians who concealed an Oriental wiliness under the veneer of Western diplomacy. With commendable prudence Byron decided to hold his hand for a time.

Meanwhile the irritations of life in Genoa threatened to rival those of life in Pisa. True, the Hunts were no longer living in his house, but they were still too near for comfort and if Hunt was not on the doorstep with some eager request about *The Liberal* he was sending up facetious little notes asking for "another 'cool hundred' of your crowns." Then no sooner had he arrived at the Casa Saluzzo than that self-righteous woman, Mary Shelley, kicked up such a terrific fuss about a sofa which she claimed had been filched during the removal that Byron was constrained to write to her:

> The sofa—which I regret is *not* of your furniture—it was purchased by me at Pisa since you left it. It is convenient for my room, though of little value (about 12 pauls), and I offered to send another (now sent) in its stead. I preferred retaining the purchased furniture, but always intended that you should have as good or better in its place. I have a particular dislike to anything of Shelley's being within the same walls with Mrs. Hunt's children. They are dirtier and more mischievous than Yahoos. What they can't destroy with their filth they will with their fingers.... With regard to any difficulties about money, I can only repeat that I will be your banker till this state of things is cleared up, and you can see what is to be done; so there is little to hinder you on that score....

The first part of his letter was not calculated to endear him either to Mrs. Shelley or the Hunts, but there is no doubt that, in the financial sense at least, Byron was extremely kind to both Mary and Shelley. Shortly before the latter's death he had lent him money and had refused to accept the £2,000 legacy the poet had left him. Since then, although he was inclined to agree with

Trelawny's opinion of her as "the most conventional slave I ever met. She even affected the pious dodge, such was her yearning for society," he had seen that the widow and her small son had a sufficiency. With regard to Hunt, Byron had paid his expenses out to Italy and had since advanced him at least £600— to say nothing of giving his brother John the copyrights of *The Vision of Judgment, The Age of Bronze,* and eight cantos of *Don Juan,* which proved to be worth many thousands of pounds.

To the multitudinous pinpricks administered by the Hunts and Mary Shelley was soon added the failure of *The Liberal.* The first number appeared on October 15, and although it sold a fair number of copies it won a storm of abuse from the Tory papers. According to the *Literary Gazette* "Lord Byron contributed impiety, vulgarity, inhumanity... Mr. Shelley a burlesque upon Goethe; and Mr. Leigh Hunt, conceit, trumpery, ignorance and wretched verses." What was worse, *The Vision of Judgment,* about which Byron had warned the Hunt brothers, aroused such ire in a body known as the *Constitutional Association* that John Hunt was prosecuted and fined for publishing it. Byron paid for his defense, but the demise of *The Liberal,* which only dragged its weary way through four numbers, hit him very hard.

It did not, apparently, affect Hunt so deeply, for on October 25th, he sent yet another facetious communication up to the Casa Saluzzo:

> Excuse all this talk, or rather excuse the excuse; but as something or other seems averse to my seeing you often, I love to chat with you as long as possible. Must we not have our ride? I thought to talk with you of "Liberals" and illiberals, of copy, of subjects, and absolute Johns, and Boswells and Spencers and all sorts of possible chattabilities. "Sir," as Johnson would say (or Scrope would say, before he became a fallen Arch-Davies), "the world has few things better than literary inter-chattation; but Byron, Sir, is milky; Sir, he is lacteolus, and has gone off to a young lady." I think I will be indecent, and try to hold you to your promise, especially as you need not go in about the house,

nor need we look at one that day. Our motto shall be "Observation with extensive View."

One can hardly blame Byron for becoming thoroughly incensed with Hunt, and while that gentleman was "walking about the stony alleys, and thinking of Mr. Shelley," he was writing savagely to Murray:

> As to any community of feeling, thought, or opinion, between L.H. and me, there is little or none: we meet rarely, hardly ever; but I think him a good principled and able man, and must do as I would be done by. I do not know what world he has lived in, but I have lived in three or four; and none of them like his Keats and Kangaroo *terra incognita*. Alas! poor Shelley! how he would have laughed had he lived, and how we used to laugh now and then, at various things, which are grave in the Suburbs!

By way of antidote Byron again made a boon companion of Trelawny, who reminded him so much of the heroes in his own earlier poems that he could never resist teasing him about the resemblance. Trelawny did not know that Byron had once said of him that if people could make him wash his hands and tell the truth they might have a hope of turning him into a gentleman. He was well aware, however, that the poet had also said it was a vast pity he should have read *Childe Harold* in his youth, and the remark had rankled. Like Hunt he was jealous of Byron and scornful of his weaknesses—his lameness, his stupid insistence on overtaxing his physical strength, his vanity, his habit of decorating his plump small hands with far too many rings—but he had no intention of voicing these opinions. Byron had been useful—had he not put him in command of the *Bolivar*? —and was going to be still more useful in the future, for all the talk about Greece had determined him that he too would go there, under Byron's wing and on Byron's money. So once again he danced attendance, and when they returned together from shooting practice, riding or swimming he would artfully encourage his patron to drink quantities of wine and spirits, noting with grim satisfaction that he had a remarkably weak head.

A succession of storms and floods accentuated Byron's feeling of depression. There was still no reliable news of what was happening in Greece, although the impetuous Pietro brought home some fresh and incredible rumor every day, and the proposed Greek Committee in London still hung fire. Old Count Gamba, who with his son had apartments in the Casa Saluzzo, complained bitterly of arthritis and dyspepsia, and Teresa, puzzled by her lover's despondency, developed a tendency to burst into tears at the slightest opportunity. Leigh Hunt was now barred as a visitor, but he came each week to collect his subsidy from Lega Zambelli, the steward, and never failed to leave an acrimonious or a jocular note, while Mary Shelley was another unwelcome correspondent.

A little light relief was provided by a visit from Wedderburn Webster, husband of that "little white penitent," Lady Frances. "He had a black wig," wrote Byron acidly to Kinnaird, "and has been made a knight for writing against the queen. He wants a diplomatic situation, and seems likely to want it." Unfortunately, he was as prosy and humorless as ever, and after some desultory conversation Byron forgot his amusement over the wig and remembered that Webster still owed him a thousand pounds.

When his guest had departed he went back to his study and his now favorite occupation—the checking of his financial affairs. On Lady Noel's death he had come into a share of Lord Wentworth's fortune, but this very considerable addition to his capital had merely served to intensify his interest in money. "Penny wise, pound foolish," he could give away large sums without turning a hair, but his mornings were spent over Zambelli's household books, in which he queried every smallest item. This task finished, he limped across to his table and sat down to his own writing—but he had lost all confidence in his work. He was, he said, "as low in popularity and bookselling as any writer can be..." and he had little wish to win back fame from a world in which the spirit of revolution and the romantic glory of Bonaparte no longer existed. Besides, it was impossible to concentrate on anything in the Casa Saluzzo. Either Zambelli would sidle in with a long explanation of a mistake he had made in some account, or old Count Gamba would come with a recital of his woes, or worst of all Teresa would appear and stand gazing at him with tear-filled, reproachful eyes.

Teresa—she was the crux of the whole sad business. She had left her husband for his sake, he was bound to her by ties of gratitude and affection, but he was too emotionally spent to be able to respond to her pathetic demands for reassurances that he still loved her. If only she would realize that love did not endure; if only she would understand the final stanza of the poem he had written for her in 1819:

> True, separations
> Ask more than patience;
> What desperations
>   From such have risen!
> But yet remaining,
> What is't but chaining
> Hearts which, once waning,
> Beat 'gainst their prison?
> Time can but cloy love
> And use destroy love:
> The winged boy, Love,
>   Is but for boys—
> You'll find it torture,
> Though sharper, shorter,
> To wean, and not wear out your joys.

But it was not in Teresa to understand such sentiments. She had given her life to Byron: she fondly believed he had given his to her. The mere idea of even a temporary separation was unthinkable. *Mio caro* Byron and she must remain together for the rest of their lives. So she consoled herself, but because she loved him truly and deeply she was uneasy at the change in him. Long afterward in her *Life*, in which she always alluded to herself in the third person, she was to write:

> But the eyes of the heart penetrate most mysteries, and she saw so unusual a preoccupation, and sometimes so great a sadness on his face, that she was very anxious. To quieten and reassure herself she tried to imagine all sorts of possible causes: the temporary nature of their stay in Genoa, the possible necessity of her return to the Romagna to assert her rights, the annoyance caused to him by Hunt, and the disapproval that all his friends felt of that unhappy collaboration....

And Byron, fuming in his study—he had reached the stage of grinding his teeth furiously when a pert communication arrived from the ubiquitous Hunt—cursed the dilatoriness of the London Committee, and developed wild thoughts of going off alone to Naples, to Nice, to anywhere. "He exhausted himself," said Trelawny, "in planning, projecting, beginning, wishing, intending, postponing, regretting and doing nothing."

But at last, in January, 1823, the London Committee was actually formed, and on February 28th it held its first meeting at the Crown and Anchor Tavern, under the chairmanship of Lord Erskine. Andreas Luriottis made a fervent appeal on behalf of the Greek insurgents and it was arranged that he and Edward Blaquière, author of several books on the Spanish revolution, should go to Greece in order to find out exactly what help was required. Then Hobhouse told the Committee that his friend Lord Byron was prepared to go to the assistance of the Greeks in person. The Committee were delighted. Whatever their personal views on Byron, they were well aware of the tremendous influence he exerted on Liberals all over Europe, and they knew that his name would swing public opinion their way. Blaquière and Luriottis were therefore instructed to call upon him on their way through Genoa, and on March 14th the honorary secretary,

Mr. John Bowring, sent Byron a copy of the report on the meeting and the following letter:

> I cannot send on the accompanying circular without adding a few lines. Mr. Hobhouse has apprised our Committee that we may hope for your kind and cordial support in the good cause. And as you, more than any living being, have been instrumental in awakening that sympathy which, I hope, will become an effective sympathy, we trust that you will lend us your talents and your influence to give our operations more success.

Had Byron received this letter at the proper time he would have been saved two months of heartache and despair. Unfortunately, just before Bowring wrote it there had been an announcement in the London press that Lord Byron had left Italy for Paris and London. Consequently both this communication and a formal resolution thanking Byron for his "generous offer" were sent to Calais and, after much re-addressing, finally reached him in mid-May.

Meanwhile he sat biting his nails in the Casa Saluzzo. He no longer wished to ride, or shoot, or swim, or sail. His liver, "that lazaret of bile," was upset by heavy drinking and his temper was so uncertain that Trelawny went off in a huff to shoot wild duck in the Maremma marshes. Byron did not regret his absence, yet it meant that his isolation was complete. Shelley was dead; Tom Medwin had left for England with a trunkful of manuscripts which recorded Byron's less discreet conversations—it had been such fun to shock the goggle-eyed Tom with highly colored accounts of his disreputable past; Hunt was beyond the pale; Teresa's air of martyrdom had so fretted his nerves that often he missed his daily call upon her and instead sent a servant to her rooms with a hastily scribbled note. Then just as he felt the tedium of his empty days was intolerable two things happened which changed his whole outlook.

❊ 4 ❊

On the evening of March 31st the inhabitants of Genoa were thrilled at sight of a great cavalcade which thundered noisily through the city and drew up with a flourish outside the Albergo della Villa. A crowd gathered around the doorway of the hotel to watch as a swarm of servants, chattering volubly in French, English and Italian, tumbled out of the carriages or from off their horses to superintend the transport of innumerable pieces of luggage up the great marble staircase. Amid the terrific hubbub the proprietor dashed down the steps and bowed low as the four occupants of the first carriage descended—the Earl and Countess of Blessington accompanied by the exquisite Count d'Orsay and Lady Blessington's sister, the mouselike Miss Power, had arrived in Genoa.

Tired as she was after a long and dusty journey Lady Blessington sat later on her balcony and wrote up the events of the day in her diary while her good-natured and indulgent lord paid his respects to Lord William Russell, who was also staying in the hotel.

And am I indeed in the same town with Byron? And to-morrow I may perhaps behold him!!! I never felt before the same impatient longing to see anyone known to me only by his works. I hope he may not be fat, as Moore described him at Venice; for a *fat poet* is an anomaly in my opinion. Well, well, to-morrow I may know what he is like; and now to bed to sleep away the fatigues of my journey.

Born Marguerite Power, daughter of an obscure squireen in County Waterford, Lady Blessington had been married off at the age of fifteen to the dissolute Captain Farmer, an officer in the 47th Foot, but had left him after three months. She was next heard of living quietly with a Captain Jenkins in Hampshire but in 1817 Captain Farmer, who had been imprisoned for debt in the Fleet, most obligingly stumbled and fell to his death from a third-floor window. Without more ado his relieved widow married the rich and kindly Lord Blessington as his second wife, and from that moment her success was assured. Beautiful to look at, with a perfect skin, large eloquent eyes, and dark hair swept back in smooth wings from a perfectly formed forehead, Marguerite possessed a quick wit, a talent for friendship, a glowing vivacity, and immense ambition. The combination was irresistible: within a very short time she was the "gorgeous" Lady Blessington, a leading hostess whose invitations were eagerly sought by people who, a year or two before, had never heard of her. That the equally gorgeous Alfred d'Orsay was her lover nobody doubted, but everyone—including her proud and devoted husband—approved the discreet manner in which the affair was conducted.

Lord Blessington, then Lord Mountjoy, had known Byron in London, where they had met at several great houses and at Watier's and other clubs. But at that time Marguerite had been tucked away in her Hampshire retreat reading *Childe Harold* and thinking what a marvelous man its author must be. More than anything, she had decided, she wanted to meet Lord Byron, and her curiosity had been further whetted by the scandals which centered about his name. Then, only shortly before her arrival in Genoa, she had met Tom Moore in Paris at a time when certain scenes witnessed in her European journeying reminded her again of Byron's verses. Only too glad to talk of his friend, Moore had spoken of his visit to Byron in Venice, but had warned her that the poet no longer resembled his more romantic portraits. One doubts, however, whether he repeated the description he had given to Isaac d'Israeli when dining with John Murray the previous autumn. D'Israeli had inquired if Byron was much altered. "Yes," Moore replied, "his face has swelled out and he is getting fat; his hair is grey and his countenance has lost that 'spiritual expression' which he so eminently had. His teeth are getting bad, and when I saw him he said that if he ever came to England it would be to consult Waite about them. . . . Besides, he dresses very extraordinarily. . . . He's very dandified and yet not an English dandy. When I saw him he was dressed in a curious foreign cap, a foreign greatcoat and had a gold chain round his neck and pushed into his waistcoat pocket."

But even if Moore had repeated that description, it would probably have made little difference to Marguerite Blessington's longing to meet Byron. All through the rest of her journey through France and Italy she had read and re-read his poems and by the time she reached Genoa she was living in a Byronic dream. Would her husband, she begged, please call on Lord Byron without delay? That affable gentleman agreed, and the following afternoon the party drove out to the Casa Saluzzo.

Lord Blessington and Count d'Orsay presented themselves at the villa, while his wife and her sister remained in the carriage. But within a few minutes thunderclouds gathered, and as rain began to fall it was hastily explained to the host that the ladies were in danger of getting wet. Immediately Byron hurried with his gliding limp across the courtyard and bowed low to Lady Blessington. "You must have thought me," he said, "quite as ill-bred and *sauvage* as fame reports, in having permitted your Ladyship to remain a quarter of an hour at my gate; but my old friend Lord Blessington is to blame; for I only heard a minute ago that I was so highly honored. I shall think you do not pardon this apparent rudeness unless you enter my abode, which I entreat you will do."

Naturally, the lady descended from her carriage with alacrity. For a long time they all sat in the big, cool study overlooking the gardens and the sea, talking of Moore, Hobhouse, Kinnaird and other mutual friends. Byron spoke wistfully of his daughter Ada, anathematized the English press for the abuse they published about him, explained the torments he had suffered during his exile from the gaping tourists who followed him everywhere. And as she listened Lady Blessington studied him in bewilderment. Was this thin effeminate little man with the wispy grayish locks and the appallingly cut Italian clothes really the author of *Childe Harold, Lara* and *Manfred?*

That evening she confided to her diary: "I have seen Lord Byron: and am disappointed. . . . Well, I will never again allow myself to form an ideal of any person I desire to see. . . ." And later, when she elaborated her impressions for the *Conversations with Lord Byron,* she wrote:

> I had fancied him taller, with a more dignified and command-ing air; and I looked in vain for the hero-looking sort of person with whom I had so long identified him in imagination. His appearance is, however, high prepossessing; his head is finely shaped, and the forehead open, high, and noble; his eyes are grey and full of expression, but one is visibly larger than the other; the nose is large and well-shaped, but, from being a little *too thick,* it looks better in profile than in front-face; his mouth is the most remarkable feature in his face: the upper lip of Grecian shortages, and the corners descending; the lips full and finely cut. In speaking, he shows his teeth very much, and they are white and even; but I observed that even in his smile—and he smiles frequently—there is something of a scornful expression in his mouth that is evidently natural, and not, as many suppose, affected. . . . His countenance is full of expression, and changes with the subject of conversation . . . I should say that melancholy was its prevailing character, as I observed that when any obser-vation elicited a smile—and they were many, as the conversation was gay and playful—it appeared to linger but for a moment on his lip, which instantly resumed its former expression of serious-ness. His whole appearance is remarkably gentleman-like, and he owes nothing of this to his toilet, as his coat appears to have been many years made, is much too large, and all his garments convey the idea of having been purchased ready-made, so ill do they fit him. . . . I had expected to find him a dignified, cold, reserved, and haughty person, resembling those mysterious personages he so loves to paint in his works, and with whom he has been so often identified by the good-natured world; but nothing can be more different; for were I to point out the prominent defect of Lord Byron, I should say it was flippancy, and a total want of

that natural self-possession and dignity which ought to characterise a man of birth and education.

But Lady Blessington's chagrin at finding Byron so different from the mental portrait she had framed of him was not strong enough to counteract her overwhelming curiosity regarding his true character. The following day he visited the Albergo della Villa to return their call, and for the remainder of their ten weeks' stay in Genoa he passed most of the time in their company. In the warm spring evening they went for long rides together, Byron jogging alongside Lady Blessington and talking... talking... talking, employing his usual mixture of confidence and evasion, hint and contradiction, truth and romance. There were many things about him which offended her sense of fitness—his monotonous insistence on his ancient lineage, the gilt trappings with which he bedecked his horse, his Gordon tartan riding jacket worn with a bright blue cap banded with gold braid, the atrocious vulgarity of his enormous bed (apparently similar to the one at Newstead), his deplorable fondness for all that was tawdry and bizarre. Yet as she listened to his interminable revelations, which always began with, "Mind you, mind you, my dear lady, I have known what it is..." and ended in dark innuendoes concerning some past episode in his life, she gradually developed a deep sympathy for him. He was so unhappy, so lonely, so misguided. Later, she was to write in her diary:

> How much has Byron to unlearn before he can hope for peace.... Byron's heart is running to waste for want of being allowed to expend itself on his fellow creatures: it is naturally capacious and teeming with affection; but the wordly wisdom he has acquired has checked its course, and it preys on his own happiness by reminding him continually of the aching void in his breast.... There was that in Byron which would have yet nobly redeemed the errors of his youth, and the misuse of his genius, had length of years been granted him.

On Byron the company of Marguerite Blessington acted like an elixir. In his seven years of exile he had almost forgotten that such women existed—brilliant, witty, informative, superbly self-assured. She took him back to the London he condemned so strenuously yet ached for in his innermost heart. Her quick bright mind in a way resembled that of Lady Melbourne, the "sort of modern Aspasia" who had been his confidante. Fortunately, he did not realize how much his outmoded Regency manners, his "decided taste" for the aristocracy, his exaggerated and foreign apparel grated on his fair companion. He was content to bask in her companionship and he was exceedingly gracious to Count d'Orsay, reading and commenting on the latter's English Journal, which he found a "very formidable production." With the amiable and tipsy Lord Blessington he was on the best of terms, and when that gentleman suggested he should buy the *Bolivar* Byron was delighted.

It was disconcerting to find, in the midst of his round of engagements with his English friends, that Teresa was wildly and most unreasonably jealous of Lady Blessington. The day of their very first call, when the ladies had been invited in out of the rain, she had been convinced that the thunderstorm was *une sorte de ruse* especially staged for the occasion. "Could Byron do less," she wrote darkly in her *Life*, "than go downstairs and ask them in? The Lady's Plot had succeeded!" As the days went on, and her lover spent more and more of his time with Lady Blessington, so Teresa's fury mounted. Byron wrote that

> *La Mia dama*, Mme la Comtesse G., was seized with a furious fit of Italian jealousy and was as unreasonable and perverse as can well be imagined. God He knows she paid me the greatest compliment ... I have long come to years of discretion and would much rather fall into the sea than in love, any day of the week.

In truth, there was no hint of any sentimental attachment between him and Lady Blessington, but Teresa was not to know that. Had she overheard Byron's remark to the lady about her, that "liaisons that are not cemented by marriage must produce unhappiness, when there is refinement of feeling, and that honourable *fierté* which accompanies it. The humiliations and vexations a woman, under such circumstances, is exposed to, cannot fail to have a certain effect on her temper and spirits, which robs her of the charms that won affection," she might well have used a stiletto on them both, for she hated her supposed rival with a deadly hatred and declared that she was doing all she could "to seduce his mind." And Teresa's simple armory contained no weapons with which to fight this witty, worldly, beautiful woman; all she could do was to voice her jealousy in innumerable scenes. She steadfastly refused to act as hostess when Lady Blessington came to the Casa Saluzzo—though she consented to sit for a sketch to Count d'Orsay. She insisted that when Byron went riding or visited the Albergo della Villa he should take Pietro Gamba with him. She wept, she cajoled, she stormed, she sat up half the night writing him passionate love letters which she tore up before bursting into tears and declaring that she only "wanted to be worthy of him." In short, she made such a thorough nuisance of herself that she merely succeeded in driving the exasperated Byron more and more into the company of the woman she detested.

One can understand and sympathize with Teresa, for in addition to Lady Blessington she had to face another menace to her peace. On April 7th Edward Blaquière and Andreas Luriottis had arrived to see Byron on their way to Greece. There was a long and excited conversation and, according to Pietro, "he [Byron] then decided on as early a departure as possible. Mr. Blaquière was to send information, and we were to be ready on the receipt of his letter." Characteristically, Byron recoiled from telling Teresa what was in his mind and asked Pietro to explain to her as gently as possible. The news very nearly turned her already distraught brain. "I know," she cried dramatically, "I know that we shall never see each other again," and in her anguish she accused Byron of sacrificing her very life so that he might selfishly retrieve his own lost reputation.

I am doing all I can to get away [he wrote to Kinnaird], but I have all kinds of obstacles thrown in my way by "the absurd womankind," who seems determined on sacrificing herself in every way.... She wants to go up to Greece too! forsooth, a precious place to go at present. Of course the idea is ridiculous. ... It is a case, too, in which interest does not enter, and therefore hard to deal with; for I have no kind of control in that way, and if she makes a scene (and she has a turn that way) we shall have another romance, and tale of ill-usage and abandonment, and Lady Caroline and Lady Byroning and Glenarvoning, all cut and dry. There never was a man who gave up so much to women, and all I have gained by it has been the character of treating them harshly.... If I left a woman for another woman, she might have cause to complain, but really when a man merely wishes to go on a great duty, for a good cause, this selfishness on the part of the "feminie" is rather too much.

So poor Teresa sobbed her heart out in her rooms, and peered from behind the curtains when she heard the Blessington carriage drive up, and wrote ungrammatical effusions to her lover. But Blaquière and Luriottis sailed away, and the Blessingtons gossiped amusedly of life in St. James's, and Pietro bustled off to inspect several possible ships recommended by Mr. Charles Barry, partner in an English banking firm which operated from Genoa, and still no word came from the London Committee. Not until mid-May, as we already know, did their long-awaited communication arrive, and Byron immediately sent a detailed and remarkably succinct answer to John Bowring. He was, he said, prepared to "go up in to the Levant in person." His information led him to believe that the principal Greek requirements were a park of field artillery, gunpowder, and medical stores. He warned Bowring that the various Greek leaders were at the moment more interested in quarreling with each other than in liberating their country. He suggested that instead of recruiting a large number of raw soldiers it would be better to secure the services of a few experienced officers, and he added:

It would also be as well that they should be aware that they are not going to "rough it on a beef-steak and a bottle of port," but that Greece—never, of late years, very plentifully stocked for a *mess*—is at present the country of all kinds of *privations*.

It was a thousand pities that this eminently sane and sensible epistle was not regarded by the Committee with all the seriousness to which it was entitled. The members were most gratified that Lord Byron was willing to go to Greece (they were even more gratified by the amount of financial help he offered), but even Hobhouse was a shade doubtful whether the project would ever materialize. He knew the poor dear fellow so well, knew his strange sudden enthusiasms and his equally sudden withdrawals, knew the moods of despair which so often succeeded ones of cheerful optimism.

Certainly Byron's final decision to go to Greece was followed by a depressing reaction, which he described to Lady Blessington:

> It is not pleasant that my eyes should never open to the folly of the undertakings passion prompts me to engage in, until I am so far embarked that retreat (at least with honour) is impossible. . . . It is all an uphill affair with me afterwards; I cannot for my life *échauffer* my imagination again; and my position excites such ludicrous images and thoughts in my mind, that the whole subject, which, seen through the veil of passion, looked fit for a sublime epic, and I one of the heroes, examined now through reason's glass, appears fit only for a travestie, and my poor self a Major Sturgeon, marching and counter-marching, not from Ecton to Ealing, and from Ealing to Acton, but from Corinth to Athens, and from Athens to Corinth.

However, he lashed himself into making preparations and wrote off to Trelawny—who was now sitting in Florence composing mendacious and ill-spelt lover letters to Claire Clairmont:

> You must have heard that I am going to Greece. Why do you not come to me? I want your aid, and am exceedingly anxious to see you. Pray come, for I am at last determined to go to Greece; it is the only place I was ever contented in. I am serious, and did not write before, as I might have given you a journey for nothing; they all say I can be of use in Greece. I do not know how, nor do they; but at all events let us go.

Meanwhile Byron was doing his utmost to persuade the Blessingtons to remain in Genoa until the time came for his own departure; but the restless Lady Blessington was anxious to move south to Rome and Naples. After all, as she gently reminded him, the object of her Italian tour was to collect "impressions" for her proposed book, *Idler in Italy*. So on May 29th there was a farewell dinner party, and three days later Byron limped up the marble staircase of the Albergo della Villa to make his good-byes.

> He seemed to have a conviction that we met for the last time, and yielding to the melancholy caused by this presentiment, made scarcely an effort to check the tears that flowed plentifully down his cheeks. He never appeared to greater advantage in our eyes than while thus resigning himself to the natural impulse of an affectionate heart, and we were all much moved. He presented to each of us some friendly memorial of himself, and asked from us in exchange corresponding *gages-d'amitié*, which we gave him. ... Should his presentiment be realised, and we indeed meet no more, I shall never cease to remember him with kindness; the very idea that I shall not see him again overpowers me with sadness, and makes me forget the many defects which had often disenchanted me with him. Poor Byron! I will not allow myself to think that we have met for the last time, although he has infected us all by his superstitious forebodings.

❋ 5 ❋

It was as well that Byron had much business to attend to after the melancholy departure of the Blessington party. So far the ardent but hopelessly inefficient Pietro had been seeing to all arrangements with lamentable results. Now Byron enlisted the aid of Captain Roberts and Henry Dunn, who kept the English shop at Leghorn. They were to keep their eyes open for a suitable ship capable of taking the party to the Morea. Charles Barry was to attend to all financial matters, Dunn was to supply certain stores (he stocked most things from books to gunpowder), and Pietro was to communicate with Dr. Vaccà at Pisa and ask him to recommend a personal physician for Byron and his staff. Having heard that Trelawny was on his way to join him, Byron then settled down to the business of designing suitable uniforms for himself, Trelawny and Pietro. These were to be made of scarlet cloth, liberally adorned with gold lace. Pietro was to wear an enormous shako of black, green and gold, but Byron and Trelawny were to have colossal plumed helmets bearing the Byron crest and made specially by Giacomo Aspe of Genoa. Then a letter arrived from Blaquière advising Byron to proceed as far as one of the Ionian islands. He added that the state of affairs on the Grecian mainland was so confused that it would be better for his Lordship to wait in Genoa until more satisfactory information about the warring factions was received, but this Byron was not prepared to do.

In his opinion far too much time had already been wasted, and when Dunn and Captain Roberts found a British brig, the *Hercules,* he immediately contracted with her owner and captain, John Scott, to collect the necessary stores from Dunn at Leghorn and then return to Genoa to embark the party. Pietro's inquiries of Dr. Vaccà had resulted in the finding of a timid and inexperienced young doctor named Francesco Bruno, and Byron decided to take with him Fletcher, Lega Zambelli, Tita Falciere, a Negro groom belonging to Trelawny, his Newfoundland dog Lion and his bulldog Moretto, and several horses.

Arrangements were well ahead when Trelawny swaggered in to upset everything. He disapproved strongly of the *Hercules*—"a collier-built tub built on the lines of a baby's cradle—she would do anything but go ahead"—for the simple reason that he had not had the choosing of her. He found fault with Captain Scott, with the stores, with poor Dr. Bruno, whom he alluded to as that "unfledged student," and when he saw the plumed helmet and the scarlet uniform he declared passionately that he would rather die than wear either of them.

Somehow everything was straightened out by the beginning of July, but on the first of that month Byron was further incensed against Trelawny when he received this typical letter from Leigh Hunt:

> I am sorry to trouble you, but will you have the goodness, by the earliest hour that is convenient to you tomorrow, to let me know your final sentiments on this matter, or whether you have any other than what you have stated? As I know that Mary, however against her inclination on account of his own demands upon him for money, will think herself obliged, under certain circumstances, to apply to Trelawny, who offered her (I also know) the use of his purse some time back. She is not aware of my saying a word to you on this point.

The matter referred to was financial aid to enable Mary Shelley, who had stayed on at the Casa Negroti in Genoa with Marianne Hunt until that lady's seventh child should be born, to return to England. Byron, who had already helped her considerably, was infuriated by this abrupt, last-minute demand, and even more infuriated at thought of Trelawny—of all people—coming to the rescue. In bitter mood he sent Hunt a savage, biting reply which was promptly communicated to Mary. She resentfully decided not to take the rather grudging help offered by Byron and did in fact turn to Trelawny.

More serious was the prolonged and heartbreaking farewell he had to make to Teresa. He was anxious to make a codicil to his will leaving her the £5,000 he had originally bequeathed to Allegra, but when he mentioned the matter she burst into a storm of protest. It was an insult to her, an injustice to Lady Byron and Ada, she would not accept a penny, she refused to return with her father to Ravenna (he had received information that his temporary exile was over) and she would either retire to a convent or remain in Genoa till Byron's return. In vain he promised that when his affairs in Greece were more settled he would send for her to join him. She would not be comforted and cried hysterically she knew his journey would lead him to his death.

She did not realize that Byron was already convinced that he would not return from Greece. He had told Lady Blessington so, he had told Tom Medwin—it was the Byronic doom, and there was no avoiding it. Besides, had not a fortuneteller at Cheltenham told his mother as far back as 1801 that her son would die in his thirty-seventh year? In a spirit of bravado he, the most superstitious of men, who had long declared that nothing would induce him to undertake anything either on a Friday or a Sunday, now announced that the party would leave Genoa on Sunday, July 13th. On the 12th he did not visit Teresa at all but busied himself the whole day with last-minute arrangements. But the following afternoon he stayed with her from three o'clock till five, when he went down to the quay and limped aboard the *Hercules*. From the terrace of the Casa Saluzzo Teresa and Mary Shelley watched the dumpy little brig lying in the bay. The idyll was over.

The next morning Teresa was carried to her carriage in a hysterical state to begin the long journey to Ravenna with her father. But within an hour or two she felt so ill that the cavalcade was obliged to stop for a while, and as she crouched on a boulder by the roadside she scrawled a line to her lover: "I have promised more than I can perform, and you have asked of me what is beyond my strength ... I feel as if I were dying, Byron, have pity on me. ..." Then the carriage jolted northwards once more.

Back at Genoa the *Hercules* still lay becalmed in the harbor, but on the 15th an American naval vessel towed her out to sea. That night a squall sprang up and the five horses were so terrified that they kicked down their stalls, with the result that a return to harbor was necessary. While carpenters were fetched to repair the stalls Byron and Pietro made their way to the now deserted Casa Saluzzo and spent a few melancholy hours in the empty, echoing house. "Where," he asked Pietro somberly over their meager luncheon of figs and cheese, "shall we be in a year?"

but when the meal was over he dismissed young Gamba and went alone into his study, where he sat for a long time before his writing table. In one of its drawers was a tress of shining red-gold hair, but although he looked at it he did not think of Teresa. His thoughts were all of Greece:

> The dead have been awakened—shall I sleep?
> The World's at war with tyrants—shall I crouch?
> The harvest's ripe—and shall I pause to reap?
> I slumber not; the thorn is in my Couch;
> Each day a trumpet soundeth in mine ear,
> Its echo in my heart....

VIII

✳✳✳✳✳✳✳✳✳✳✳✳✳✳✳✳✳✳✳✳✳✳✳✳✳✳✳✳✳✳

The Land of Honorable Death

At Leghorn, which the *Hercules* took five days to reach, they were joined by a Greek naval officer named Vitali, who had requested a passage to his native land. He and a M. Schilizzi, a relation of the Mavrocordato family who was also on board, seemed pleasant men, but a group of "Greek patriotic merchants" rushed aboard with the news that Vitali was in the pay of the Turks and Schilizzi an agent of the Russian Government. "This," wrote Trelawny acidly, "was our first sample of the morality of the modern Greeks"; but Byron took the matter casually and refused to disembark his two Greek passengers. Instead he busied himself with interviewing Dunn and Barry's partner. In addition to quantities of stores he provided himself with 10,000 Spanish dollars in cash and bills of exchange for a further 40,000, and he also met and made friends with a young Scot called Hamilton Browne, who was anxious to sail with them. Because of his strong Hellenic sympathies, Browne had been dismissed from British Government service in the Ionian islands, but Byron quickly saw that with his knowledge of the Grecian character and the Romaic tongue he would be a most useful companion, so he too joined the company in the *Hercules*, and it was on his advice that Byron

decided to land at Cephallonia—where the redoubtable Colonel
Napier was Resident—rather than at Zante, the island recommended by Blaquière.

The *Hercules* finally sailed from Leghorn on the 23rd, and
soon they had left the glimmering white façade of the Carrara
Mountains behind them and were moving down the Italian coast
towards the Straits of Messina. For the first few days Byron
kept aloof from his shipmates and lay most of the time on a
rough couch Fletcher had improvised in the stern. Here he
pretended to read, but more often than not he could be seen
gazing at the distant coastline. He was no longer the libertine of
Venice, the *cavaliere servente* of Ravenna and Pisa, the irascible
recluse of the Casa Saluzzo: he was a man of destiny who walked
in the shadow of a grim companion, death; he was a man who,
with that dread knowledge always with him, must strive for
the time which remained to him to justify the admiration of the
world that had so recently condemned him—for already the press
and the public had taken up the song—"Byron is going to Greece.
... *Childe Harold* is pledged to the cause of Liberty...." The
fame he had once longed for had come back at him with all
the force of a boomerang, and in a flash of honesty he knew that
he was incapable of living up to what was expected of him. All
he could do was to die.

Yet despite himself his spirits revived a little as the *Hercules*
sailed south under cloudless skies. By the time they passed
Stromboli he was working out a fifth canto for *Don Juan* and
from that night on he took part in the life of the ship, fencing
with Pietro, boxing with Trelawny, teasing Captain Scott. "I
never was on shipboard," wrote Trelawny virtuously, "with a
better companion than Byron. He was generally cheerful, gave
no trouble, assumed no authority, uttered no complaints, and
did not interfere with the working of the ship..."

Not that Trelawny's words were ever to be wholly relied
upon. Had he not, before leaving Italy, written to Claire Clairmont that hitherto he had been deterred from going to Greece

...by the fear that an unknown stranger without money, etc., would be ill received. I now go under better auspices. L.B. is one of the Greek Committee; he takes out arms, ammunition, money, and protection to them. When once there I can shift for myself— and shall see what is to be done.

In other words, Trelawny was merely making use of Byron, and did not care what sort of shipmate he was.

Still, certain passages in his account of the voyage have a definite Byronic ring. There was, for example, the episode of the much befogged green riding jacket which Trelawny had had specially made for himself. When he tried it on it proved far too small, and while he cursed the tailor, Byron, who was sitting near him on the deck, picked up the offending garment. Perhaps remembering those scarlet uniforms so scorned by Trelawny he asked Fletcher if he had a suitable jacket to wear when landing in Greece. "Only your old plaid one, my Lord," answered the valet; so his master promptly donned Trelawny's, which was pronounced by the admiring Fletcher to be a perfect fit. Now, over a hundred and thirty years later, that jacket is still visible in the Byron Museum at Newstead, a pathetic relic of the Missolonghi tragedy.

But while Byron regained considerable interest in what was going on around him, he was still obsessed by the premonition of death. "If Death," he said to Trelawny, "comes in the shape of a cannon-ball and takes off my head, he is welcome. I have no wish to live, but I can't bear pain. Mind you, Trelawny, don't repeat the ceremony you went through with Shelley—no one wants my ashes."

Trelawny protested swiftly that his fame entitled him to burial in Westminster Abbey, but Byron shook his head. "No, they don't want me, nor would I have my bones mingled with that motley throng. There is a rocky islet off Maina—it is the Pirate's Isle; it suggested *The Corsair*. No one knows it; I'll show it to you on the way to the Morea. There is the spot I should like my bones to lie."

When Trelawny reminded him that if he wished to rest near the Morea some instruction should be left in his will, Byron said that he would attend to the matter and added: "If you are with me when I die remind me, and don't let the blundering, blockhead doctors bleed me, or when I am dead maul my carcase—I have an antipathy to letting blood."

Neither Byron nor Trelawny knew how soon that antipathy was to be proved, and with an effort Byron turned the conversation into lighter channels. Indeed, as their voyage drew to a close and the *Hercules* wallowed slowly between the glorious islands of the Heptanesos he became quite exuberant; and when at last he saw the lovely mountains of the Morea rising against the horizon he experienced a sense of homecoming he had never known before. "I don't know why it is," he murmured in a low voice, "but I feel as if the eleven long years of bitterness I have passed through since I was here were taken off my shoulders, and I was scudding through the Greek Archipelago with old Bathurst, in his frigate."

❋ 2 ❋

On August 3rd the *Hercules* dropped anchor in the harbor of Argostoli, at that time the garrison town of Cephallonia. Unfortunately, Colonel Napier was away and his secretary, a Captain Pitt Kennedy, gave Byron a rather gloomy account of the perpetual squabbles with which the rival insurgent groups on the mainland were occupying their time. He also handed over a note from Edward Blaquière which sent Byron into a towering passion. In it Blaquière stated shortly that circumstances obliged him to hurry back to England for a time—a palpable lie, since Byron was well aware that the only reason behind this hurried departure was a desire to get his book on Greece published before the English public lost interest in the War of Independence.

Fuming to Trelawny that he would buy an island from the Greeks or the Turks and conduct his own campaign rather than serve any longer under a Committee which clearly did not appreciate his efforts in the Greek cause, he limped to his cabin, where he remained all day brooding on the perfidy of man.

The next happening did much to restore his confidence—although it scared the wits out of Zambelli and Dr. Bruno. Early the following morning the Souliots, who had fled from the mainland and sought refuge with the British, swarmed aboard clamoring to see "Lord Veeron." Tall, fierce, unkempt, they were a savage-looking crowd, but Byron was delighted to see them for he had greatly admired them on his earlier visit. They wanted money, they wanted to join his expedition, they wanted all manner of things; and the more he conceded the more rapacious they grew until, according to Trelawny, Byron "stood at bay like a hunted lion, and was glad to buy them off by shipping them to the Morea."

All the same Byron was heartened by the visit of the Souliots; and he was further cheered by the return of Colonel Napier, that excellent soldier who was to conquer Sind some twenty-two years later. Napier knew and loved the Greeks although, like Byron, he was perfectly aware of their many shortcomings, and it was he who provided the first accurate account of the situation. It was true that the insurgents had conquered practically the whole of the archipelago, but they had made no attempt to implement their victory. Both military and civil leaders were fighting violently among themselves; there was no money; the shipowners refused to allow the Greek fleet to put to sea unless a large down payment was made; the Turks, either out of ignorance or indolence, were making no attempt to seize back the Morea, though it would be uncommonly easy for them to do so. He agreed that Byron would be wise to stay in Cephallonia until the future was more clear, and he promised to help the expedition to the best of his ability, despite the fact that his official position obliged him to maintain a strictly neutral attitude.

Had Napier joined forces with Byron there and then, the course of events might have been very different. But the job of Resident was not one which could be given up at a moment's notice, and it was not until the following January that the man who afterwards stated that he "would rather have finished the roads of Cephallonia than have fought Austerlitz or Waterloo," presented himself before the London Committee armed with a letter of introduction from Byron—and by then it was too late.

Napier was, however, of the greatest assistance throughout the summer and autumn of 1823; and Byron was also delighted to find that the young officers of the 8th Regiment of Foot, then stationed at Argostoli, wished to meet him because they were all fervent admirers of *Don Juan*. To a man who had wrongly believed himself at the very nadir of popularity this news was overwhelming, and when Colonel Duffie invited him to a banquet to be held in his honor in the mess he was as excited as any schoolboy. The dinner was a huge success and on his elated return to the *Hercules* he drew up a dispatch to Marco Botzaris, a Souliot chief highly recommended by Mavrocordato, and sent it off by messenger to Missolonghi.

Since some time was bound to elapse before he received any answer, Byron then decided to revisit Ithaca—that lovely island he had once so nearly purchased. With Trelawny, Pietro, Hamilton Browne and Dr. Bruno, he stayed there eight days, and it was during this time that he had one of the epileptiform attacks which were presumably caused by the Little's Disease he had suffered from birth. The party were staying with Captain Knox, the Resident, at Vathy where another guest was a Mr. S————, an English lawyer who subsequently told the author of *Medora Leigh* the story:

> The next morning about nine o'clock, the party for the Fountain of Arethusa assembled in the parlour of Captain Knox; but Lord Byron was missing. Trelawny, who slept in the room adjacent his lordship's, told us that he feared he had been ill during the night, but that he had gone out in a boat very early in the

morning. At this moment I happened to be standing at the window, and saw the object of our anxiety in the act of landing on the beach.... I never saw, and could not conceive the possibility of such change in the appearance of a human being as had taken place since the previous night. He looked like a man under sentence of death, or returning from the funeral of all that he held dear on earth. His person seemed shrunk, his face was pale, and his eyes languid and fixed on the ground. He was leaning upon a stick, and had changed his dark camlet-caped surtout of the preceding evening for a nankeen jacket embroidered like a hussar's —an attempt at dandyism, or dash, to which the look and demeanour of the wearer formed a sad contrast....

The attack passed without leaving any apparent ill effects, although Dr. Bruno was much agitated by his temperamental patient's insistence upon swimming, boating, and drinking quantities of gin and water. Before he left the island Byron adopted a Patras family named Chalandritsanos and arranged for them to accompany him back to Cephallonia; and also presented Captain Knox with a donation of two hundred and fifty dollars for his Greek refugees.

On their return to Cephallonia the party spent a night at a monastery on the hill of Samos, where the Abbot welcomed them with a long and incomprehensible speech and much ceremonial. It seems likely that Byron was not fully recovered from his Ithaca attack, for all of a sudden he burst into a torrent of Italian imprecations and then shrieked to his companions: "Will no one release me from the presence of these pestilential idiots? They drive me mad!" The poor monks thought he was indeed insane and according to Mr. S—— a terrible night followed:

> Lord Byron retired almost immediately from the *sala*. Shortly afterwards we were astonished and alarmed by the entry of Dr. Bruno, wringing his hands and tearing his hair.... It appeared that Lord Byron was seized with violent spasms in the stomach and liver, and his brain was excited to dangerous excess, so that he would not tolerate the presence of any person in his room. He refused all medicine, and tore all his clothes and bedding like a maniac.... Trelawny at once proceeded to the room, but

soon returned, saying that it would require ten such as he to hold
his lordship for a minute.... The doctor asked me to try to bring
his lordship to reason: "He will thank you when he is well," he
said, "but get him to take this one pill, and he will be safe."...
There being no lock on the door, entry was obtained in spite
of a barricade of chairs and a table within. His lordship was half
undressed, standing in a far corner like a hunted animal at bay.
As I looked determined to advance in spite of his imprecations
of "Back! Out of my sight! Fiends, can I have no peace, no
relief from this hell? Leave me, I say!" he lifted the chair nearest
to him, and hurled it direct at my head. I escaped as best I could,
and returned to the *sala*....

It was Hamilton Browne who eventually induced Byron to
swallow two pills, and the next morning he apologized profusely
for all the trouble he had caused. But it is certain that his general
health was by no means good and the news which greeted him
on his return to Argostoli did not tend to alleviate the physical
and mental distress he was enduring. First, there was a pompous
letter from John Bowring which opened with the assurance that
the Committee were convinced that Byron's presence in Greece
was of inestimable value to the cause, but ended with a wail of
despondency. "We have not made the progress we expected. The
Spanish cause has absorbed attention, and we begin to fear un-
worthily." Secondly, the Turks had sent a force under Omar
Pasha to Western Greece, and Turkish ships blockaded the coast
from Missolonghi to Navarino, while the Greek fleet, still without finance, lay idle in the harbors of Hydra, Psara, and Spetsai.
Lastly, the three chief leaders of the Grecian factions, Mavrocordato in Western Greece, Koloktronis in the Morea, and Odysseus in Eastern Greece all sent emissaries to implore his help and
to warn him that their own especial army was the only one which
could save the country, while lesser leaders sent demands for
funds and stores.

It was a weary Byron who wrote in his journal:

As I did not come here to join a faction but a nation, and to
deal with honest men and not with speculators or peculators,

(charges bandied about daily by the Greeks of each other) it will require much circumspection to avoid the character of a partisan, and I perceive it to be the more difficult as I have already received invitations from more than one of the contending parties, always under the pretext that *they* are the "real Simon Pure." After all, one should not despair, though all the foreigners that I have hitherto met with from amongst the Greeks are going or gone back disgusted.

Whoever goes into Greece at present should do it as Mrs. Fry went into Newgate—not in the expectation of meeting with any special indication of existing probity, but in the hope that time and better treatment will reclaim the present burglarious and larcenous tendencies which have followed this General Gaol delivery.

When the limbs of the Greeks are a little less stiff from the shackles of four centuries, they will not march so much "as if they had gyves on their legs." At present the Chains are broken indeed; but the links are still clanking, and the Saturnalia is still too recent to have converted the Slave into a sober Citizen. The worst of them is that (to use a coarse but the only expression that will not fall short of the truth) they are such damned liars; there never was such a capacity for inveracity since Eve lived in Paradise. . . .

Byron was still living aboard the *Hercules*, undecided whether to try to reach the Morea or to disembark at Argostoli and await events, when he received an answer from Marco Botzaris, dated August 18th:

Your letter, and that of the venerable Ignazio, have filled me with joy. Your Excellency is exactly the person of whom we stand in need. Let nothing prevent you from coming into this part of Greece. The enemy threatens us in great number; but, by the help of God and Your Excellency, they shall meet a suitable resistance. I shall have something to do to-night against a corps of six or seven thousand Albanians, encamped close to this place. . . .

In the encounter with the Albanians Botzaris was killed by a shot in the head. Mavrocordato meanwhile had fled to Hydra; so there was nobody left in Western Greece on whom Byron could count. He decided therefore that his only wise move was to disembark, send the *Hercules* back to England, and wait until the situation had clarified itself. He wisely determined not to accept the hospitality offered him by Colonel Napier and rented a villa at Metaxata, a village four miles from Argostoli.

Before he left the *Hercules*, however, he had engaged forty Souliots as a personal bodyguard. It was one of those theatrical gestures he never could help making, and it led to endless trouble. The three local chieftains among the Souliots demanded all sorts of perquisites and distinguished themselves by embezzling the four dollars a day Byron had offered each of their men. The men themselves then turned out to be a mixed bag of dishonest characters who owed allegiance to nobody and Colonel Napier advised Byron to give them all two months' pay and ship them to Missolonghi, where they were eventually to prove a source of serious trouble.

Sick and exhausted, Byron again fell prey to nightmare, and every evening the faithful Fletcher had to examine every inch of his portmanteau bed in order to be sure it concealed no hidden danger. But no precaution sufficed. Even during his afternoon siesta he was pursued by horrors and one day he cried out to Trelawny, "I have had such a dream! I am trembling with fear. I am not fit to go to Greece."

But Trelawny had already decided to "shift for himself." Ever since their arrival at Cephallonia he had been irritated by Byron's inaction, and when he learned of the proposed move to Metaxata he was furious. "I well knew," he wrote spitefully, "that, once on shore, Byron would fall back on his old routine of dawdling habits—plotting, planning, shilly-shallying, and doing nothing." Not without subtlety he suggested that he and Hamilton Browne should endeavor to run the Turkish blockade and reach the Morea from whence they could report on the true state of affairs. Byron was against this move, thinking it better to delay until the whole party could proceed together, but Trelawny was adamant. On September 6th, Byron, with Gamba

and Bruno, went to Metaxata, and on the following day Trelawny and Hamilton Browne left for the Morea.

And at Metaxata Byron remained for four long months.
While he was there he was again pestered by innumerable dele-
gations from the various Greek leaders, and by stupid communi-
cations from the London Committee, with which body he was
rapidly losing patience. None of them, not even his old friend
Hobhouse, seemed to realize that it would be fatal to proceed to the Grecian mainland until the expedition was properly
organized.

> I shall continue here till I see when, and where, I can be of use,
> if such a thing at last be practicable. I have hitherto only contra-
> dictory accounts. If you send out a military man, he will have
> every co-operation from me; or if you send out any other per-
> son, I have no objection to act as either his coadjutor, or
> subordinately, for I have none of those punctilios.

So Byron wrote in a letter to John Cam, but the real truth
was that he could not bring himself to accept the responsibility
which must fall upon him if he assumed active control of a
military force. He had not the makings of a soldier; he was not
gifted in diplomacy; he shrank from the idea of having to make
decisions. And behind and beyond his own weakness towered
public opinion, which he both venerated and feared. From all
over Europe and America had come letters extolling his bravery
in rushing to the aid of the Greeks: if he rushed still further
and failed in his mission then public opinion would promptly
hurl him from his pinnacle and the resultant fall would be such
as to make his previous débâcle the merest tumble by comparison.

But from the security of Metaxata there was one thing he
could do; and that was to provide the Greeks with financial
assistance. "Get together," he told Kinnaird, "all the means and
credit of mine we can, to face the war establishment, for it is
'in for a penny, in for a pound,' and I must do all I can for the
ancients"; and when Hamilton Browne reappeared in November
with the two Greek deputies who were on their way to London

to arrange a loan for the immediate payment of the fleet, he offered to advance them the sum of £4,000 for the purpose. There was much acrimonious argument with bankers over the raising of the money, but finally Mr. Hancock of Barff and Hancock, who operated in Cephallonia and Zante, agreed to furnish the necessary amount.

Apart from the complications of politics and finance Byron's life at Metaxata was peaceful enough. He rode over the mountains with Gamba, entertained the officers from Argostoli, argued about religion with the sturdy and Scottish Dr. James Kennedy —who was attached to the garrison—and welcomed several visitors including Lord Sidney Osborne, who was State Secretary at Corfu. Then in November a "tall, delicately-complexioned, rose-cheeked, dandy boy of simpering and affected manners" named Dr. Julius Millingen, arrived to find Byron "on the balcony of the house, wrapt in his Stewart tartan cloak, with a cap on his head, which he affected to wear as the Scotch bonnet, attentively contemplating the extensive and variegated view before him. . . ."

It is not clear why Byron should have been wearing the Stewart tartan when he belonged to the Gordon clan; but then nothing about Millingen's writings is either clear or accurate. He was an Edinburgh medical student and had been selected by the London Committee to convey to Greece medical stores provided by the Society of Friends; he was, like Trelawny, an adventurer and a liar; and eventually, after deserting to the Turks, he ended his inglorious career in Constantinople, where he was personal physician to no fewer than five successive Sultans, though it is doubtful whether he had ever attained a medical degree.

But in Metaxata he proved an entertaining enough companion, and Byron felt sorry when he left for Missolonghi. However, there arrived only a few days later the long-awaited emissary from the London Committee, Colonel the Honorable Leicester Stanhope, C.B. This gentleman, although he had seen active service in South America and India, was a great deal more interested in politics than in the Army, and was an ardent disciple of Jeremy Bentham. It was soon to be made clear that his real purpose in coming to Greece was to bring "culture" to the Grecian masses; but he listened attentively to Byron's explanation of the situation and agreed that this had brightened considerably in the past few weeks.

The various leaders were still fighting among themselves, but thanks to Byron's money, the Greek fleet were preparing to leave the island of Hydra. They finally did so at the beginning . of December, followed by Mavrocordato, and after violating the neutrality of the Ionian islands by running two Turkish ships ashore at Ithaca, they proceeded in triumph to Missolonghi, where Mavrocordato was received enthusiastically. The Turkish fleet retired to the inner Gulf of Corinth and on December 12th the bustling Colonel Stanhope joined Mavrocordato. A week later he sent to the London Committee just the sort of heartening letter they liked to receive:

> Your agent has now been at Missolonghi one week. During that period a free press has been established, a corps of artillery has been decided on, the funds furnished for its maintenance during nine months, and a person despatched to assemble it; means have been furnished to prevent the Greek fleet from dispersing, and a proper house and grounds have been procured for the establishment of a laboratory. This is a very encouraging commencement of our labours.

By this time the situation in the Morea had degenerated into civil war, and in Eastern Greece Odysseus ruled as a virtual autocrat, scorning any connection with leaders in other parts of the country. But in Western Greece the Souliot chiefs were willing to serve under Mavrocordato, now firmly established in Missolonghi from where attacks could be made on Patras and Lepanto, the two fortresses remaining in Turkish hands. It was clear, therefore, that any aid from the London Committee must be given to Western Greece, and by the middle of December Byron was uncomfortably aware that he had no reason to defer his departure for the mainland.

On December 28th he set sail for Missolonghi. The last adventure had begun.

❋ 3 ❋

It was surely a final vicious twist on the part of that malignant fate which had always dogged him that sent Byron to die in Missolonghi.

The little town rises crazily, on rotten piles and mudbanks, above a three-mile-wide lagoon of filthy, scum-covered water; and is protected most effectively from the clear and lovely Gulf of Patras by a sandy bar. The houses are dilapidated affairs of stone and plaster, and everywhere there are sinister green puddles all too obviously used as latrines. The streets are just narrow lanes fringed with small squalid shops from which drift odors rivaling those from the puddles, and under the stunted pepper trees outside the café down by the lagoon miserable fowls and mangy goats search the slimy ground for garbage. All around the town stretch stagnant, colorless marshes; and behind it rear the Ætolian and Akarnanian mountains, their forbidding limestone cliffs a cold gray in winter and a dun brown in summer.

For various reasons—invasions, earthquakes, and the gradual sinking of the houses into the mud which sucks perpetually at their foundations—Missolonghi has been wholly or partially rebuilt several times in the past hundred and thirty years; but since the inhabitants seem to have replaced existing buildings with exactly similar ones, the present-day visitor can gain a pretty accurate impression of the town as it was in Byron's day. True, the house belonging to the primate of Argostoli, in which he lodged, has long since been demolished and a smaller one erected in its place; but when one studies the records left by those who were with Byron this seems to be the only major change.

A sort of miasma broods over Missolonghi. A week—even a day—in the place induces an apathy hard to describe. The very air is thick and sluggish; the mists rise from the marshes till the sun shows only as a distant lemon-colored ball; the ground is so dank that even in summer the muddy open spaces never quite dry up. Occasionally at dawn or sunset—as though to tantalize the dwellers in this purgatory—the skies clear and it is possible to gaze across the lagoon to the shimmering island of Cephallonia set like a jewel in the dark Ionian sea; then the prospect closes again.

Yet once, for a brief space, Missolonghi came vividly, gloriously, to life.

The date was January 5th, 1824. The town swarmed with Souliot troops, whose chieftains had been holding a protracted and noisy series of conferences with Mavrocordato and Colonel Stanhope. For almost a week everyone had been in a state of wild anxiety, owing to rumors that the famous and excessively rich "General Veeron," the noble Englishman who was coming to aid their cause, had been captured by the Turks and taken to Patras. Fortunately, the rumors had proved false. Lord Byron's own vessel, a light sailing ship known as a mystico, had evaded the enemy by putting into Dragomestri; and it was the bombard, which carried members of his entourage led by the young Pietro Gamba, that had been captured by a Turkish frigate and, by some mysterious chance that all were too relieved to ask much about, suddenly set free after a few days. To the Souliots this news was an omen that their arms would prevail; and their excitement mounted to fever point when, at noon on the 4th, Gamba actually arrived accompanied by Lega Zambelli, several servants, Trelawny's Negro groom (now transferred to Byron's service), five horses, and such vast quantities of stores that it took the entire population the rest of the day to transport them to the primate's house.

And now the supreme moment for which Missolonghi had been waiting was at hand. As a canoe made its way to the mystico anchored at the entrance to the lagoon, the guns boomed out from the fort; the soldiers blazed away with their muskets; every man, woman and child in the place ran helter-skelter to the edge of the lagoon. Most of them had not the faintest notion of who Lord Byron was; but they had been told he was come to deliver them from the Turks, from the rival factions which warred so bitterly within Greece, from poverty—and that was enough. They roared such a full-throated welcome that Pietro Gamba "could scarcely refrain from tears."

The din grew even louder when a slight erect figure in scarlet regimentals (borrowed for the occasion from Colonel Duffie, but the population were not to know that) stepped into the canoe and was paddled toward the heaving, swaying multitude. "Veeron!" they shouted, "Veeron!" and Byron's hand went up in salute, and all the cares and disillusionments of the past eight years fell from him. He had come back to Greece, the country he had loved ever since his stay there as a young man, the country which would surely give him back "The love of brighter things and better days."

He stepped ashore and was swept by the cheering, laughing crowd to the doorway of the house where he was to lodge. Here he was greeted warmly by Mavrocordato, Stanhope and a large group of Greek and foreign officers. Again and again, as he turned to enter the house, he was forced to pause on the steps and acknowledge more cheers, more bursts of musketfire, more thunderous salvos from the guns. Around him, reaching out to touch the skirts of his coat, surged the Souliots; and behind them pressed a crowd so thick that for once the muddy spaces, the evil green pools, the heaps of rotting garbage were hidden from view. All that Byron could see was a host of eager, friendly faces. Intensely moved, he stood there gazing down upon them. "Hope and content," wrote Gamba afterwards, "were pictured on his countenance"; and had he been an Englishman he might well have added Marlowe's lines: "Is it not passing brave to be a king and ride in triumph through Persepolis?"

For Byron, no less than for Missolonghi, the moment was supreme. He did not know, as he gave a final wave and stepped across the threshold, that he had reached the point of no return.

✳ 4 ✳

The Byron who had lingered so long in Cephallonia was the man of common sense who had, as we know from the entries in his journal, no illusions about the people he had come to help. The Byron who landed at Missolonghi was suddenly transformed by his tumultuous welcome into the man of action determined to save the land he had dreamed of for thirteen years. For the moment the inner exultation of this second Byron rendered him immune to fear of failure. His mission was to save Greece, and if this entailed the sacrifice of his own life on the field of battle, then he would go proudly to a glorious death. While Fletcher decorated the stained walls of his upstairs sitting room with a frieze of arms—swords, pistols, blunderbusses, daggers, trumpets and helmets—he plunged straightaway into discussion of military details with Mavrocordato and Stanhope. The Sultan had removed all his troops from Western Greece; but the Turks still held the Patras and Lepanto forts, also two castles guarding the Gulf of Corinth, and when the spring came it seemed inevitable that there would be an attack on Missolonghi. With much eloquence, his eyes blinking behind his gold-rimmed spectacles, Mavrocordato explained how necessary it was that Lepanto should be seized from the enemy with the least possible delay. He did not add that its capture would be a large feather in his own cap; he laid stress on the fact that the only suitable leader for such an important expedition was the noble English lord. Furthermore, he pointed out, the garrison of the fort consisted of mercenaries, mostly of Albanian origin, who were ready—indeed eager—to throw down their arms after the merest show of defense, provided they were given some small financial reward.

Whether by accident or design (one suspects the latter), Mavrocordato had propounded the very scheme to appeal to Byron. Lepanto, with its historical associations, was a name to reckon with, and the man who succeeded in wresting the fortress from the Turks would surely be acclaimed the world over. At once he agreed with enthusiasm to the proposal and retired to make copious notes on the planning of his campaign.

On paper it all looked absurdly easy. Mr. Parry, who, according to John Bowring, was a "very intelligent firemaster who was General Congreve's right-hand man, and understands the manufacture of every species of destructive missiles," was already on his way to Missolonghi with "a small body of labouring artificers, with forges, laboratories, and every implement necessary for the fabrication of the *material* of war"; therefore an efficient artillery brigade must be formed. Then the Souliots must be banded together and trained as an infantry force. Finally, the fourteen ships of the Greek fleet must provide naval support.

But within twenty-four hours of Byron's arrival the whole magnificent project began to go wrong. The trained soldiers from European countries, who had come to Greece asserting fervently that they were true Philhellenes, showed a strange reluctance to take up commissions in the artillery brigade. Many had succumbed to the sickness which emanated from Missolonghi's fever-ridden swamps; others complained that they had been entirely misled by the persuasive gentlemen who had coaxed them to Greece and demanded immediate repatriation; only two officers and a handful of raw recruits volunteered to join, so Byron had to fall back upon the Greeks—which soon led to violent troubles as the foreign officers were Germans who considered themselves infinitely superior to these semioriental savages.

Next, nine of the twelve Greek ships had again sought sanctuary in Hydra and had no intention of emerging from their base because they were quite certain they would be asked to serve without pay. This belief was echoed by the crews of the five Spetsiot brigs remaining near Missolonghi, and it was only when Byron agreed to pay them out of his own pocket that they consented, albeit sulkily, to stay with him.

The worst troubles of all, however, occurred among the Souliots, those brave, ruffianly characters for whom Byron had far too soft a spot. They lived in a chronic turmoil of tribal and family feuds—and they brought all their problems to "General Veeron" at any hour of the day or night. No sooner had he soothed one chieftain than another would come storming up the stairs bawling unintelligible complaints; and at last Mavrocordato wrote Byron a terse history of the Souliots, pointing out that it was impossible to rely on such lawless, greedy, quarrelsome people.

Byron's answer was to take five hundred Souliots into his service, making himself responsible for their pay—he was already beginning to suspect the smooth-tongued, eternally blinking "Greek Prince" who had taught Mary Shelley; and to distrust Colonel Stanhope, that disciple of Jeremy Bentham who was so absorbed in "educating" the Greeks that he had no time for his legitimate job of soldiering; and to despair of making an efficient aide-de-camp out of loyal, stupid, blundering Pietro Gamba. There was indeed nobody who was capable of taking any decision except himself, and at the thought all his old diffidence returned with a rush.

By way of solace he concentrated on the Souliots. For their part they were only too willing to enlist under his banner. To begin with he was rich (that was the important thing) and they quickly learned how to wheedle him into supplying them with this, that or the other: to end with, every least thing about him intrigued their childish minds. The way he walked with a curious half-limp, half-glide; his habit of grinding his teeth when he was angry; the green jacket he wore with a gold-trimmed blue cap; the manner in which he dressed his servants; the quantities of food he gave his two dogs; the weapons hanging on the sitting-room walls; the tiny lacy handkerchief he always carried in his small beringed hand. To oblige a leader who paid them good money and provided such fascinating entertainment into the bar-gain, the Souliots were perfectly ready to learn any new-fangled methods of warfare he might care to teach.

Each day, therefore, the artillerymen maneuvered their anti-quated cannon onto the mudflat in front of the former Seraglio, in which tumbledown building they had been housed; while those Souliots who were to form Byron's personal force drilled in the courtyard of his house. The noise was terrific, but as the men could scarcely keep foothold because of the mud, and as personal brawls broke out every few minutes, it is doubtful whether much progress was made by anybody. But to Byron, standing at his second-floor window, it was a sight which never failed to stir the blood. So soon now, so very soon, he and these brave Souliots would launch their triumphant assault on Lepanto!

January 18th marked the prelude to disaster. After a day of torrential rain the Souliots and the townsfolk decided to have a fight. They kept up the battle for an hour or two while Byron and his party stood guard in the house with their muskets, wait-ing for an attack from one side or the other. Gradually, however, the din subsided, and they were wondering if it would be safe to retire for the night when Mavrocordato's secretary rushed in to tell them that the Spetsiot brigs at the entrance to the lagoon had sailed off because the Turkish fleet had left Patras and was bear-ing down on Missolonghi. Two days later the shapes of the enemy warships showed ghostly through the mist—the blockade of Missolonghi had begun.

There was much agitated discussion about attacking the ships by boat, and Byron was all for putting this idea into force at once. Fortunately, he was overruled, and by the eve of his thirty-sixth birthday he was again so wrapped in his dream of Lepanto that he composed the famous poem, *On This Day I Complete My Thirty-Sixth Year:*

> The sword, the banner, and the field,
> Glory and Greece, around me see!
> The Spartan, borne upon his shield,
> Was not more free.
>
> Awake! (not Greece—she *is* awake!)
> Awake, my spirit! Think through *whom*
> The life-blood tracks its parent lake,
> And then strike home!
>
> If thou regrett'st thy youth, *why live?*
> The land of honourable death
> Is here:—up to the field, and give
> Away thy breath!
>
> Seek out—less often sought than found—
> A soldier's grave, for thee the best;
> Then look around, and choose thy ground,
> And take thy rest.

Pietro Gamba wrote that:

> We perceived from these lines, as well as from his daily conversations, that his ambition and his hope were irrevocably fixed upon the glorious objects of his expedition to Greece, and that he had made up his mind to "return victorious or return no more." Indeed, he often said to me, "Others may do as they please—they may go—but I stay here, *that is certain....*" He one day asked his faithful servant, Tita, whether he thought of returning to Italy. "Yes," said Tita, "if your Lordship goes, I go." Lord Byron smiled, and said, "No, Tita, I shall never go back from Greece—either the Turks, or the Greeks, or the climate, will prevent that."

The last words are significant, for hitherto Byron had always stressed his hope that he would die in battle. The dire spell cast

286

by Missolonghi was beginning to destroy even his inner exalta-
tion. Besides, despite Pietro's repeated assertions that he had
enjoyed "excellent health" ever since leaving Italy, Byron was
an exceedingly sick man. Up to mid-February, however, he was
probably unaware of the seriousness of his condition; he was
conscious only of an overwhelming lassitude and to conquer it
he summoned every ounce of will power. He forced himself to
ignore the constant squabbles going on around him; the subtle
slyness of Mavrocordato's behavior; the unpleasant habits of
Colonel Stanhope who, when he was not writing odious articles
for his *Greek Chronicle* was forwarding deprecatory little notes
about Lord Byron to the London Committee; the incredible
foolishness of Gamba in ordering a bolt of red cloth wanted by
nobody. He tried to concentrate on his final plans for action when
Mr. Parry, that "master of all the improvements in gunnery and
of the maritime service of war," should have arrived to perform
his miracles.

Sure enough, when he and Mavrocordato returned from a
visit to the Archbishop of Anatolikon on February 3rd, they
found that Parry's stores had arrived and were lying on the quay
in the pouring rain because the following day was a public
holiday and the Greeks had already begun celebration of it. This
infuriated Byron so much that he limped down and started man-
handling the heavy boxes himself, a procedure which effectively
shamed the soldiers and townsfolk into helping him. Watching
the stores being packed into the Seraglio so exhilarated him that
his worries were momentarily forgotten, and he wrote off eagerly
to Charles Hancock, his Cephallonian banker:

> It is perhaps best that I advance with the troops; for if we do not
> do something soon, we shall only have a third year of defensive op-
> erations and another siege.... As for personal safety, besides that it
> ought not to be a consideration, I take it that a man is on the whole
> as safe in one place as another; and, after all, he had better end
> with a bullet than bark in his body. If we are not taken off with
> the sword, we are likely to march off with an ague in this mud-

basket; and, to conclude with a very bad pun, to the ear rather than to the eye, better *martially* than *marsh-ally*—the situation of Missolonghi is not unknown to you. The dykes of Holland when broken down are the deserts of Arabia for dryness, in comparison.

Four days later the redoubtable Mr. Parry appeared: a bluff, hearty man with an unquenchable thirst for strong liquor and a fund of Rabelaisian stories—most of them directed against the members of the London Committee. In his first interview with Byron he stated bluntly that his only practical experience had been as a firemaster in the Navy; that he knew nothing of the making of the famous Congreve rockets since he had been a mere civilian clerk while working at Woolwich; that it would be extremely difficult to manufacture any artillery munitions at Missolonghi since the Committee had failed to send out any coal; and that Colonel Stanhope had flatly refused to advance any pay for the four officers and eight mechanics he had brought with him.

Despite this alarming list of troubles Byron took an immediate liking to Parry. Crude and ignorant though he was, his uncompromising directness was a welcome contrast to the smooth duplicity of Mavrocordato and the crack-brained schemes of Colonel Stanhope. Parry was a practical man too, and took the arrangement of many matters off Byron's shoulders. Besides, he was a most amusing companion and, when primed with grog, would give excruciatingly funny accounts of his interviews with Jeremy Bentham and John Bowring. But while Byron made a boon companion of the firemaster everybody else, from Mavrocordato to Fletcher, detested him. Inside a week he had picked violent quarrels with Stanhope, with Bruno, with Millingen, and even with the Greeks, while a German officer who was in the artillery brigade resigned his commission rather than serve under him. To all the mutterings of dissension Byron paid no attention, but went on blindly with his preparations for the Lepanto assault, and by February 13th Gamba and a force of Souliots were ready to depart; and it was arranged that they should act as an advance guard and leave Missolonghi on the following evening.

But in the Morea, Koloktronis had got wind of the expedition and, fearing it would bring far too much fame to Mavrocordato, he sent all the Souliots he could find in the Peloponnese to Missolonghi, with instructions to stir up revolt. Consequently, at the very hour Gamba and his men were supposed to leave, a deputation waited on Byron and told him insolently that unless nearly half the force were granted commissioned rank and a great deal more pay they would refuse to budge. Byron immediately flew into a rage and declared he would have nothing more to do with any of the Souliots; but after days of haggling it was agreed that those who were willing to obey Lord Byron's orders would band together into a new corps. But the harm was done. Owing to the necessary delay there could be no assault on the fortress, and Byron realized he would never fight the Lepanto of his dreams.

The blow crushed him utterly. Lying on the divan in his uncomfortable room he told Gamba he did not feel well, but even while that concerned youth was running around the house trying to find Bruno or Millingen, Byron ordered Fletcher to bring him a beaker of cider. Parry, who had meanwhile entered, saw that he looked very flushed and recommended brandy punch instead, but Byron insisted on swallowing the cider, rose to his feet, staggered, and collapsed into Parry's arms. The latter promptly administered brandy, and in a moment Byron was in a violent convulsion. Bruno and Millingen dashed in to attend to him, and after a short time he regained his senses and his speech but seemed so weak that Tita and Fletcher carried him up to bed. Half an hour later word came that the still disgruntled Souliots were planning to steal the arms and ammunition in the Seraglio, whereupon everyone except Bruno tore out of the house. In their absence two very drunk Germans—who later turned out to have incited the Souliots to revolt—blundered up the stairs and forced their way past the terrified Bruno, shouting that the arms raid had been successful and that they had come to protect their adored leader. To the semiconscious Byron they appeared like the creatures who infested his nightmares, but this was by no means all he was called upon to endure during a fateful week.

The next day, despite his protests, Bruno and Millingen insisted upon bleeding him, but in their usual bungling fashion they applied the leeches too close to the temporal artery and had the utmost difficulty in staunching the blood. By the time they had succeeded in doing so Byron had fainted. This, on top of his seizure, so weakened him that he was forced to stay in bed and the following morning, when news came that a Turkish brig was stranded on the coast, he was unable to go with Parry and Gamba to capture it. Alas, it was not captured, and on the 19th the Souliots actually did rise and succeeded in murdering the Swedish lieutenant Sass, one of the best of the artillery officers. After this distressing episode six out of Parry's eight mechanics demanded to be repatriated forthwith and Byron, who had tottered from his bed to mete out justice to the Souliot chieftains, was obliged to send them to Zante with a request to his banker there to furnish them with their passages home. Finally, there was a severe earthquake on the evening of the 21st, and Byron remarked mournfully to Parry: "In one week I have been in a fit; the troops mutinied; the Turkish brig burned; Sass killed; an earthquake; thunder, lightning, and torrents of rain—such a week I never witnessed. My situation here is unbearable. A town without any resources and a Government without money; imprisoned by the floods, unable to take any exercise, without the means of satisfying them or doing anything either to relieve them or myself."

The only pleasant thing which happened was that Stanhope departed for the Morea and Athens.

* 5 *

Byron struggled on trying to reform the artillery brigade, but soon an envoy arrived from Athens, bearing a request from Odysseus that Lord Byron should attend a conference at Salona. Behind this polite invitation was that astute person Trelawny, who some time previously had gone on to Athens from the Morea and attached himself, limpet-wise, to the Eastern Greek leader. It was not difficult for the wily Odysseus to prejudice Trelawny against Mavrocordato, and Trelawny retaliated by telling his new patron all about the rich Lord Byron and the immense funds controlled by the London Committee. Between the two of them they concocted the idea of the Salona conference, at which they hoped to drag Byron into their net; but they had no sooner dispatched their invitation than the obliging Colonel Stanhope arrived in Athens. He was easy meat, so easy that within four days he was writing assuring Byron that Odysseus was a magnificent leader, "a most *extraordinary* man" with a heart of gold and a "strong arm." This opinion, it may be stated, was formed entirely because Odysseus allowed the gallant Colonel to set up a printing press; but although Byron trusted neither Stanhope, Trelawny nor the Greek leader, he decided it would be policy to go to the conference.

The month of March passed without incident. The Salona meeting had been postponed, since floods made the roads impassable; the rain still poured down; the inhabitants of Missolonghi implored "General Veeron" to repair the defenses of the town; and the members of the artillery brigade started quarreling among themselves over the punishment meted out to one of their number who had been found guilty of robbing a peasant.

At this moment [wrote Parry] there was a combination of circumstances, all tending to irritate the naturally sensitive disposition of Lord Byron and to weaken his hopes of a great and glorious result. He was more a mental being, if I may use the phrase, than any man I ever saw.... As his hopes of the cause of Greece failed—and they seem to have been the last and perhaps the greatest his mind was capable of forming—he became peevish; and, if I may say so, little-minded. Losing hope, he lost enthusiasm, and became gloomily sensible to his situation. There was no mental stimulus left to make him bear up against his increasing perplexities and nerve his body to resist the noxious effects of a bad climate.

It was true that the blow to Byron's hopes of a glorious outcome to the Grecian campaign had been severe. It was also true that the climate of Missolonghi and the ceaseless demands of Mavrocordato for money had rendered him peevish. But the real cause of his melancholy state was the rapid decline in his physical health. All through March he suffered attacks of giddiness, and at least once he had a slight recurrence of convulsions. Miserable, oppressed by nervous fears, he was thrown into a further mood of despondency by the news early in April that Djavalla, a Souliot chief, and Karaïskaki, a minor Greek leader, had joined forces and were marching upon Missolonghi. The townsfolk panicked and the day that Djavalla took possession of the fort of Vasiladi, which commanded the approach to the lagoon, the Turkish fleet again appeared. It seemed that the town was doomed, and on April 6th Byron bravely rode out into the countryside in an effort to reassure the frightened peasants. His personal guards, clad in their white fustanellas, led the way. Behind them he rode in solitary state, a slim, white-faced figure in his little green befrogged jacket and nankeen trousers. Behind him again rode Gamba, Bruno, a page in scarlet livery, Tita in blue and bold, and Trelawny's Negro groom. The cavalcade made a brave sight and the following morning, when the people heard that other Souliot chiefs were on their way to relieve the town and fight Djavalla, they told each other that this turn of events was all due to their "General Veeron."

Djavalla fled from Vasiladi, the Turkish fleet vanished, and the situation was momentarily saved. But Byron knew that through all the troubles since the beginning of the year the Government of Western Greece had suffered a moral defeat they would find hard to overcome. His mission had failed, lamentably and completely.

* 6 *

On Friday, April 9th, reassuring letters were received from England. The Committee wrote that the negotiations for the Greek loan were proceeding apace, and Byron also heard that his small daughter Ada, who had been ailing, was fully recovered. This news came in a letter from Augusta and so cheered him that he suggested to Gamba that they should go out riding. For once it was a dry morning, but before they had ridden three miles the rain began to fall and soon they were soaked to the skin. Byron's usual practice was to return by canoe to Missolonghi; but Pietro implored him on this occasion to ride the whole way, saying that he was less likely to catch cold on horseback than sitting still in a boat. Touchy as ever where fussiness over his health was concerned, Byron refused to consider the suggestion; and two hours after returning home he developed a severe chill accompanied by shooting pains in his limbs and back. Despite this he again went riding the following day and by the evening was obliged to call for Bruno, complaining that he had cold shuddering fits followed by burning intervals and pains all over his body. He slept little that night and in the morning said he thought that the pains were caused by his having ridden on a damp saddle the previous day. "I ordered him a hot bath, and on the top of it two ounces of castor-oil," reported Bruno afterwards. "... I begged him to let me bleed him, since I found that his pulses were strong and irregular, but he refused categorically. Instead, he agreed to take six doses, one every hour, of fifteen grains of antimony powders, and during the evening he perspired a little and slept in snatches throughout the night."

Strangely enough it was Parry, rather than Bruno, who first grew anxious about Byron's condition and urged him to cross to Zante, where Dr. Thomas could treat him. Byron agreed and told him to make all arrangements; but he would not take the brandy which the firemaster pressed upon him, and he still refused querulously to allow Bruno to bleed him. This was in no way surprising, since in addition to his strong antipathy to being bled he had suffered that disastrous experience on the night of his convulsion. By the afternoon of the 13th his temperature rose sharply, and Bruno called Millingen into consultation. He had no further treatment to suggest; and that evening the sirocco descended on the town making the idea of sailing to Zante quite impossible. The next morning Byron declared he felt much better, and he walked into another room to discuss some business with Pietro. "I was afraid," he told him lightly, "that I was losing my memory, and, in order to try, I attempted to repeat some Latin verses with the English translation, which I have not endeavored to recollect since I was at school. I remembered them all except the last word of one of the hexameters."

He seemed childishly pleased with this achievement; but when Bruno and Millingen appeared at noon he turned on them furiously when they again suggested bleeding. "It was not possible," wrote Bruno, to convince him. He even burst into a fit of irritation, saying that he knew well that the lancet had killed more people than the lance. He agreed to take one of his usual pills, and to swallow some black currant tea. The latter rendered him violently sick, and his sleep was disturbed and restless.

One can scarcely blame either Bruno or Millingen for failing to realize at once the serious nature of their patient's illness. They were young, deplorably inexperienced, and justifiably frightened of Byron's temper. But by the afternoon of the 15th, when Byron developed a raging fever and implored Millingen

to find a witch to exorcise the spell cast upon him by the Cheltenham fortuneteller, they became seriously alarmed. Late that
night Byron at last yielded to Bruno's entreaties and said he
would consent to being bled the following morning, but when
the time came and the doctors produced their lancets he announced that a more peaceful night had induced him to change
his mind. At this Millingen (and it seems about the only sensible
thing he did throughout the illness) warned him that unless he
allowed himself to be bled "the disease might operate such a
disorganization in his cerebral and nervous system as entirely to
deprive him of reason." Byron immediately thrust out his arm,
scowled at the doctors, and said: "Come; you are, I see, a damned
set of butchers; take away as much blood as you will; but have
done with it."

At this first bleeding they drew a pound of blood, although
Byron kept commanding them to close the vein. Nevertheless,
his pulses still raced and the fever mounted and he was unable to
get any proper rest. Two more bleedings were achieved, but at
neither would he let them draw sufficient blood, and on the night
of the 16th he suffered a period of such wild delirium that Tita
wisely took away the pistols which were kept by his bedside. By
this time the doctors, Pietro, Parry and the servants were all in
a state of near-hysteria. None of them had any idea of what to
do for the best and, to add to the general confusion, none of
them could fully understand any language save their own.
Bruno's English was hopeless, so was the Italian of Millingen
and Fletcher; Parry used little but his native swear words; Tita
could not make out what anyone said unless they spoke his Venetian dialect; and the Greek servants gabbled frantically among
themselves. On the 17th Byron insisted fretfully that his bed
must be made and Fletcher and Tita half-carried him into the
next room, Byron crying to the former that he could exist no
longer without sleep. "I know," he said, "that without sleep a
man must die or go mad. I would sooner die a thousand times. . . ."

Meanwhile, Bruno had told Mavrocordato's doctor, Lucca

Vaya, and Dr. Treiber, who looked after the health of the artillery brigade, about Byron's illness and his treatment of it; and now he asked permission for them to pay a visit, emphasizing the fact that Mavrocordato would be mortally offended if they were not allowed to do so. "Very well," muttered Byron, "let the man come in; but he must only look at me and keep silent." It is doubtful if he realized that two doctors, not one, stood by his bedside, because he was by then alternating between delirium and fainting spells. However, the two new doctors and Millingen did not agree with Bruno that Byron's condition was extremely grave, nor did they consider that it would lead to cerebral inflammation. They were against further bleeding as the patient seemed so weak, and advised a concoction of cream of tartar, boracic, and sugar.

"Very well," exclaimed Bruno dramatically, "since I find myself in opposition to all three of you, it is obvious that I must give way, and the responsibility for the life of so great a man will fall upon your own shoulders. It may be that I am mistaken; if this is so it can only be that the unspeakable affection which I have for the gracious person of my Lord, and the awful fear that he may die, have made me see things in a more serious light than necessary...for my own part, since you have taken from me the remedy of bleeding, I judge my Lord already doomed and dead."

A few moments later there was a change in Byron's condition. His extremities became deathly cold, his pulse weakened, and he was semiconscious. In a frantic effort to revive him the doctors applied blisters to his neck and thighs and poured a mixture of laudanum and ether down his throat. But these remedies produced little change. All through the night they listened to his moaning, and in the morning Bruno persuaded his colleagues to let him apply leeches to the temples. In his own words the effect was so miraculous that it "gave the illusion to those who loved that noble person that he could still recover from the fatal danger in which he found himself"; but one cannot really believe that at that stage of Byron's illness the leeches made the slightest difference to his condition.

It was Easter Sunday; but the townsfolk, who were as concerned as the household, did not hold their usual processions. Millingen and Bruno watched by the bedside, and in a conscious moment Byron turned to the former: "Your efforts to preserve my life," he said, "will be in vain. Die I must: I feel it. Its loss I do not lament; for to terminate my wearisome existence I came to Greece. My wealth, my abilities, I devoted to her cause. Well, there is my life to her. One request let me make to you. Let not my body be hacked, or be sent to England. Here let my bones moulder. Lay me in the first corner without pomp or nonsense."

In the afternoon, mail arrived from England—three letters from Hobhouse and one from Kinnaird. The business of the Greek loan had been successfully concluded ... the Committee sent Byron a vote of thanks and gratitude. ... Hobhouse declared that his "present endeavor is certainly the most glorious ever undertaken by man" and besought him to care for his health. ... Had those letters arrived but a few hours earlier Byron would have been overjoyed. But when they came he had lapsed into unconsciousness and the household had gathered around his bed. Suddenly he rallied and asked for Parry, but by the time the firemaster came he was raving in delirium. At five o'clock, however, he seemed momentarily to regain his senses and spoke to Fletcher, who later recorded what followed:

> I then said, "Shall I go, my Lord, and fetch pen, ink and paper?"—"Oh, my God! no, you will lose too much time, and I have not it to spare, for my time is now short," said his Lordship; and immediately after, "Now, pay attention!" His Lordship commenced by saying, "You will be provided for." I begged him, however, to proceed with things of more consequence. He then continued, "Oh, my poor dear child! My dear Ada! My God, could I but have seen her! Give her my blessing, and my dear sister Augusta and her children—and you will go to Lady Byron, and say—tell her everything—you are friends with her." His Lordship appeared to be greatly affected at this moment. Here my

master's voice failed him, so that I could only catch a word at intervals; but he kept muttering something very seriously for some time, and would often raise his voice and say, "Fletcher, now if you do not execute every order which I have given you, I will torment you hereafter if possible." Here I told his Lordship, in a state of the greatest perplexity, that I had not understood a word of what he said; to which he replied, "Oh, my God! then all is lost, for it is now too late! Can it be possible you have not understood me?" "No, my Lord," said I; "but I pray you to try and inform me once more." "How can I?" rejoined my master; "it is now too late, and all is over!" I said, "Not our will, but God's be done!" and he answered, "Yes, not mine be done—but I will try——" His Lordship did indeed make several efforts to speak, but could only repeat two or three words at a time—such as "My wife! my child! my sister!—you know all—you must say all—you know my wishes!" The rest was quite unintelligible.

The doctors decided to give him a dose of quinine and this was administered by Parry, who also loosened the bandages around his head. Byron seemed more peaceful for a time; but still muttered about Augusta and Ada. "Why," he suddenly exclaimed in a loud voice, "was I not aware of this sooner? Why did I not go home before I left for here? ... Poor Greece—poor town—my poor servants...."

At six o'clock he relapsed into a stupor and the blood discharged by the leeches streamed down his face. His breathing became intensely labored and throughout the night the watchers kept raising his head from the pillow in an effort to ease it. All Monday he remained in the same condition until a quarter past six in the evening when they saw him open his eyes then close them again.

"Oh, my God!" cried Fletcher, "I fear his Lordship is gone."

Bruno and Millingen bent above the still figure and nodded silently. George Gordon Noel, sixth Lord Byron and the most famous poet of his age, lay dead.

Epilogue

✳ ✳

Epilogue in Missolonghi, April, 1824

A T THE moment of Byron's passing the thunder pealed from across the lagoon and the rain came down with torrential force. But within the squalid stuffy bedroom, with its litter of basins, dirty towels and medicine bottles, the six men stood irresolute, staring down at Byron's blood-streaked face. There was so much to be done—but how to set about the doing of it? Worn out with the strain of the past forty-eight hours they could not bring their tired minds to bear on the problem; they could only remember that the man who had been so alive, so vital, was dead.

But one of the servants appeared with lamps, and Mavrocordato's voice came echoing up the stairway, and suddenly everyone began to bustle about with a great air of busyness. Fletcher and Tita cleared the room of its more horrid contents; Gamba went off to sort out his friend's many papers and Parry to tell the sad news in the town; Bruno and Millingen retired to consult with Vaya and Treiber about the autopsy which was to be held the following morning; two men arrived to lay out the body—exclaiming as they did so at its smooth whiteness. Letters had to be sent to Stanhope, to Hancock, to Napier, to Hobhouse, to the London Committee, to Lord Sidney Osborne, to Lady

Byron, to Augusta, to Teresa and to innumerable other people, and everyone was still working when dawn broke and the cannon from the fort rolled out a last salute.

The body was embalmed before the four doctors started on what proved to be a most interesting post-mortem examination, for they found that the sutures of the skull had clamped together, a state commonly found only in people of extreme age. The *dura mater* was firmly attached to the inner wall of the cranium and its membranes were suffused with blood. The heart was enlarged and the liver—as might have been expected—was diseased; but the lungs and other organs were healthy. When they had finished they put poor Byron together again as best they could, packed the lungs and viscera into earthenware jars, and placed the body in a long, tin-lined packing-case, the only suitable receptacle to be found in Missolonghi. When all this was done they sat back and began to argue fiercely with each other over what was to be done with the remains.

Trelawny, who had heard the news on his way from Athens, and hastened on to Missolonghi ostensibly to mourn his friend but really to examine the lame foot (of which he had only caught glimpses during swimming expeditions), was of the strong opinion that Byron ought to be buried in the Acropolis at Athens. Stanhope agreed with him and one cannot help feeling that they were actuated more by the wish to further the cause of Odysseus than to do Byron honor. Millingen then immediately explained how Byron had asked him not to let his body be hacked and to see that he was laid to rest in "the first corner without pomp or nonsense." (Considering that he himself had assisted in the hacking there seemed no reason for him to emphasize the second part of the request.) Lord Sidney Osborne mildly suggested that there should be a provisional interment at Zante until Lady Byron expressed her wishes. Pietro Gamba, Parry and Fletcher were vehemently certain that Byron had desired an English burial. The local authorities at Missolonghi asserted that it was only right that the noble Lord should lie in the town for which he had done so much.

As they wrangled, so the news of Byron's death traveled far and wide. In Bologna Teresa lay prostrate with grief; in distant London Hobhouse and Kinnaird stared dully at letters from Obsorne, Gamba, Mavrocordato and Bruno; all over Europe people whispered to each other, "Byron is dead!" Tom Medwin, Leigh Hunt, Trelawny, Millingen, Lady Blessington and many others started rather furtively to shuffle through their papers and diaries for material for the only *true* book about the dead poet; and somewhere in England Annabella and Augusta sat silently with their memories.

After the most regrettable scenes, it was decided that Byron's body should be shipped to Zante; and that the lungs in their earthenware should be buried in Missolonghi. A most extraordinary document was then drawn up and signed by the local authorities, stating that they had closed and sealed the body into the packing case and that the "honored intestines of the said noble and respected Lord Byron" had been deposited in four sealed jars. The document added that the lungs had been buried in the Church of San Spiridone at Missolonghi "in the hope that the most noble and respected family of the Illustrious Lord would grant them to Missolonghi, of which town my Lord had accepted the honorary citizenship."

In that fetid, miserable town a grand funeral service was held on April 22nd; and five days later the packing case was banded round with iron hoops and enclosed in a huge barrel filled with spirit. But even when the body reached Zante on May 3rd the arguments and fights over its ultimate disposal continued, and it was not until May 25th that it was transferred to the brig *Florida*, which then sailed for England with Stanhope, Bruno, Fletcher, Zambelli, Tita and—for some obscure reason—Trelawny's Negro groom. The *Florida* reached the Thames on June 29th, and after the body had lain in state for seven days in Sir

Edward Knatchbull's house in Great George Street, it was buried in the Byron family vault at Hucknall Torkard.

But the squabbles of the little men; the spiteful writings of those who had claimed his friendship; the agitated controversy concerning his morals which was to go on for well over a hundred years—and still goes on today—could not destroy Byron's essential greatness. By his verse he influenced the whole trend of nineteenth century romantic literature; by the manner of his dying he restored freedom to the land he loved above all others, Greece.

✳✳✳✳✳✳✳✳✳✳✳✳✳✳✳✳✳✳✳✳✳✳✳✳✳✳✳✳✳✳✳✳

Bibliography of Principal Books Consulted

Byron—Ethel C. Mayne (2 vols.)
Byron: A Self-Portrait: Letters and Diaries 1798–1824—ed. Peter Quennell (2 vols.)
Byron in Italy—Peter Quennell
Conversations with Lord Byron—Lady Blessington
Greece in 1823 and 1824—Leicester Stanhope
Idler in Italy—Lady Blessington
Journal of the Conversations of Lord Byron—Tom Medwin
Last Attachment, The—Iris Origo
Last Days of Lord Byron, The—William Parry
Last Journey, The—Harold Nicolson
Lord Byron—Lord Macaulay
Lord Byron and Some of his Contemporaries—Leigh Hunt
Lord Byron's Correspondence—ed. R. E. Prothero (Lord Ernle) (6 vols.)
Lord Byron's Life, Letters and Journals—Thomas Moore
Lord Byron's Letters and Journals—ed. John Murray

Pilgrim of Eternity, The—John Drinkwater

Recollections of a Long Life—Lord Broughton (John Cam Hobhouse)

Recollections of the Life of Lord Byron (1808–14)—A. R. C. Dallas

Records of Shelley, Byron and the Author—E. J. Trelawny

Works of Lord Byron, The—ed. E. H. Coleridge (7 vols.)

Years of Fame, The—Peter Quennell

Index

Index